# FROST

## A Literary Life Reconsidered

# FROST

## A Literary Life Reconsidered

### William H. Pritchard

*Second edition, with a new preface*

The University of Massachusetts Press

AMHERST

Library of Congress Cataloging-in-Publication Data

Pritchard, William H.
    Frost : a literary life reconsidered / William H. Pritchard. —
2nd ed.
        p.   cm.
    ISBN 0–87023–838–8
    1. Frost, Robert, 1874–1963.
    2. Poets, American—20th century—Biography.   I. Title.
PS3511.R94Z89   1993
811'.52—dc20
[B]                       92–36872
                    CIP

Acknowledgment is made for permission to quote from the following sources:

Unpublished material from the Frost collections at Dartmouth College and at
Amherst College is quoted by permission of the Estate of Robert Lee Frost.

*The Poetry of Robert Frost* edited by Edward Connery Lathem. Copyright 1916,
1923, 1928, 1930, 1934, 1939, 1947 © 1969 by Holt, Rinehart and Winston.
Copyright 1936, 1942, 1944, 1951, © 1956, 1958, 1961, 1962 by Robert Frost.
Copyright © 1964, 1967, 1970, 1975 by Lesley Frost Ballantine. Reprinted by
permission of Holt, Rinehart and Winston, Publishers.

*Robert Frost: Poetry and Prose*, edited by Edward Connery Lathem and Lawrance
Thompson. Copyright © 1972 by Holt, Rinehart and Winston. Reprinted by
permission of Holt, Rinehart and Winston, Publishers.

*Photographs courtesy of the Jones Library, Inc., Amherst, Massachusetts,
with the exception of the photograph on page 259, which is reproduced by courtesy of
the Amherst College Library.*

*To Theodore Baird*

# Contents

# Preface to
# the Second Edition

*Frost: A Literary Life Reconsidered* was first published nine years ago. In calling the book "A Literary Life," I meant the words to apply to Frost in a more than perfunctory sense, since his way of taking things seemed to me, from first to last, incorrigibly literary—"poetical," he might have said. The word "reconsidered" was by way of underlining the revisionist nature of my endeavor, the work to be revised being Lawrance Thompson's three-volume biography of Frost which had so confidently and—as it appeared to me—so wrongheadedly offered up a portrait of a vengeful, malicious, grossly selfish, opportunistic man and poet. My introduction considers a few egregious examples of Thompson's explanatory simplifications, even as it acknowledges dependence on him for the factual core of my book.

While still convinced that Thompson's uncongenial portrait of Frost needed to be set straight, at least argued with, I regret somewhat the way most reviews of *Frost: A Literary Life Reconsidered,* both in this country and in England, concentrated on that issue to the relative exclusion of what I cared most about: the fact that, along with T. S. Eliot and Wallace Stevens, Frost was one of the great American poets of this century. Oxford University Press decided that a good way to sell the book would be to play up the issue of the poet's moral character, so after a few favorable reviews were in they ran an advertisement headed by the following catchy questions: "Benign sage or monstrous megalomaniac? Which was the *real* Robert Frost?" When I saw the ad I winced at its melodramatic, all-or-nothing challenge, as if the matter were to be settled by an applause meter. I knew that the answer to the question was *neither* and that there was no "real" Frost who could, finally, be exactly measured and understood. My book attempted rather to demonstrate that the most real, most compelling Frost was to be found only in the poetry.

In rereading, it looks to me that the book's densest, most useful and original sections are chapters 3 and 4, "Not Undesigning" and "Forms of Guardedness." These seventy-five pages take Frost from his landing in England in 1912 through the publication of his first two books, then back to America in 1915 and the beginning of his career as a public performer of his poems and as a teacher at Amherst College. In some ways the most exciting years of his life, they are the ones in which his finest work appears, both in the published poems and in the poetics he formulated in letters and interviews. His publication of *North of Boston* and the "sound of sense" verse theory he constructed to accompany it; his practices as a poet compared with those of the Georgian poets and with Edward Thomas; his educational assumptions and prejudices, and the way they clashed with those of Amherst's president Alexander Meiklejohn—these matters are at the heart of Frost's life as a man and a poet, and I managed to say some things about them that hadn't been said previously.

A few reviewers complained that in my eagerness to correct the Thompson portrait of Frost I had gone to the other extreme by striving too hard to put a "benign" interpretation on actions and motives that Thompson was right to have judged otherwise. At least one reviewer said that in so doing I had reduced the stature of Frost by making him into a less intractable and difficult—even tragic—figure than in fact he showed himself to be. Rather than taking issue with these charges, which probably have some truth to them, I will point to two important books about Frost which succeeded my own and which, in the course of their arguments, confirm, amplify, and occasionally correct my sense of the poet. The books are Stanley Burnshaw's *Robert Frost Himself* (1986) and John Evangelist Walsh's *Into My Own: The English Years of Robert Frost* (1988). Burnshaw was an editor at Frost's publisher, Henry Holt, late in the poet's career, and he supervised the publication of *Selected Letters of Robert Frost*, which was edited by Thompson and appeared in 1964, the year after Frost's death. Burnshaw gives a blow-by-blow account of his increasing consternation at the amount of negative, unfavorable commentary Thompson directed at his subject in this edition of the letters. Feeling that he could no longer work with Thompson on the biographical volumes to follow, Burnshaw removed himself from the scene but kept watch over what happened as the books came out. Some years previously, in 1959, Frost had implored him in the following terms with respect to Thompson: "I'm counting on you to protect me from Larry." Burnshaw's book, especially its chapter titled "The Fabrication of the 'Monster' Myth," is a convincing, if somewhat belated effort to do just that.

Two years after *Robert Frost Himself,* John Evangelist Walsh, in a book combining sturdy research with an excellent critical sense of the poems, provided a fresh account of the years Frost spent in England. Walsh's conviction that Thompson came to entertain a fairly strong personal bias about his subject, followed from Burnshaw's and my own treatment. But Walsh went further, suggesting that some of what passed for "fact" in Thompson's narrative might just as well be termed "the piling up of mere assertion based on unverifiable anecdote." Interestingly, Walsh pointed to the notorious incident in Thompson's biography when Frost, then a farmer in Derry, New Hampshire, one night wakened his six-year-old daughter Lesley and led her down into the kitchen where her mother was sitting at the table, crying. Lesley remembers that her father pointed a revolver first at his wife, then at himself, exhorting Lesley to choose one or the other since "before morning one of us will be dead." Thompson writes that Lesley wondered whether she might have dreamed the whole thing (she was prone to childhood nightmares); but, says the biographer, "There was evidence enough to make her certain that this experience had not been a dream." A footnote reveals that the incident was communicated to Thompson by Lesley soon after her father died. When I dealt with this matter in my book, I was accused by reviewers of callousness because I called it a bad theatrical performance, while admitting that as a melodramatic gesture it was also a terrifying one. Walsh's book convinces me I should have been more skeptical toward the whole business. He puts it this way:

> To begin with, the anecdote should not have been presented in such a bare and downright fashion, dropped into the text as if its truth were beyond question. Thompson never cited, never even said whether he had sought and studied, the unspecified "evidence" claimed by Lesley, that made her so certain, sixty years after the fact, that her childhood experience had been real and not a dream.

The *way* a biography presents what it assumes as fact is something we need to consider in attempting to assess just how much the "fact" should count for—an obvious truth, but it is useful to be reminded of it.

## PREFACE TO THE SECOND EDITION

The not-too-distant future holds two exciting prospects for those who care about Frost. The first is Margot Feldman's edited transcripts of his prose notebooks from the Dartmouth College Library. These span a half century, from around 1903 to the early 1950s, and until now have been mainly untouched. Their publication is certain to affect in significant measure our understanding of Frost. The second, tentatively scheduled for publication in 1994–95, is a Library of America Frost edited by Richard Poirier and Mark Richardson. This volume will contain the poems, newly edited, and freed, it is to be hoped, from the tinkerings and "improvings" of Frost's punctuation that characterized E. C. Lathem's 1969 edition, *The Poetry of Robert Frost*. In addition the new volume will contain Frost's complete prose and a selection from his letters having more or less exclusively to do with poetic theory. With these volumes to look forward to, I am pleased to have *Frost: A Literary Life Reconsidered* back in print.

*September 1992*                                                    W.H.P.

# Author's Note and Acknowledgments

I invite the reader to read with a volume of Frost at hand, using the poems to check up on me, as well as rereading them for their own sake. While I have many misgivings about and disagreements with Edward Connery Lathem's editorial emendations in his text of the complete poems (*The Poetry of Robert Frost,* 1969) I have quoted from the edition throughout. Quotations from Frost's letters reproduce his sometimes erratic or designedly humorous spellings. Most passages quoted may be traced to their source in the Notes at the end of this book.

A number of people have been generous in directing me to relevant Frost material, and I should like in particular to thank Philip Cronenwett of the Dartmouth College Library, John Lancaster of the Amherst College Library, and Dan Lombardo of the Jones Library in Amherst, the last of whom was especially helpful in putting photographs at my disposal. Alfred Edwards, Frost's literary executor, has been most kind in his assistance. Jack W. C. Hagstrom supported me from the outset, and Newton McKeon has been both bibliographically and sympathetically contributory. A grant from the American Council of Learned Societies is gratefully recognized here. Chapter VIII of this book appeared in *The American Scholar,* Fall 1984.

Francis Murphy, Roger Sale, and, as always, Marietta Pritchard read the manuscript and helped make it less porous. I should also like to thank Curtis Church and Susan Meigs of Oxford University Press for their editorial help. My teachers, Reuben Brower and G. Armour Craig, were the two readers of Frost from whom I learned most, first in their classrooms and later in my colleagueship with them. The person to whom this book is dedicated has been ever ready, insistently so, to talk with me about Frost, as he has been to talk about books generally. His particular contribution to my discussion of Frost at Amherst College in the fourth chapter is but one instance of what he has given me over the past thirty years of friendship.

*Amherst, Mass.*                                                                          W.H.P.
*April 1984*

# Introduction

In calling this book a "literary life," I intend a doubleness of reference: to the subject of the book, Robert Frost, and to the book itself. My original aim was to write a reasonably short biography of Frost—a "life," as most biographers these days name their product. But Frost lived for almost ninety years, and the official biography by Lawrance Thompson runs to almost 2000 pages, many of them devoted to long, fact-filled, or speculative footnotes. A short biography following in its wake must be ruthless in what it chooses to leave out (the recently published one-volume compressed edition of Thompson's book still runs to over 500 pages and omits all the footnotes). One of the things left out may have to be the poetry, at least any extended discussion and criticism of it; so the writer who is unwilling, as I am, to leave it out, must therefore be extremely selective in the materials of the life which are included. For the reader who wants to follow the events of Frost's life from year to year, Thompson's biography is the essential work and is unlikely to be replaced.

That work—which more people have heard about than read through—effected a striking change in the way people thought about Frost's character. In 1966 when the first volume appeared, a critical redefinition of his poems had already occurred; the popular view of them as essentially spirit-warming tributes to man and nature had been replaced by a presumably more sophisticated view of them as "dark" parables rather, ironic meditations played out behind deceptively simple surfaces. Thompson's biography led to a similar all-or-nothing reversal, as the man who had been placed on a pedestal and worshipped in schoolrooms all over America was now seen—so the presumption went—for what he had really been all along: a species of monster in human form.

The phrase is no exaggeration on my part. When Helen Vendler reviewed the second volume of Thompson's biography in 1970, she accused him of "criminal blandness" in his (for her) too unjudgmental account of Frost's lack of "sustained affection" for his son, Carol. "What is a father who has no 'sustained affection' for his son but a monster?" she asked. And when the final volume of the biography was completed and published in 1976 after Thompson's death, by his research assistant R. H. Winnick, one reviewer, David Bromwich, felt confident in proclaiming that "a more hateful human being cannot have lived" than Frost. The attitude lingers. Such a civilized, moderate writer as Howard Moss, poetry editor of the *New Yorker,* referred to Frost, after reading Thompson's biography, as a "mean-spirited megalomaniac" who represented "one of the worst examples of a common strain in American literary life." And just recently, when the *New York Times Book Review* invited certain writers to name and describe the literary figure they found most obnoxious, a novelist named Harold Brodkey eagerly volunteered Frost's name, ascribing to him a "demonic vileness" and claiming that it "showed in his face."

It is certain that the intemperateness of such language was brought on by the earlier idealization of Frost it attempted to displace. I began to think about the present book by asking myself what responsibility, if any, Thompson's biography bore for such subsequent judgments. After all, it was not he who used terms like "monster," "hateful," or "vile" to describe his subject. He was, rather, a scholar who devoted a large portion of his life to gathering all the facts about Frost, talking to him over long periods of time about countless subjects, following up every lead that might put him in closer relation to the man he had committed himself to understanding. It is possible that after this labor of decades a state of mind hostile to Frost ensued; at least there is a commonplace that it sometimes happens to assiduous biographers who spend years with their subject. After the Bromwich review was published, one of Frost's defenders, Dorothy Van Doren (Mrs. Mark Van Doren), said in a letter to the *Times* that by the end of Thompson's second volume "it seemed to me that he had learned to dislike his subject." Yet explaining things that way doesn't explain much—or it explains too much—and we owe Thompson the decency of taking seriously his aim as he defined it in the introduction to his second volume. That aim was to "offer a balanced delineation of Frost's character which would mingle sympathy with critical detachment," and thus bring out the man's complexity, not his simple goodness or simple awfulness. Thompson set out to show his subject warts and all: nothing to be extenuated, but nothing set down in malice either.

These intentions, we may agree, were admirable; in one of his letters to Frost, Thompson even assured him, "But the simple truth is that I love you," and the assurance was doubtless heartfelt. In practice, however, he had to express his caring in sentences and paragraphs, had to find a style appropriate to present the subtle, playful Frost. And it is fair to say that, for all his tireless fact-gathering, Thompson as a writer was not adequate to that subject. Both reviewers mentioned earlier, Vendler and Bromwich, highly intelligent critics, were unhappy with Thompson's writing: Vendler characterized his prose as "doughy," and Bromwich, while allowing that the books were "tolerably well written" also judged them to be "without subtlety or penetration." Yet they both went on to speak in no uncertain terms about the Frost they saw *by means of* those unsubtle doughy words. And here their confidence seems to me quite misplaced.

After reading the three volumes of biography, my feeling was that despite Thompson's scrupulousness in ascertaining and recording facts about what Frost said and did and wrote, his biographical style made Frost into a particularly unattractive presence, so much at variance with what many who knew him (including myself, briefly) remembered of him, that something had perhaps gone amiss. Thompson seemed overeager to fix Frost in explanatory categories that imposed upon the life a rigid scheme, as when in the introduction to the second volume he tried to speak to the heart of his understanding of the poet. His idea was that "early disappointments"—by which he meant the child's experience of a stern, sometimes violent father and a compensatorily over-protective mother, or Frost's inability for some time later on to persuade Elinor White to marry him, or his uncertain stays at Dartmouth and Harvard and his shiftings about from one line of work to another—that these experiences "had caused him to become self-protectively arrogant" to the extent of confusing himself with the Old Testament God who said it was right to punish your enemies by striking back at them. And he described Frost's vengeful makeup as follows:

The imagined forms of retaliation kept changing, even as the actual forms of humiliation changed. In Salem, when he became the best pitcher on his grammar school team, he dreamed he would some day achieve renown as a hero in the major league of his choice—and even a baseball could serve as a lethal weapon if carefully aimed at the head of an enemy batter. Later, in high school, where his baseball dreams were spoiled, he achieved excellence as a scholar, and thus found a successful way of scornfully triumphing over those who were better than he at baseball. As soon as he began publishing poems in the high school literary magazine, he began to dream that some day his reputation as a literary hero would provide him with another way of triumphing over his enemies.

At this point the credulous reader is evidently prepared to believe that the reason to write poems or to graduate first in your class (as Frost did) is in truth to get back at your enemies by surpassing them or wiping them out. The reason to want to excel at being a pitcher is that it provides you with a "lethal weapon" to throw at somebody's head, perhaps permanently dispatching him. What look on the surface to be benign, time-honored ways for a young man to distinguish himself— in scholarship, in aesthetic creativity, in athletics—turn out under the Thompson microscope to be in fact ways of "retaliation"—ways expressed by the biographer in melodramatic terms. Though nothing in Thompson's actual account of Frost as scholar and poet and pitcher bears out the "lethal" nature of his performance (he didn't become a beanball expert, and the scholarship by which he "scornfully triumphed" may have been superior only because he was very intelligent), the grounds are laid for the reader to distrust Frost's surface motives in doing anything—and to assume that he was "really" operating at a deeper level which is available for inspection only to the biographer.

Having thus committed himself to seeing through anything Frost did and finding something a good deal more sinister, or at least obsessive, Thompson was in a position to explain everything as yet another example of retaliation, or vindictiveness, or arrogant, "spoiled-child" behavior. So he provided a special index of sixty-three topical subheads for use in "illuminating the complicated and contradictory responses of Frost as man and artist." For example, under "vindictiveness" may be found a list, in alphabetical order, of Frost's "vindictive gestures against" people ranging all the way from "Arnold, Matthew" to "Zabel, Morton D.," and including along the way most contemporary poets, as well as Frost's wife, son, and sister. The assumption is of course that at one point or another in his life he was "vindictive" toward all these people, and that the biographer has found the right word to label, in each individual case, what went on. A selected list of Thompson's subheadings includes the following: "Anti-intellectual," "Baffler-teaser-deceiver," "Brute," "Charlatan," "Cowardice," "Depression, Moods of," "Enemies," "Fear," "Gossip," "Hate," "Insanity," "Jealousy," "Misunderstanding," "Murderer," "Pretender," "Puritan," "Rage," "Retaliations, Poetic," "Revenge," "Self-Centeredness," "Spoiled Child," and finally the aforementioned "Vindictive." On the opposite side of the ledger, one finds "Friendship," but no headings like the following: "Bravery," "Exhilaration, Moods of," "Hope," "Intellectual," "Love," "Loyalty," "Sanity," "Understanding." Though Thompson would surely not have denied that Frost on occasion showed these traits, either he did not feel they were worth indexing, or he was carried away by his systematic impulse to classify his subject's vices.

I dwell at some length upon Thompson's style because it has been so important in promoting a notion of Frost still current. Further, that biographical style was rooted in a certain literalness of mind which made Thompson, to say the least, uncomfortable with the playful, complicated, devious Frost—even as he was sure he "loved" the man. He knew well enough words Frost had written in "Education by Poetry": "It is touch and go with the metaphor, and until you have lived with it long enough you don't know when it is going. You don't know how much you can get out of it and when it will cease to yield. It is a very living thing. It is as life itself." Yet as can be seen from any number of instances, only one of which I will point to here, Thompson was plainly not at home in the metaphor. He had little sense of humor; his command of irony was not subtle. At one point, discussing some of Frost's later poems, he says that many of them reflected "murderous thoughts." Then, in a series of footnoted references to people Frost presumably "could remember" wanting to do away with, we are taken on a tour of the potential victims, from a boyhood enemy in San Francisco, to an opponent in a fight he had as a young man in Lawrence, Massachusetts, to more recent candidates:

> In England, there came a day when he would have taken pleasure in murdering Ezra Pound. Not long after he returned to the United States, he had thought of killing his old enemy, Ellery Sedgwick, editor of the *Atlantic Monthly*. As for Ernest Silver [Principal of the Plymouth Normal School where Frost once taught] . . . he had used razor words in public to achieve a murderous revenge.

The difficulty is evident. For Thompson there is really no difference—or hardly any—between word and thing, between a way of talking and a way of acting. If Frost one day "would have taken pleasure in murdering Ezra Pound" (as anybody who knew Pound well probably felt like doing at one time or another) he was just one step away from carrying it out. If Frost was filled with rage, as he was, at Ellery Sedgwick's lordly treatment of him, then he had "thought of killing him" (quite ready to put his promising literary career in jeopardy) by stomping into the office of the *Atlantic* and gunning Sedgwick down, frock coat and all. If he used "razor words" in public to achieve a "murderous revenge" on his old boss Silver, then that was really about the same as cutting Silver's jugular.

These adverse criticisms of Thompson are also, in one sense, ungenerous, since they are an instance of biting the hand that has fed me. His biography is indispensable, a mine of facts on which I have constantly drawn. When he turned, on the other hand, from the life to the poetry, he approved of what he saw but was comfortable mainly with relating a particular poem to some incident in the life from which it may have sprung. There is no conviction in his own sentences that Frost was a remarkable poet because he used language in remarkable ways. "I have made a life study of what I can say," Frost wrote in one of his notebooks. But Thompson devoted little energy to that "saying." For him, the goodness of the poetry was evident and nearly went without saying, even as the not-so-goodness of the life had to be illustrated again and yet again.

My decision to write a "literary life" of Frost came out of the belief that whatever he did, for better or worse, was done poetically, was performed in a style which must not be pushed out of the way in order to get at the "real" or "deeper" motives that supposedly underlay it. Since we care about the life because of the poems which came out of it, a literary life of Frost could only be written by someone—so I flattered myself—who had an informed inwardness with that poetry. (By "poetry" I mean not just the poems, but also the prose reflections: essays, interviews, notebooks—above all, the letters.) One of Frost's favorite words for poetry was "Play," and everything he did or wrote could be thought about in the light of that notion. One of his notebooks contains perhaps his deepest word on the subject: "Play no matter how deep has got to be so playful that the audience are left in doubt whether it is deep or shallow." That "audience" also includes the writer of a literary life, thus a certain reticence or diffidence may creep in at times, as I attempt to understand him in his poems, in his life.

When I find myself in doubt whether I have deeply or shallowly responded to a particular moment, or poem, I console myself by noting that the response is probably neither one nor the other—a mixture, rather.

In any event, a spirit of play should animate both the reader of and the writer about Frost, whether at the end of "Directive"—"Here are your waters and your watering place. / Drink and be whole again beyond confusion"—or in the following little dialogue from one of his notebooks entitled "Crash there goes another young ideal":

BOY   You say you hate the word gem
MAN   Not the word at all except as applied figuratively to a poem or picture
BOY   What's your favorite word?
MAN   I have no favorite words.
BOY   My favorite words are silver & twilight. Some people think pavement is the most beautiful word in the language. Pav-e-ment.— pav-e-ment. A boy at the Poetry Center last night had a set of poems all filled with the words silver & twilight & frosted. I never heard anything I liked better.
MAN   The first thing frosted taken alone brings into my head is cake.
BOY   Don't!

Frost added, "The question is is it right to educate young people by shock. They are an undeniable temptation to teachers." No poet of this century, one ventures to say, spent more energy in and out of classrooms, educating young people by shock, or by whatever method seemed appropriate at the moment. But it was not only young people who, throughout his life, provided Frost with the "undeniable temptation" he speaks of in respect to the little dialogue. In the lecture hall, in the living room after dinner, interviewed by students at Harvard or by Lawrence Spivak on *Meet The Press,* he was, first to last, an "educator." As with love or with poetry, the work of education was—in the words from "Two Tramps in Mud Time"—"play for mortal stakes." And he once insisted, "I am never not working," proving his point with an energetic formulation to jog the mind.

In the pages to follow, I am concerned to identify and describe Frost's play of mind as it reveals itself in an art which is notable for the amount of felt "life" it contains, and in a life which is notably artful, constantly shaped by the extravagant designs of his imagination. My procedure is to move back and forth between life and art, often blurring the distinctions in the interest of telling a story of a literary life. As noted earlier, much is left out: whole areas of his experience like his teaching at Michigan, his long association with the Bread Loaf School of English, details of the houses and towns in which he lived, his travels as an old man to Brazil, Israel, and the Soviet Union, are treated only briefly or not at all. There is probably also a relative lack here of "memorable" portraits of faces and farms and New England nature; plenty of such portraits are there to be consulted in writings on Frost by Thompson, Sidney Cox, Kathleen Morrison, and others.

As for the poetry, one acknowledges at the outset three large pairs of footsteps not to be avoided: Randall Jarrell's pioneering essays on Frost in *Poetry and the Age;* Reuben Brower's *The Poetry of Robert Frost,* distinguished for the delicacy of its particular insights into voice and speaker in the poems; and most recently, Richard Poirier's superb *Robert Frost: The Work of Knowing,* an extended, meticulous, and daring commentary on the work. Rather than trying to compete with these critics by offering longer, fuller, more "definitive" analyses of individual poems, I have attempted instead to concentrate on the individual volumes, in sequence as they appeared, from *A Boy's Will* (1913) to *In The Clearing* (1962). It has long seemed to me that the ideal way to read Frost is to encounter his poems in their original, first habitats; especially such wonderful collections as *North of Boston, New Hampshire* and *A Witness Tree,* which are much more than receptacles containing discrete, individual efforts. My methods of dealing with these volumes and the particular poems in them, are the hardly novel ones of description, comparison, evaluation. To locate the individual writings within the larger sequence of intention, of the willings and sufferings which the man enacted and underwent, is the challenge that has kept me alert.

The act of treating life and work in a chronological, rather than (as in the Brower and Poirier books) a topical or thematic fashion, seemed essential to me. Only in the opening chapter is there a departure from chronology, in that it begins with speculation about Frost's move to England in 1912, then jumps back into his life to consider two earlier moments of impulsive self-assertion, then proceeds to a discussion of *A Boy's Will,* his first published book. In giving the poetry a prominent place early in my book, I want to emphasize that although for convenience we speak as if life and work were separate compartments yoked together by the critic, we also know better. For Frost, probably for any serious poet, the most important part of life is the work, is the Art. That is another thing meant by speaking of a "literary life." In the first chapter, "Guessing At Myself," I attempt to present that life in capsulated form, after which I go back to the beginning and present it at length in the remainder of the book.

The first chapter's title also points up my distrust of explanatory terms which attempt to fix and "explain" Frost too quickly or for too long. I have a related disinclination to lecture him about his behavior, or to lecture the reader as to how that behavior should be construed. Above all, I am wary about entering, without embarrassment and misgiving, something called the mind of Robert Frost in order to say how he really felt in one or the other situation. It is probably true that such biographical reticence or scepticism will not satisfy anybody eager to be let in on the *true* story of what happened. But I trust that as a literary life, it may be a more stylish way to treat a master of style who made a life study of what he could say.

# FROST

A Literary Life Reconsidered

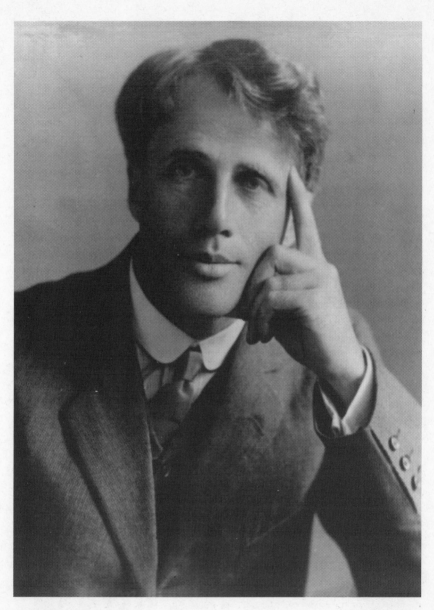

In England, 1913.

# I

## Guessing at Myself

I must have been asked once years ago what I was doing in England, and I had forgotten what I was doing . . . I said to somebody—I saw it in print somewhere—that I said that I had come to the land of *The Golden Treasury*. That's what I went for. One of my theories was that I went to live under thatch . . . I'm guessing at myself, you know; guessing at ourselves. The beauty of it is the lambent way the mind plays over that guessing.

This remark, made during a talk at the Bread Loaf School of English nearly forty-four years after Frost had sailed with his family from Boston to Glasgow and begun the great adventure of his life in England, might be understood as the forgetful uncertainty of an old man looking back on his younger self. More strategically, it might be taken as Frost's attempt at fending off any definitive account of why he did something, anything. Thus to go to the land of Palgrave's anthology of poems, *The Golden Treasury* (1861), or to live "under thatch," would be no more than spurious reasons, diversionary tactics to throw dust in the eyes of the too curious. But these ways of understanding him, whether patronizing or cynical, are less than he deserves, since the truly interesting movement of mind in this passage occurs at its end, where Frost hits upon the word "guessing" and is propelled by it into an elegant statement: "The beauty of it is the lambent way the mind plays over that guessing." In other words, it might be that with sufficient play of mind—sufficient unto the needs of a poet—any significant choice can and must be imagined and successively reimagined, not to cover the real truth with veils of comforting

3

illusion, but to tell a story about the self which stays fresh. Like Wallace Stevens's "Supreme Fiction," it must change. An account of Frost's motives and desires in moving to England in 1912 should remind itself at the outset that it, too, is "guessing," and should refuse to settle on any single explanation which explains everything, thus doesn't explain enough.

His decision to pull up stakes came after he and Elinor Frost had been married for nearly seventeen years and had produced six children, two of whom died at early ages. Frost had tried poultry farming in Derry, New Hampshire, the farm purchased for him at Elinor's urging by his paternal grandfather, and the indifferent results probably had a good deal to do with the very qualified way he would later characterize himself as a farmer. When William Prescott Frost died in 1901, he gave his grandson free use of the farm for ten years, after which it would belong to Frost. There was, as well, an annuity of five hundred dollars for each of the first ten years; it would then become eight hundred for the rest of the grandson's life. Meanwhile, in 1906, Frost began full-time teaching at Pinkerton Academy, in Derry, and in 1911 taught for a year at the Plymouth Normal School, in Plymouth, New Hampshire. In 1911, the farm having become his to do with as he pleased, Frost sold it, and the proceeds, in addition to the enlarged annuity which was now his, made the possibility of living away from New England for a time—with no responsibilities except literary and familial ones—real and attractive.

In retrospect the move looks like a canny professional decision on Frost's part to spark a poetic career which had not quite gotten off the ground. His acquaintance to be, Ezra Pound, was to rail against the thickheaded American editors who refused to publish the poet, speaking as if Frost came to England so as to be discovered by Pound. But Frost, by that time, had published a number of poems, and in 1912— the year of departure for England—such good ones as "October," "My November Guest," and "Reluctance" appeared in the *Forum* and the *Youth's Companion* which, if not prestigious magazines like the *Atlantic Monthly,* were still reputable places to appear. To decide despite these small victories to throw in one's lot with another country, without the literary connections there which might help in getting noticed and published, was surely not expedient nor obvious good sense, even though it worked out magnificently well. There must have been some guessing involved. And the situation was further complicated since he and Elinor were uncertain whether to go and live in

England, or in Vancouver, British Columbia, where his friend and former pupil John Bartlett had taken up residence. Presumably, so goes the story, things were settled by the toss of a coin: "The coin chose England," said Frost later on.

This story of impulse obeyed owed everything to the poet's need to see the event as somehow guileless, unforeseen and unpragmatic, even miraculous in its nature. Lines from "The Trial by Existence," which he had published six years previously, insist that the essence of life is to "choose greatly," and then to get "nothing but what we somehow chose." Another poem, written while he was in England, asserts that its speaker would someday "set out for somewhere" and "make the reckless choice" ("The Sound of Trees"). Both poems are intent on widening and making less tame the act of choice: not just choosing, but "somehow" choosing; not a choice that is measured and thoughtful, but a "reckless" one. As further instances of the "lambent way the mind plays over that guessing," they convert choice from the prudential into the poetic realm.

The most reckless choice Frost had previously made in his life occurred in 1894 when he "set out for somewhere" and wound up in the Dismal Swamp in Virginia. He had set out just before that, recklessly enough, for Canton, New York, where Elinor was in her second year of studies at St. Lawrence University, a situation about which Frost was full of dissatisfaction. Jealous of her college friends, fearful of other possible suitors, and unable to deter Elinor from completing her education (even though she planned to complete the degree in three years after which, if he had "established" himself, they would be married), Frost went about trying to win her by the most extraordinary, poetical means. Having assembled four of his earliest poems, including "My Butterfly" (which he had just sold to the sympathetic William Ward and his sister Susan, who ran a New York magazine called the *Independent*), he had them printed in Lawrence, Massachusetts, in what may have been one of the smallest printings ever made—just two copies. He would present this book to Elinor, and the gift, magically, would somehow turn everything around, would open her eyes in fresh ways to his virtues. As it turned out, Elinor was most unreceptive when Frost showed up at her lodgings at St. Lawrence. Refusing to discuss any matters with him, she accepted his copy of *Twilight* but without comment, and suggested that he leave town on the first train, after which she closed the door.

What happened subsequently has not only the attributes of lyric pathos, but of comedy, even burlesque. Thompson spends many pages in his biography admirably tracking down as best as he can Frost's journey from Lawrence to Boston to New York by train, then to Norfolk, Virginia, by steamer, then into the Dismal Swamp itself, on foot. The biographer's supposition about Frost is that "It may have crossed his mind that he could secretly arrange death by plunging into the very heart of some such Slough of Despond as the Dismal Swamp in Virginia," from which disastrous event news of his demise would filter back home only mysteriously and incompletely. It is impossible to know just how seriously, if at all, the thought of suicide crossed Frost's mind. But if we consider the fabulous venture he embarked on it may be hazarded that a mere plain old-fashioned suicide, like cutting your throat or swallowing pills, would have been, for Frost, much too abrupt and final a gesture, lacking in imaginative possibilities. Whether the comparison of his projected journey with Bunyan's *Pilgrim's Progress* actually occurred to him—it is hard to imagine that it didn't—his very choice of the Dismal Swamp for a possible exit from the world was a blatantly literary thing to have done.

Here then went the heroic, rejected lover, dressed in street clothes and carrying a satchel, plodding into the Dismal Swamp and waiting for something to happen (the scene brings words from the song "Chloe" to mind—"I'll roam through the dismal swampland"). What happened in Frost's roaming was that sometime in the middle of the night he saw a light, heard voices, and walking toward them came upon what turned out to be the Dismal Swamp Canal. A party of men was raising a boat in one of the locks; duck hunters, headed for Nag's Head, they were about to indulge in a pre-hunt celebration with copious food and drink. During the ensuing celebration, in which he was invited to participate, Frost slipped off alone, walked to where he could hear the Atlantic surf, and met a stranger on the beach, an officer in the Life Saving Service on patrol from Kitty Hawk. In conversation the man told him of how Aaron Burr's daughter, Theodosia, supposedly met her death off the Outer Banks. Then Frost returned to the hotel and at dawn heard the hunters as they opened fire on their prey.

Thompson's treatment of this whole episode (from which I have selected a few details) is a tour de force of reconstruction, made on the basis of listening to Frost's story of what happened and visiting the Dismal Swamp himself. Yet it is also rather hard to believe, or at least to take seriously the Frost presented to us who, as the gun-fire rattled away, "listened, and thought bitterly that if Elinor White learned how her beloved had accidentally met death at the hands of drunken duck-hunters at Nags Head in North Carolina—and all for love of her—it would serve her right. But again nothing happened . . ." I doubt that we can respond sympathetically to Frost's presumed "bitter" feelings here. For the whole scene feels so beautifully orchestrated in its juxtapositions and incongruities—youthful, sensitive, would-be self-destroyer meets garrulous, bibulous, would-be duck-destroyers—that we lose the hero's sufferings in the larger grotesque (or providential) design of the whole. But sixty or so years later he put the experience into the words of a long poem, "Kitty Hawk," in which full of a song he might have sung but didn't, he falls in by chance with some hunters ("Some kind of committee / From Elizabeth City, / Each and every one / Loaded with a gun") and reflects on the event as follows:

> Getting too befriended,
> As so often, ended
> Any melancholy
> Götterdämmerung
> That I might have sung.

So that whatever song got sung, then or later, would be something other than a death knell, would be delivered in a less sincerely full-throated way—a way which might even make a line out of a single resplendent word like "Götterdämmerung," then just for fun have it rhyme with the end word of the next line. As is usual with Frost, the fun lies in how the poet, years later, guesses at himself way back then. He might have taken a flight "into the sublime," even anticipating the Wright brothers, so says the poem; instead he remained to grow old, to write about himself when young by constructing a romantic image of that self, then hedging it round with befriending and unromantic duck-hunters.

In other words, Frost did not succeed in carrying out the reckless choice of doing away with himself in the Dismal Swamp, but stayed around rather to tell, and to stimulate others to tell, a fabulous story about the event. Yet at no moment, it seems, did he prudentially decide to save rather than lose himself: there were just, suddenly, those lights, those human voices toward which he may have moved with as much disappointment as relief, but with surely some curiosity. The beauty of his discovery—or his being discovered—is that it wasn't part of his stated plan; it wasn't exactly what he chose, but—again in the words of "The Trial by Existence"—what he "somehow chose."

It involved a lucky correspondence between the individual mind—"too poor- / Spirited to care," in words from "Kitty Hawk"—brought suddenly into a society larger than that mind, impervious to or insensible of its deep distress, or of the song that might have been sung out of it. Still, that society was not unresponsive to the young man alone, lost and out of sorts with fate; indeed, through the offices of one Ed Dozier, owner of what he called "the best goddam bar in Elizabeth City," Frost was offered slabs of fried chicken, ham, potato salad, and liquor if he wanted it. Looking ahead to his move across the ocean eighteen years later, we see that England was to prove equally hospitable.

———————

Frost and his family arrived in London in September of 1912 and a week later settled themselves in Beaconsfield, Buckinghamshire, one of the "'ome counties" as it was attractively advertised to him through the speech of a one-time policeman turned columnist whom Frost sought out in the offices of a newspaper called *T. P.'s Weekly*. From the beginning he approached the land of the *Golden Treasury* in the proper poetical spirit. The finding of a place to live—"The Bungalow," a small house in Beaconsfield—satisfied at least initially his literary expectations of what it would be like to live in the mother country, not too far from "where Milton finished Paradise Lost on the one hand and a mile or two of where Grey lies buried on the other and within as many rods as furlongs of the house where Chesterton tries truth to see if it won't prove as true upside down as it does right side up." He noted England's lack of drinking fountains and converted it to a piece of wit in a letter home to his young friend and teaching colleague Sidney Cox; with reference to the alcoholic poet, Ernest Dowson, Frost wondered what Dowson would say today "if he were alive as he might have been with a little less liquor and a little more of the water one sees so seldom over here—never a drop of it in lunch rooms, railroad stations, or streets." In fact the water came plentifully, but from nature rather than fountains, and to celebrate this fact Frost enclosed a poem "In England," perhaps the first he had written since his arrival. It began as follows:

> Alone in rain I sat today
> On top of a gate beside the way,
> And a bird came near with muted bill

And a watery breeze kept blowing chill
From over the hill behind me.

I could not tell what in me stirred
To hill and gate and rain and bird,
Till lifting hair and bathing brow
The watery breeze came fresher now
From over the hill to remind me.

What he was reminded of, as the rest of the poem makes out, is that England is surrounded by a sea from which the breezes blow always fresh (and often wet) and that English country life "is never far from sailing."

This graceful, neatly-turned poem, never published during his lifetime, was probably written too recently to have been considered for the book of poems he had by this time already contracted to publish, but of which he made no mention in the letter to Cox that included the new poem. More than a month before however, in response to the request of a Maine book collector, Thomas Mosher, who wanted to publish Frost's poem "Reluctance" and offered to do his first book in the Lyric Garland Series of poets, he confessed that the book was already spoken for. As he explained to Mosher, "I came here to write rather than to publish." But if that were the case, a funny thing had rather quickly happened along the way. Only a month after having settled in Beaconsfield, Frost had gone to London with the manuscript of a book brought over from America "in the bottom of my trunk," as if he were afraid of finding it too easily. He told Mosher that he had three other books of poetry "somewhere near completion" (one of which bore the curious title "Melanism," another, "The Sense of Wrong") and that he had planned to work on them at his leisure: "But see how little I knew myself. Wholly on impulse one day I took my MS. of A Boy's Will to London and left it with the publisher . . ." Notable here once again is the insistence that the trip to David Nutt, who was to be his first publisher, was not thought out in advance and had nothing to do with firm-willed persistent resolve. He had "expected" that anything he published would be through an American publisher, and now look what has happened! A boy's will is the wind's will: just as something in him "stirred" when the watery English breeze blew on him, or as something just somehow happened in the Dismal Swamp which lifted him back into rather than out of life, so a poetic career was begun, just like that.

On Christmas day of 1912 he wrote to Ernest Silver, his employer

of the previous year at Plymouth Normal School who had persuaded
Frost to move there from Derry and to teach English and Psychology.
Silver was sceptical about Frost's plans to move to England, not wanting, naturally, to lose so powerful a teacher as he had proven himself
to be. Failing to dissuade Frost from his plan, Silver asked him to
write home a "literary letter," as evidence that England was doing
something important for the ex-teacher. It may have been a combination of that demand, plus Christmas high spirits, which set Frost off
on the sort of letter he was to write more and more frequently: high-
spirited, almost manically so; playful to the point of giddiness, with
every sentence working hard to bring off a turn of wit, to create some
further, new, verbal effect. He tells Silver to reread *Lorna Doone* for
verification of the impression that English winters are real ones, then
says it's all false, a piece of "unrealism" which ignores the fact that
the winters consist really of mud. There follows a fantasy about a
farmer and his horse in which the latter, stuck in the mud and having
to be dug out, is compared in its docile patience to the English lower
classes. Then Frost announces that

> We have had ice (a few times) on the rain barrel if that constitutes
> winter. And one morning early in December the papers were out with
> scare heads like this:

### ENGLAND IN THE GRIP OF FROST

> I accept the omen, says I, I accept the omen. Better so than that Frost
> should be in the grip of England.

There follows some further information about meteorological conditions, then an apology for not being "literary" enough in the letter—
only after which he reveals the news of his about to be published book
of poems.

Admittedly Ernest Silver had asked for it, and one hopes he appreciated the literary effort he received. But it would be wrong to write
off the letter as hyperbole, the "mere" joking of harmless exaggeration. For the "omen" here, in Frost's treatment of it, is not something
to be passively noticed and respectfully saluted. If by strenuous verbal
means, a silly "scare" headline can be converted into personal literary
capital by a young man's will—a young man who is approaching his
thirty-ninth birthday—then who knows what wonders may follow? He
was later to insist, more than once, that he was never more serious
than when humorous, and this Christmas day annunciation, made but

a few months after he had landed in the new old world, should be understood as emanating from a source of power and insistent belief.

Either through advice from the same London ex-policeman who had helped him find a house, or through researches of his own, Frost approached the firm of David Nutt with the manuscript of *A Boy's Will* and in October, 1912, Mrs. Nutt (the daughter-in-law of David Nutt) accepted it for publication. By the following April when the book appeared and was "going the rounds" as Frost put it, he had himself gone some rounds in the London literary world, having attended (in particular) the opening of Harold Monro's Poetry Bookshop in Bloomsbury the previous January. There, in a story he took great delight in repeating, he made the acquaintance of a young and now pretty much forgotten poet, F. S. Flint. As Frost tells it, Flint spotted him as an American, and when asked how he knew replied, "Shoes." Flint told Frost about Ezra Pound, offering to speak to Pound about his fellow countryman, then later sent Frost a copy of his book of poems *In the Net of the Stars*. Obviously flattered and anticipating more good things to come, Frost wrote back to Flint, admitted to being "childishly happy" at having met such a company of poets at the bookshop opening, and took a sharp backward glance at the land whence he had come: "I have lived for the most part in villages where it were better that a millstone were hanged about your neck than that you should own yourself a minor poet."

He went on at length to praise Flint's poetry, which, as the title of his book might suggest, was rich in inexpressible yearnings. (Flint later embraced more austere, Imagist principles of composition.) The influence of early Yeats is everywhere felt in the book (though Flint seldom achieves a Yeatsian music). A typical poem, "The Heart's Hunger," begins

> I have the heart of the sea within me, the
> strange wild heart of the sea,
>
> The restless longing, the song and sob and wash of
> the wave;
> And I desire and desire not the silence and calm of
> the grave
> To quench and still the passion and storm of soul
> in me.

Frost told Flint that he loved the "beautiful sad figure of the title," and he praised the metaphorical character of the poetry: "If that is

old-fashioned make the most of it." His only demur came when he
hinted that, in Flint's poetry "the image finds its word and phrase . . .
more nearly than it finds its cadence"—a telling though politely delivered criticism. In describing the letter, Thompson uses words like
"flattering," "cultivate," and "ingratiated," suggesting that it should
be understood as among the earliest of many Frost would write
devoted to buttering up people who might have literary influence. But
it could also, more generously, be seen as the sincere response of an
aspiring poet to someone who had been nice to him—a fellow practitioner whose work, whatever its merits, authentically rang with
accents of the poetical.

The critical observation that Flint's work was perhaps lacking in
"cadence" points up, by comparison, the flowing cadences to be found
in *A Boy's Will* as well as Frost's emerging preoccupation with the
"sound of sense." But at the end of the letter to Flint he alluded rather
to the myth around which his own book was organized:

> When the life of the streets perplexed me a long time ago I attempted
> to find an answer to it for myself by going literally into the wilderness,
> where I was so lost to friends and everyone that not five people crossed
> my threshold in as many years.

He added, with more than a touch of the sardonic, that "I came back
to do my day's work in its day none the wiser." What must Flint have
made of this talk about "going literally into the wilderness"? Frost
was referring in fact to the six years beginning in 1900 when he and
his family moved to the farm near Derry, and ending (though he still
lived on the farm) with his appointment as a full-time teacher at Pinkerton Academy, in town. This "wilderness" period would vary in
length, as time went on. In the 1930s he told his first biographer, Robert Newdick, that for an eight-year period he and Elinor had no call-
ers, and Newdick ends the period with the birth and death two days
later in 1909 of his sixth child, Elinor Bettina. One of the notes in
Newdick's fragment of a biography (it had barely been begun when
Newdick died) says, unbelievably, that Frost was "Out twice after
eight o'clock in eight years"—though perhaps "Out" meant something more than a walk about the property before bed. But even if the
facts do not live up to this myth of wilderness isolation (there *were*
visitors to the farm, and at one point in 1903 Frost took his family to
live in New York City for a month) there is no reason to question the
depth of his aloneness during those years, even as his wife was bearing

him four children. Nor should we underestimate his eagerness to capitalize on the literary possibilities of such isolation by seeing it in retrospect as enriching, soul-extending solitude.

So when he wrote to Susan Hayes Ward in May, 1913 with reference to poems from his first book, that "The beauty of such things as Into My Own, My November Guest, A Dream Pang, Mowing, and Reluctance is that they are not just post-graduate work, nor post-postgraduate work, but the unforced expression of a life I was forced to live," he managed gracefully to turn his past life, which centrally included the years on the Derry farm, into a fortunate passage. The slighting reference to "post-graduate work" is appropriate, coming from someone who had not graduated from college; but he was probably distinguishing his book from those of other younger and more callow writers whose art he thought owed less to the life—however "forced"—out of which his own had come and from which it had sprung free and "unforced" in the poems. Although the proof of this assertion can only lie in *A Boy's Will* itself, it is worth a moment's pause to ask how those poems are "the unforced expression of a life [Frost] was forced to live." It would be too simple to see him as a sentimental victim of circumstance, "forced" by his domestic situation, or by the lack of response on others' part to his poetry, or by the cruel circumstances, familiar to many, of having to earn a living. When he reviewed *A Boy's Will,* Pound contributed to the sentimental myth by announcing—indeed because Frost had untruthfully told him it was so—that the poet had been disinherited by his grandfather and uncle and left to rot in poverty because of his poetic ambitions (Pound quoted the little poem "In Neglect" by way of proof). The story was nonsense, in fact was shockingly at variance with his grandfather's purchase of the Derry farm for Frost; but it neatly fitted Pound's melodramatic tale about the neglected poet driven to England because unappreciated at home, and in telling it to him, Frost had himself fallen prey to melodrama or worse. Understood in such terms, "the unforced expression of a life I was forced to live" sounds close to a self-serving whine, something Frost usually tried hard to avoid.

A better way to understand it is to agree that any life is "forced" in a number of connected senses, driving the green root through the flower of Dylan Thomas's poem, or in Frost's own "West-Running Brook" instancing "the universal cataract of death / That spends to nothingness . . ." What poems do is not so much "express life" as express *from* life; not put into words the tribulations of "the stream of everything that runs away" but make their way in words out of the stream and into another time and space. Again, in the language of "West-Running Brook," they are a "sending up," a "backward motion," and they may be described by innumerable metaphors, many of which Frost delighted to invent over the years. But it is certain he knew that "forced" and "unforced" expression existed in the most intimate of relations, and that he believed he had demonstrated this relation in the poems from his first book.

A final sense of what "unforced expression" means in relation to the book of poems Frost had venturesomely submitted for publication, may be gathered from a sonnet he wrote sometime during his time at Derry and never published, though he sent it along with others to Susan Hayes Ward. (No copy of this poem was found in his papers after his death, but Thompson recalls him quoting the whole poem from memory about a year before he died.) "Despair" is a sonnet which begins with the annunciation that "I am like a dead diver after all's / Done, still held fast in the weeds' snare below," then paints through its octave a lurid picture of his condition, then proceeds to its close:

> I am like a dead diver in this place.
> I was alive here too one desperate space,
> And near prayer in the one whom I invoked.
> I tore the muscles from my limbs and choked.
> My sudden struggle may have dragged down some
> White lily from the air—and now the fishes come.

Why didn't Frost include "Despair" in *A Boy's Will?* Thompson wants us to see it, along with "The Subverted Flower" (not published until after his wife's death) and another never-published poem, "Flower Guidance," as expressions of "puritanical guilt," importantly connected to Frost's feelings about his own unworthiness in relation to his mother and his wife. But, aside from some formal awkwardness in the technique, the real trouble with "Despair" is that nothing happens in it; the "I" remains the same "dead diver" at the end of the poem as he was in its first line—with the addition of a "white lily" he may have dragged down with him. Accordingly its tone is monotonous, portentous, humorless throughout. The emotional situation it creates is like the one Matthew Arnold had spoken of a few decades previously in the 1853 preface to his poems where he described the condition of certain works as one from which "no poetical enjoyment can be derived": "those in which the suffering finds no vent in action; in which a continuous state of mental distress is prolonged, unrelieved by incident, hope, or resistance; in which there is everything to be endured, nothing to be done." Arnold used the adjectives "morbid" and "monotonous" to characterize these painful (but not tragic) situations, whether in life or in art. "Despair" found no place in *A Boy's Will* therefore because its expression was "forced," its protagonist too passively in the grip of circumstances from the contemplation of which no "poetical enjoyment" could be derived. And poetical enjoyment was the quality Frost sought above all others, whether in life or in literature.

By contrast to "Despair," the poems in *A Boy's Will* were arranged in a sequence which would show that the grip of circumstance had met its match in the grip of Frost. He wrote his American friend John Bartlett, early in 1913, that the book "comes pretty near being the story of five years of my life. In the first poem I went away from people (and college); in the one called A Tuft of Flowers I came back to them actually as well as verbally for I wrote that poem to get my job at Pinkerton . . ." The phrase "pretty near" is an appropriately vague measure of the way such a collection of lyrics—mainly of elegiac, wistful remembrance and regret at the passing of seasons and places—could add up to a "story" of anything. More specifically, to think of the opening poem from the collection, "Into My Own," as somehow about going away from "college," is to indulge a pleasant fiction which only the poet and not the poem itself could suggest to us. Yet Frost's effort to give a shape to the whole collection and provide a sort of beginning, a development through various moods, then a turning into new resolution, is of a piece with his attempts to provide such temporal shapes within individual poems. Probably he was more successful in the smaller than in the larger unit; he must at any rate have been uncertain enough whether the poems as arranged in his first book would actually tell a "story" of progress from solitude to society, that he decided to call in aids by writing brief explanatory glosses to each poem in the manner of Yeats in *The Wind Among the Reeds*. These glosses would serve as indicators of what "the youth"—the protagonist of *A Boy's Will*—is musing about. "The youth is persuaded that he will be rather more than less himself for having forsworn the world"; "He is in love with being misunderstood"; "He resolves to become intelligible, at least to himself, since there is no help else"— so run typical ones. In their wistful utterance these glosses (removed in later collections of his poetry) provided both a teasingly suggestive and gracefully reticent atmosphere in which to read the poems. If any possibly unfriendly critic were moved to cry sentimentality or self-indulgence at a poet luxuriating in moods of sadness, Frost could point to the glosses as proof that the poet was not wholly taken in by them, had kept an ironic distance from his youthful hero.

In its original state, *A Boy's Will* consisted of thirty-two poems divided into three parts, the majority of poems contained in part one. The movement in them from private reverie to less visionary, more social impulses (in "Mowing," for example, "He takes up life simply with the small tasks"), coincides with the changing of the season into spring and summer; while in the final poems from part three, which include "October" and "Reluctance," the autumnal mood comes back, if "with a difference," as one of the glosses puts it. The sense of transience in *A Boy's Will,* that things grow older and pass from view, is exceptionally strong: "He sees days slipping from him that were the best for what they were" ("October"); "There are things that can never be the same" ("My Butterfly"). But not a great deal should be made of any presumed progress from subjective dreaminess to social responsibility, either in the glosses or in the poems themselves. What remains constant is the quality of sadness, the wistful recognition of things passing and of it being beyond our power to do anything about arresting them. "My November Guest" is the third poem in the book; "October" the third from its end; but they are each delicate instances of a temperament embodied in an individual way of using language, an identifiable manner. It is this manner which remains attractive, rather than any "story" the poems in sequence might be thought to tell. Indeed even with the aid of the glosses, no reviewer of the book felt there was a progression in it worth mentioning. And today, even if the poems from *A Boy's Will* are read as a volume, they are likely to be done so without the glosses, without the division into parts, and without three of the poems that were originally included.

Although the first notices of *A Boy's Will* were brief and verging on the perfunctory, later ones were more substantial and encouraging, especially the two written by Flint and Pound. Flint had suggested that Frost meet Pound, and the two men did come together, though after some delay. Frost's account of it, as set down in his *Paris Review* interview decades later, was that Pound sent him a postcard with the information, "At home, sometimes," an invitation Frost felt was less than warm. Eventually he took it upon himself to visit Pound in his flat in Church Walk, Kensington, at which visit Pound asked him for a copy of the new book. Frost tells us he had not yet seen a copy himself, so he and Pound proceeded to walk to Frost's publisher (though David Nutt's offices were miles away, in Bloomsbury) and procure a copy of *A Boy's Will*. They then, presumably, walked back to Pound's flat, and Frost sat quietly while Pound read through the volume, pausing once to laugh out loud at something. Frost later said he knew "where that was in the book, what Pound would laugh at." The meeting ended with Pound saying "You don't mind our liking this," to which Frost replied "No, go ahead and like it": Pound then dismissed him, announcing "You better run along home, I'm going to review it." "And I never touched it," says Frost. "I went home without my book and he kept it. I'd barely seen it in his hands."

As one can see from even this abbreviated version of the meeting, Frost has managed to transform whatever really happened into a humorous, fabulous version that feels too good to be true. But the important fact was that Pound followed up on his threat to review it, and not once but twice, first for the *New Freewoman* (later the *Egoist*) in England, then for *Poetry* in America. In looking at all the reviews of *A Boy's Will*, particularly Pound's (about which Frost had decidedly mixed feelings), one notes their stress on the poems' simplicity. A two-sentence notice in the *Times Literary Supplement* said that the poet was "not afraid to voice the simplest of his thoughts and fancies," while Flint singled out "simplicity of utterance" as the truest mark of Frost's book—"a simplicity that proceeds from a candid heart." The anonymous reviewer in the *Academy* liked *A Boy's Will* because it was "simple," while Pound used the word to point at what he felt was a relative absence of simile and metaphor: "He is for the most part as simple as the lines I have quoted in opening ["I had withdrawn in forest, and my song / Was swallowed up in leaves," from "A Dream Pang"] or as in the poem of mowing." For Pound, this simplicity was a measure of Frost's sincerity, his freedom from "sham and affectation." We read him, Pound said, for his "homely" tone. Underneath various "infelicities" and some "rawness"—which he did not go so far as to specify—the book had the "tang of the New Hampshire woods." In the eyes of Pound and of others, then, Frost had come from over the seas bringing a welcome sincerity and directness, a simplicity of heart and tone and sentiment, to an English poetry which all too often (so the assumption seemed to be, certainly behind Pound's review) showed artifice and therefore insincerity.

Another praiser of *A Boy's Will* as superior to the usual American product was Yeats, to one of whose "evenings" Frost had been taken by Pound. Elinor Frost reported that Yeats called it "the best poetry written in America for a long time," although she wished that he had said so in print. Even if one wonders how carefully Yeats kept up with American poetry, or thinks Pound's wholesale condemnation of it must have overstated the case, a brief look through the first *Oxford Book of American Verse,* edited by Bliss Carman in 1927, is a depressing experience. Admittedly Bliss Carman's taste was old-fashioned (he included a single, tiny poem by Pound, none by T. S. Eliot, Hart Crane, Wallace Stevens or William Carlos Williams), but by any standards the bulk of the book, stretching from Whitman to Frost, is a wasteland marked all too infrequently by isolated talents like Emily Dickinson and E. A. Robinson. Even with tolerant, disinterested, historical spectacles on it is difficult to hear much besides uplift and ever more uplift, a monotony of elevated tone, and reverence for Poetry and The Poetical. Richard Hovey was speaking about his country in the concluding stanza of his "Unmanifest Destiny"—

> I do not know beneath what sky
> Nor on what seas shall be thy fate;
> I only know it shall be high,
> I only know it shall be great . . .

—and such a strutting dignity (which as Dr. Johnson remarked about Gray's odes "is tall by walking on tip-toe") is present everywhere in the *Oxford Book.* As an alternative to the "high" and the "great," to the elevated sentiments and diction characterizing most of the poems, there is the broad humor of a James Whitcomb Riley or a Eugene Field. Or there are exercises in dialect by Thomas Nelson Page and John Hay; or historical tales by Edmund Clarence Stedman; or there is the single fine illumination of William Vaughn Moody's "Gloucester Moors." But it is an especially sharp surprise to come upon Frost in this context and hear the distinctiveness of the voice which was heard first in *A Boy's Will.*

Bliss Carman began his Oxford selection of six Frost poems with "Storm Fear," from that first volume, which opens with wind and snow "working" all night against the house in which a wakeful person proceeds to address his chances against the natural elements:

> I count our strength,
> Two and a child,
> Those of us not asleep subdued to mark
> How the cold creeps as the fire dies at length—
> How drifts are piled,
> Dooryard and road ungraded,
> Till even the comforting barn grows far away,
> And my heart owns a doubt
> Whether 'tis in us to arise with day
> And save ourselves unaided.

These are the last ten lines of one of the poems that readers of *A Boy's Will,* including Pound, might naturally have thought of as simple: there are only two words of more than two syllables in the whole of it, while the feeling of helplessness and fear is an easily available one. Indeed, the named circumstances of "Storm Fear" are as familiar, even as comforting, as the barn used to be until the snow made it seem far away. But almost immediately one is struck by how the disposition of words and line lengths and rhymes is not simple at all, is certainly much more complicated than what passed for "technique" in most of the writers from the 1927 *Oxford Book of American Verse.* It is the expressive use of materials which makes the overall pace of the poem so interesting and satisfying; for example the way the short line "Two and a child" *looks* like not much protection when compared with "How the cold creeps and the fire dies at length," a line which takes as long to say as it did to feel the creeping cold and dying fire. The rhymes create continuity and suppleness of movement by never quite coming when you expect them; by having the last word of "Those of us not asleep subdued to mark" rhyme with the ends of lines much earlier in the poem; by having the key word "doubt" in the third from final line go all the way back to an early line, "Come out! Come out!"; by deferring over the course of five lines the unobvious rhyming pair of "ungraded" and "unaided." There is also an effect, for which "simplicity" will hardly do as a name, gained by the use of the surprising "subdued," placed as it is quite daringly after "asleep," and in its refined way naming a state of acute yet feeble awareness.

Subtlety of rhythm and movement goes along here with subtlety of rhyme, the attempt not to do the expected, not take the obvious way out. And it goes with the subtlety of feeling introduced by the word "subdued" or in the nice gesture by which the barn is called "comforting" even as it "grows far away" in the isolating storm. As with so many of Frost's poems, "Storm Fear" moves at its end a little beyond the particular isolation felt by the husband or the wife, there with the child, worked on by a natural process into a worried "doubt" about "Whether 'tis in us to arise with day / And save ourselves unaided." It is not just that they may need to be plowed out, but that the situation inspires a tremor of metaphysical worry, no more nor less than that, as real but perhaps as transient as the storm itself. What one might call the movement from the level of sense to that of spirit is unpretentious and unobtrusive, but from the very beginning it lay at the heart of Frost's enterprise as a poet and there was nothing the least bit "simple" about it.

In a journal Frost kept in England, he noted that "A poem would be no good that hadn't doors. I wouldn't leave them open though." This remark may suggest the sense in which these early poems (and many later ones as well) both invite us to imagine a life or lives behind them, yet exclude us from intimate knowledge of that life, those lives. Since the poet is male, it is natural to assume (as with "Storm Fear") that they are spoken by a man, a husband, a concerned being, and that the "you" who appears in many of these poems is a woman, a wife, the object of his concern. Yet this "you" is never specifically identified as a wife, nor even as a woman, nor does she ever speak. Nor are there any references to children in the poems from *A Boy's Will*. So it is rash to think we can move securely from words on the page to assuming that they attach to or are "about" Elinor and Robert Frost; yet at the same time the temptation to do so is real—the poems have the ring (some more than others) of a personal revelation, a sharing with us of an intimate relationship. In dealing both with these early poems and with Frost's life generally, my inclination is to be wary of trying to open the doors he left shut; for the poems in *A Boy's Will* both are, and are *not* about the life Frost as a man lived with his wife Elinor during their married years on the farm at Derry.

Consider "A Dream Pang," which of all the poems in his first book could most fairly be called one with "doors" that tempt us to open them:

> I had withdrawn in forest, and my song
> Was swallowed up in leaves that blew alway;

And to the forest edge you came one day
(This was my dream) and looked and pondered long,
But did not enter, though the wish was strong:
You shook your pensive head as who should say,
"I dare not—too far in his footsteps stray—
He must seek me would he undo the wrong."

Not far, but near, I stood and saw it all,
Behind low boughs the trees let down outside;
And the sweet pang it cost me not to call
And tell you that I saw does still abide.
But 'tis not true that thus I dwelt aloof,
For the wood wakes, and you are here for proof.

"A Dream Pang" recalls the opening poem in *A Boy's Will,* "Into My Own," where the youth indulges a dream-wish about how he should steal away into the dark trees, if those trees became sufficiently dreamlike to accommodate him, and were "stretched away unto the edge of doom." In a sentimental though charming fantasy, he imagines how he would never turn back but would also be pursued by the friends or loved ones who missed him, and that they would not only find him, but find him unchanged "from him they knew— / Only more sure of all I thought was true." In "A Dream Pang" too, the youth has "withdrawn in forest" (Frost rather awkwardly and parenthetically emphasizes that it was a dream) to the edge of which the "you" comes but goes no farther. Hidden in the forest, he watches her, imagining her to be reproaching him for some "wrong" he has committed, vowing to make him seek her out should he wish to make restitution. But he remains silent, meanwhile suffering a "sweet pang." Then with a wave of the magic wand, and in the final couplet, everything turns out happily, the woods (and his withdrawal into them) disappear ("wakes") and the "you" is now "here" instead of someplace outside.

For all its mawkish apologies (the "sweet pang" and the complacent final couplet), a more interesting psychology is at work here than in "Into My Own," and one could make out a case that in "A Dream Pang" Frost explores his guilty feelings about withdrawal into self— the egotistical sublime which seems necessary for the writing of poetry, to the neglect of that "objective" world of work, domestic and marital responsibility, and love for another person. Yet "explore" is probably too solemn a word for the easy, casual way in which the poem gracefully reverses its situation and comes out all right. We may be tempted to talk about "guilt," either as felt by the poem's speaker, or by Frost in his life with Elinor; but since "A Dream Pang" simply indicates it as "the wrong," there is precious little to go on for anyone who would attempt to open doors. "I wouldn't leave them open," he said, and he didn't. The poem is a teasing invitation to investigate behavior; but it will not follow through on that invitation, for its "simplicity" is really a refusal of serious moral probing on the part of the lyric poet. Rather, its grace consists in the traditional, Elizabethan transformation of the mutabilities of life into the eternal shape of a sonnet, in which the "proof" that the loved one is "here" is manifested by the fourteen lines of poetry. Frost has not often been admired for the wit in his first book, but it is surely there in "A Dream Pang."

It is there, too, at various moments in other poems, so as to make emphasis on the simplicity of *A Boy's Will* too simple an emphasis. In fact one of Frost's most attractive characteristics as a poet is the surprise and elegance of his "turns," of the sort which are visible, for example, in "My November Guest." This poem tells of how "My Sorrow"—the speaker's tragic muse, or perhaps the "you" personified— loves "the bare, the withered tree" and thinks that such an appreciation is hers only:

> The beauties she so truly sees,
> She thinks I have no eye for these,
> And vexes me for reason why.

Then comes the turn, indeed two or three turns:

> Not yesterday I learned to know
> The love of bare November days
> Before the coming of the snow,
> But it were vain to tell her so,
> And they are better for her praise.

The first line of this poem's final stanza is given power by the understated, subdued idiom of "Not yesterday I learned to know," slightly old-fashioned and poetical in its ring. The voice speaks as if it could a tale unfold, but won't, and we are asked to trust the depth of its love for both the bare November days and for the way in which his "sorrow" loves them. Coming across such a turn one understands what Pound meant in his review when he said that we read *A Boy's Will* for its "tone," even though "homely" and "pleasing" (the adjectives he used to describe it) don't touch the muted elegance Frost so often shows.

Such elegance is there at midpoint in "October," whose gloss reads, "He sees days slipping from him that were the best for what they were"—in itself a model of not claiming too much. As with "A Prayer in Spring" or "Rose Pogonias," the speaker in "October" asks nature to suspend or retard the ways in which days pass, seasons change, flowers wither. A completely traditional theme, therefore all the more difficult to make fresh and appealing:

> O hushed October morning mild,
> Thy leaves have ripened to the fall;
> Tomorrow's wind, if it be wild,
> Should waste them all.
> The crows above the forest call;
> Tomorrow they may form and go.
> Oh hushed October morning mild,
> Begin the hours of this day slow.
> Make the day seem to us less brief.
> Hearts not averse to being beguiled,
> Beguile us in the way you know.

We are willing to be beguiled by the October morning, our hearts are open, and the rest of the poem acts out the imagined retard ("Slow, slow") which the poet will conduct. But what makes "October" so successful at its own beguilement of a reader, is the phrasing in which the plea is made:

> Hearts not averse to being beguiled,
> Beguile us in the way you know.

The implied "we have" before "Hearts" is the better for its being merely implied, not written out; while beginning the line with "Hearts" gives it the authority of compression and makes for an emphasis on the unobvious word "averse." To be not averse to being beguiled, is to be at heart a poet and to know just how much to say, or not say, to the October morning which is supplicated. Though not a couplet, these two lines have the memorable force and beauty of one of Marvell's out of "To His Coy Mistress" or "The Garden," while the sequence of "being beguiled, / Beguile" does exactly to us, in its sound, what it asks to have done.

There are other kinds of surprises, of sudden wit and graceful turning of words into original combinations, which show an accent more studiedly artful than Poundian phrases like "utter sincerity" or "tang of the New Hampshire woods" suggest. This way with words is playfully and ingeniously combined with a wonderful sense of cadence and (in the acute words of one reviewer) "an ear for silences." By their very artfulness, the poems make it that much more difficult to pretend they are the utterances of a "youth" who is supposed to be feeling this or thinking that, or who is being led through a series of poetic experiences by which he moves from isolation to society. Instead, we are conscious of the literary artist and his skill.

But as the title of this chapter suggests, my intent is to claim that in Frost's first book of poems, as in selected, representative moments from his life, there is an aspiration toward freedom, play, toward guessing at oneself rather than knowing once and for all. One of the anthologized favorites from *A Boy's Will,* "The Tuft of Flowers," is instructive for what it reveals about how a poem can change in significance, in "meaning," depending on the circumstances of the poet's changing life. In his editor's, E. C. Lathem's, copy of the book there is a note by Frost which places it as written "After a summer job in Salem [Windham?] N.H. This was submitted as a theme in English A at Harvard." Frost began to attend Harvard as a special student in the fall of 1897. His English instructor was a man whom he found less than congenial and who did not like "The Tuft of Flowers" when it was submitted to him as part of Frost's work in the course. Nothing more is heard about the poem for nine years, when Frost decided he would cease being a farmer and teach school instead, perhaps at Pinkerton Academy in Derry. On the suggestion of a Congregational minister in Lawrence, he was put in touch with another Congregational minister in Derry, also a trustee of the academy, who suggested that he read some of his poems before the Men's League of the church. Extremely nervous at such a prospect, Frost asked the minister, Charles Merriam, if he would be willing to introduce him by reading one of his poems. The poem he gave Merriam to read (and which was well-received by the audience, some of them teachers at Pinkerton) was "The Tuft of Flowers."

Seven years later, from England in 1913, he wrote home to Bartlett in the letter about *A Boy's Will* mentioned earlier, saying that he had gone away "from people and (college); then in the one called A Tuft of Flowers I came back to them actually as well as verbally for I wrote that poem to get my job in Pinkerton as little Tommy Tucker sang for his supper, and Brer Merriam read it for me at a Men's League Banquet in Derry Village because I was too timid to read it myself." If he had already submitted the poem to his Harvard instructor, he could scarcely have written it nine years later in order to get a job. But that matters less than the way he continued to alter the poem's significance to meet the needs of his career at a given moment. By the time *North of Boston* was published in 1914, "The Tuft of Flowers," along with "Mowing," is mentioned in an epigraph to the volume as containing a "theme" which the new book will pick up and develop. A final twist to the poem's changing identity comes with a remark Frost made many years later at a public reading at Amherst College in 1957, where, before he read the poem aloud, he said that it was about "exhibitionism"—that it was "against the idea that you write poetry just to show yourself off."

It is of course amusing to note that the poem which late in his life came to be against exhibitionism was one which on at least two occasions he had used with varying degrees of success to show himself off. Furthermore, in speaking about the poem at the 1957 reading, Frost chose to emphasize not its final utterance about how "Men work together ... / Whether they work together or apart," or about how "fellowship" (which the original gloss for the poem said it was about) is dependent on something more spiritually wide-ranging than physical proximity. Instead he singled out as crucial lines the following:

> The mower in the dew had loved them thus,
> By leaving them to flourish, not for us,
>
> Nor yet to draw one thought of ours to him,
> But from sheer morning gladness at the brim.

In this sense the poem was against exhibitionism, against believing that the mower had left the flowers or the poet had written his poem, "for us," with the intention of drawing our thoughts to him. The poem says rather that the act was done from something else, "from sheer morning gladness at the brim." How does the youth in "The Tuft of Flowers," and how does Frost in his later comment on the poem, come to know this truth?

Here we touch on as deep a conviction as is to be found in the life or the poetry; for the importance of this insistence on a "free" action, unmotivated by reasons of prudence or foresight or sentimental feeling, is not a message peculiar to "The Tuft of Flowers" but something Frost believed centrally about his own life. What was his real intention in heading into the Dismal Swamp in 1894, or in going to and then away from Dartmouth and Harvard Colleges, or in becoming a farmer, then a teacher, then a man on the loose headed for England with a book away down at the bottom of his trunk? Frost's effort was always to imagine, and to help others imagine, that these things were done somehow for themselves, from "sheer" something or other, be it morning gladness, or sadness, or whatever the impulse. To know, or believe, or passionately insist that something is done "from sheer morning gladness at the brim" is to make a metaphor, to say one thing while meaning another, to see one thing in terms of another (as he was later to put it). So it would not be too ingenious to argue that "The Tuft of Flowers" brought Frost back to the world of other people, as it brings the youth in the poem back, by confirming him in his imaginative vocation: by helping him believe that one writes poems, or makes beautiful things, or spares flowers from the scythe's stroke, just and only because it is a beautiful thing to do.

"The Tuft of Flowers" is explicit about the way in which things suddenly take a turn, in this case—and as is usually the case in Frost's poems—for the better. At the poem's opening, the youth appears "to turn the grass" after the mower has left it to dry. He views the "leveled scene," listens and looks for the mower, hears and sees nothing. He is alone as all men must be alone, he tells himself, "Whether they work together or apart." At which point the butterfly enters, sensitively imagined by the youth to be

> Seeking with memories grown dim o'er night
> Some resting flower of yesterday's delight.

The youth thinks of unanswerable questions and "would have turned to toss the grass to dry; / But he turned first . . ." What the butterfly turns his attention to is the tuft of flowers spared by the mower. From preparing to turn the grass, to the butterfly's natural "turning" in his flight, to the spiritual, poetic turn which the youth experiences—courtesy of the poet's artful turning of phrases and lines—the poem asks us to believe that things do come together in wonderful and surprising ways. They overturn our generalizations, our attempts to make the world behave as we say it should. And to have the finished poem interpreted by its author as both a symbolic and a real "turning" in his life outside the page, shows how strong was Frost's will that there be a correspondence, Wordsworthian in its dimension, between the individual mind and the world.

That "fit" is more compactly and effortlessly expressed in "Mowing," the best poem in *A Boy's Will* and surely the one in which not a line, a word could be altered. Frost recognized its specialness, writing to Sidney Cox in 1914 that he guessed there was no doubt it was the best poem in the book, while saying elsewhere that in it he had come so near to what he wanted to get that he almost despaired of coming any nearer. Invariably he put "Mowing" in lists of his favorite poems from the volume (lists which also included "Reluctance" and "My November Guest"). Compared with it, "The Tuft of Flowers" sounds old-fashioned, even a trifle labored and poetical. But there is harmony between the two poems in that they both reject exhibitionism: the pretense that a sensitive mind, like a youth's or a poet's, can commune with nature in privileged ways; the pretense that nature is sensitive and ready to satisfy the dreams and questions of a boy's will. Such a "fit" would be too easy, and by insisting that the flowers were spared by the mower "not for us,/Nor yet to draw one thought of ours to him," "The Tuft of Flowers" rejects cozy ways of making oneself at home in the universe. "Mowing" develops the insistence along similar lines, in response to the mower's question about his scythe, "What was it it whispered?" Why would anyone ask such a question? Only because the poem's opening lines announce that

> There was never a sound beside the wood but one,
> And that was my long scythe whispering to the ground.

If scythes "whisper," says the poetical mower to himself, they must be whispering *something,* must have something to tell just me and nobody else in the silent world around. He speculates that

> Perhaps it was something about the heat of the sun,
> Something, perhaps, about the lack of sound—

yet whatever the scythe whispered "It was no dream of the gift of idle hours, / Or easy gold at the hand of fay or elf":

> Anything more than the truth would have seemed too weak
> To the earnest love that laid the swale in rows,
> Not without feeble-pointed spikes of flowers
> (Pale orchises), and scared a bright green snake.
> The fact is the sweetest dream that labor knows.
> My long scythe whispered and left the hay to make.

Of the many fascinating effects in these lines, there is none more so than the connection, or lack of it, between the final two. Remembering how the poem began, with the mower wondering what the scythe was whispering—as if a secret confidence were being bestowed upon his ears only—one is momentarily tempted to hear the secret revealed in the next-to-last line: "The fact is the sweetest dream that labor knows—so *that's* what my scythe was whispering!" But of course the period at the end of that line doesn't permit us to make it the object of the scythe's whispering; it is, instead, an imaginative utterance, more intricate, less obviously metaphorical than was "sheer morning gladness at the brim," but equally as sheer and equally untranslatable into meaning less gnomic than itself. For the more one repeats this strong truth ("Anything more than the truth would have seemed too weak") the stranger and more purely aural it becomes, as fact, dream, labor, and knowing, all merge in the perfect oneness of a satisfying rhythm. After all, "Mowing" is about an achieved rhythm, a moment of clarity and fullness and even happiness, so it is important that, in the poem's final line, all the scythe "whispers" is the regular repetition of its own sound.

A passage from the introduction to Emerson's *Nature* may or may not have been in Frost's mind when he wrote "Mowing" and the other poems in *A Boy's Will:*

> Undoubtedly we have no questions to ask which are unanswerable. We must trust the perfection of the creation so far as to believe that whatever curiosity the order of things has awakened in our minds, the order of things can satisfy. Every man's condition is a solution in hieroglyphic to those inquiries he would put. He acts it as life, before he apprehends it as truth.

Frost does not often share this bold confident talk about trusting the order of creation to satisfy us; but the priority he gives to acting a "solution" as life before apprehending it as truth, seems another way to talk about his insistence, in "The Tuft of Flowers" and "Mowing" especially, on the truth of "fact" which is really the truth of metaphor, uttered most trenchantly by poets. And uttered not so as to be exhibitionistic, but to give the sense rather—as with Frost speculating about why he went to England in the first place—that one is always guessing at oneself and that poetry is the harvest of such guesswork. My effort at the outset of this book has been to suggest, with a few examples, how similar principles and motives may be observed in his life and in his poems. To write a literary life of Frost is to enter the realm of guesswork.

# II

## *Life Before England*

The life of a supremely interesting poet inevitably has a claim on our attention out of proportion to any particular explanatory use we can make of it. To note, as in the previous chapter, that Frost was rejected by Elinor White and subsequently set out into the Dismal Swamp, or that he spent years in relative isolation on the Derry farm, may not help us to understand a whit better any single poem from *A Boy's Will,* nor the volume as a whole. Yet our sense of Frost is enlarged, we are led to imagine him in different ways, we know more of him than we did before; that knowledge should make us less, rather than more willing to explain him too quickly, to assume that we "understand" him. One place where such understanding temptingly offers itself is in the matter of the child's relationship with his parents.

To say the least, Frost had an interesting childhood and was never in any danger of ignoring either his father or his mother. The former, William P. Frost, Jr., was by all accounts a man of passionate impulse, a Phi Beta Kappa graduate of Harvard whose diversionary activities included cards, alcohol, and sex. William Frost decided to make his career in journalism and to do it by heading across the country to San Francisco. But first he had to raise the necessary funds by working for a year as principal of a small academy in Lewistown, Pennsylvania. There he met Isabelle Moodie, a teacher at the school and the woman he was to marry. By February of 1873, William Frost had proposed to her in a letter which takes as an epigraph a stanza from a poem about the necessity of putting things to "the touch / To win or lose it all." He assured her that he was aware of possible reasons which might be urged against their union: their disparity in ages (she was six years older); the fact that she was a Christian and he was not (although he insisted that with him "It is rather lack of belief than unbelief"); and her expressed opinion that she would never marry. Against these possible drawbacks he offered her himself as a "support in the rugged ways of life," and as giving her a love "than which, if more worthy, I am sure you can at least find none more devoted." He ended by insisting that this was a turning point in his life: "A person of my character cannot transfer his love at will. What is yours now is yours for life. You cannot reject it. You can only refuse to reciprocate it. Whatever your answer may be, you can lose nothing, but I—I—*everything*, I know; then, you will think well before you reply." It is a fine theatrical letter, and she thought well enough of it to accept him.

Twelve years later he died of consumption, his attempts at both journalism and politics less than successful, although for nine years he was city editor on the San Francisco *Post*. His efforts as a campaigner for the presidential race of Samuel Tilden and his service as a delegate to the 1880 Democratic convention which nominated Winfield Scott Hancock, led to no effective political career on his own part. As for his domestic affairs, they were, not surprisingly, unable to live up to the early idealism professed in his letter of proposal to Isabelle Moodie. After Robert Frost was born in 1874, just over a year after the marriage, his father slipped back into the dissipated habits he had acquired in college. He refused to take any interest in, and was indeed actively hostile to, the Swedenborgian religion in which Isabelle believed, and when he made an unsuccessful run for Tax Collector in 1884 stayed away from home for days after the outcome, then appeared, drunk and furious that (he said) the minister of the Swedenborgian church had voted against him. In 1952, Frost was asked by an interviewer what he remembered most about his father, and replied that "He was a long-distance swimmer, he could walk over six miles an hour, he was very ambitious in politics, and he was cut off in everything too young. I remember him swimming out San Francisco Bay out of sight till he appeared again on a buoy or something out there in the evening." Recalling that he spent much time with his father rather than going to school, Frost spoke of riding with him in a horse and buggy, campaigning with him in the year "that elected Grover Cleveland for the first time." The son's retrospectively mild and balanced judgment of his father was that "He was severe but informal. He was a regular fourth-of-July American."

William Frost's reckless impulsiveness, as in his penchant for long-distance swimming, combined badly with a love of whiskey and with the pulmonary complaint that ended his life at thirty-four. There is little in the portrait that cannot be assimilated to familiar stories of domineering fathers and sensitive long-suffering mothers: William Frost was preoccupied, severe, and short-tempered, a man who believed in discipline and in wasting no words; a man of action rather than contemplation; a drinker, with the conviction that the real things of this world were public ones—the wars of politics and journalism. His inadequacies, his failure even, were—like Walter Morel's in D. H. Lawrence's *Sons and Lovers*—brought out more sharply through their juxtaposition with a woman surely as spiritual, idealistic, and powerful in her moral goodness as could be imagined. Years later one of Isabelle Frost's students recalled her presence as a teacher at the private school she ran in Salem, New Hampshire: "Her frame was angular, rather loosely knit, the type of figure we associate in a man with Lincoln . . . the large broad brow of the thinker; the eyes deepset, somewhat cavernous . . . There was that disregard of the trivialities of dress, characteristic of those whose minds are concerned with other values, with matters of the spirit. That spirit, lofty, kindly, sympathetic, and understanding, also registered on the mind and heart of the child."

So it must have registered on her son's, and must also—in its forbearance or quiet disapproval of William Frost's vagaries—have provided an affecting image of another Anglo-American archetype: the "fine" woman whose higher values do not meet correspondence in the man she has married. Born in Scotland, Isabelle Moodie came to the United States at age twelve to live with her uncle in Columbus, Ohio. Fond of reading and writing poetry, of singing hymns, her spiritual proclivities were particularly expressed in the conviction, fostered in her by her grandparents, that she possessed powers of second sight. Her devotion to the philosopher-mystic Emanuel Swedenborg also suggests the sense of specialness and the ardor of her religious aspiration. As with Charlotte Stearns Eliot, another gifted, literarily inclined mother of a famous American poet, Isabelle Frost wrote poetry, publishing some of it in a San Francisco newspaper. The longest of her poems is titled "The Artist's Motive," and though not easy to read through with any pleasure, its religiose atmosphere suggests how compelling and perhaps oppressive must have been the effect of her personality:

> Oh! Such a fire doth burn within my soul
> That it must be consumed, did not it give
> Unto the world the light and warmth thereof.

> The scene is a most holy one.
> 'Twas thou, oh Truth, that led my soul
> To lean upon the heart of God
> Which burst in sacred light before mine eyes
> Whence flowed to me the spark divine
> Upon my canvas here.

It proceeds in this vein, occasionally reminding us of Browning's "Andrea del Sarto" ("Ah, but a man's reach should exceed his grasp / Or what's a heaven for?") though without any of its complexities of syntax or shades of feeling.

Remarking on his mother's religious activities at the First New Jerusalem Church, Frost remarked to Louis Mertins in 1947 that all the church-going may have had a bad effect on him, since he'd done so much of it when young that he felt no call to continue it in later life; he added that his father was truly a "counteracting influence," notable for a "voluble profanity" (Mertins's words) which made Isabelle Frost extremely unhappy. Again, conflict between the high-toned Christian woman and the pagan whiskey-drinker is a staple of American domestic myth. As it concerned the young and the older Robert Frost, it may suggest that there is more than one way to talk about the situation. Thompson's biography gave us the brutal father, and the overcompensatory, too indulgent mother; with the result, Thompson says, that "In later life Frost was never quite able to understand or fully to resolve some of his inner conflicts, which seemed to mirror the opposed attitudes of his parents," and in which "self-inflicted punishments were mixed with self-gratification." Does this analysis really tell us much about Frost as distinguished from other artists, or from the rest of us with our unresolved inner conflicts in which are mirrored opposed attitudes traceable to our parents? Is there anyone who would not, in the psychological atmosphere surrounding us like the weather, admit to the gratifications involved in punishing oneself?

Frost may have become a more interesting man, and a richer poet, not in spite but because of his "unresolved inner conflicts"; that is, the opposing principles of his father and mother helped to generate a more troubled and complex person than might have been the case had they lived in blissful unity and brought him up under a common code of values. If, as is very likely, William Frost's unpredictable and sometimes brutal behavior with his children (Robert's sister Jeanie was born in 1876) influenced Isabelle Frost toward excesses of solicitude and protectiveness, who can say with surety how much mother love is too much for a poet to bear? When Mrs. Frost sent her son, at age five, to a private kindergarten conducted by a lady named Madame Zitska, the boy developed a stomach ache and never returned after the first day. This ache recurred numbers of times, as Frost was enrolled in different public school grades where he never lasted long, always returning to the tutorship of his mother. Such indulgence and capitulation were doubtless dangerous for the son's social and personal health; yet the mother was a very literary woman, convinced of her own and of Frost's specialness, so perhaps his homemade education was a more stimulating thing to have undergone than the routines of a public grade school.

At any rate he was wholly educated at home for the remainder of his years in San Francisco. An important part of that education was connected to the peculiar spiritual power his mother believed she possessed—that of "second sight" in which future occurrences or things at some distance from us are perceived as if they were actually present. One of Mrs. Frost's favorite authors was the "visionary" Scottish novelist George Macdonald, and her interest in fairy tales, in the merging and confusion of dream and reality, showed itself in the stories she read to her children. The young Frost developed his own capacities in this direction, particularly when, as a child, he began to hear voices which penetrated his consciousness even after he put his hands over his ears. "Sometimes he would hear whole sentences. At other times the words were so indistinct that he understood only such meanings as were conveyed through the tones of the voice," says Thompson, and adds that at other times the voice or voices would repeat something said earlier, but in a different tone so as to create an ironic, mocking effect. Frost communicated this information to his official biographer not only a great many years after the childhood happening, but many years after he had, from England, written home a number of letters to his friend Bartlett and others in which he developed a theory of tones of speech, heard independently from any particular words, as if through a curtain or from behind a closed door. Later on we will take up the theory of poetry Frost worked out in these terms; for now it is enough to note the relation between the boy who was visited by voices, sometimes mocking ones, and the man who wrote to Bartlett that "the sentence sound often says more than the words. It may even as in irony convey a meaning opposite to the words." Of course it may also be possible that in his later recallings of childhood memories, Frost read back into them a formulation with respect to the writing of poetry which he arrived at only later.

At age two he had been taken on a visit to his paternal grandparents in New England where Isabelle Frost, temporarily separated from her husband, gave birth to Jeanie. When William Frost died in 1885 the mother moved her two children once again across the continent to Lawrence, Massachusetts, and took up residence with her husband's parents in a stiff and highly regulated atmosphere. During that summer it was suggested that mother and children live with an uncle in the country across the New Hampshire border near Amherst; later, after Mrs. Frost tried to find a teaching position in a district school there, the family went back to live in Lawrence with another uncle. Finally, in the winter of 1886, she succeeded in finding a position in a district school in Salem, New Hampshire. These abrupt changes of residence were frequent, and I mention an example of them only to avoid recounting them henceforth, along with descriptions of the various boarding houses or apartments in which they lived.

Of more interest is the way Frost began to exhibit some daring and persistence in the reading he initiated. A letter from Elinor Frost written to Edna Romig in 1935 says this about what he was reading in his early teens:

> He never read [all the way through] a book of any kind to himself before his 14th year. His mother read aloud constantly. Poe and Shakespeare, George McDonald [Macdonald]—old fashioned romances, like the Romance of Dollard. In his 14th year he read Jane Porter's Scottish Chiefs, Mysterious Island by Jules Verne, Tom Browne's School Days, first volume of Scott's Tales of a Grandfather, Prescott's Conquest of Mexico, and also The Last of the Mohicans, and Deerslayer . . . Read first poetry in 15th year . . . In that year he read a little of Shelley and Keats in Christmas gift books. Almost learned all of Poe by heart. Keats and Arnold only other poets he ever found he knew as large a proportion of.

Notable for their absence from Elinor's list, and from her husband's memory which provided her with it, are any references to Emerson or Wordsworth or William Cullen Bryant, poets whom his mother had read to him and who (particularly Emerson) were of importance to him later. Longfellow, from whom he took the title for his first book of poems, would also become a favorite. In other words, the reading that shaped him was pretty thoroughly nineteenth century in its origin. At age twenty, writing to Susan Hayes Ward and thrilled that she had agreed to publish his "My Butterfly," he told her that his favorite poems were Keats's "Hyperion," Shelley's "Prometheus Unbound," Tennyson's "Morte d'Arthur," and Browning's "Saul"—

"all of them about the giants." Clearly poems and poets shifted about in their importance to him, but they shared a common origin in the Anglo-American romantic tradition.

His program of academic study at the high school was the "preparatory" or classical one, and his grades in Latin, History, and Algebra were spectacular. (Later on he took pride in announcing that he hadn't taken English courses since they were perceived to be less distinctive and less severe.) But his "unofficial" course of independent reading in literature and romance was at least as important as the official certified record. Prescott's *Conquest of Mexico,* one of the books cited by Elinor in her letter about Frost as a youthful reader, was the source of his first published poem in the Lawrence High School *Bulletin,* April 1890. He had been taken with the section from Prescott's *Conquest* describing the death of Montezuma and the retreat of the Spaniards by night from Tenochtitlan. Frost's sympathies may well have been with the Aztecs, as Thompson says; but how could he have read Prescott attentively and not felt more than a pang for Cortes, "dismounted from his jaded steed" and "gazing mournfully on the broken files as they passed before him . . . their shattered mail and tattered garments dripping with the salt ooze, showing through the rents many a bruise and ghastly wound; their bright arms soiled, their proud crests and banner gone . . ." In Prescott's history, Cortes—"as he looked wistfully on their thinned and disordered ranks, sought in vain for many a familiar face"—proceeds to weep. In Frost's poem, "La Noche Triste," "he" views the retreat and is lifted up by the young poet in the following lines:

> Surrounded and alone he sits,
> Upon his faithful steed;
> Here Alvarado clears a space,
> But none might share the deed—
>
> For darkness of that murky night
> Hides deeds of brightest fame,
> Which in the ages yet to come,
> Would light the hero's name.

It is the heroic, elegiac tone which especially thrilled the young Frost, who found that—along with writers like Prescott—he, too, could command it.

Toward the end of his life, in his fascinating *Paris Review* interview with Richard Poirier, Frost responded to a question about how poets write by speaking of that far distant day when "La Noche Triste" came to him:

> Very first one I wrote I was walking home from school and I began to make it—a March day—and I was making it all afternoon and making it so I was late at my grandmother's for dinner. I finished it, but it burned right up, just burned right up you know. And what started that? What burned it?

Rather than answer his own question directly, he scoffed at the popular notion that one could only write poetry out of agony, through suffering: "How could I, how could anyone have a good time with what cost me too much agony, how could they? What did I want to communicate but what a *hell* of a good time I had writing it?" Seventy years after the event something had stuck from that March day when he began to "make" the early poem, and it had nothing to do with suffering. The "burn[ing] right up" was its own reward; the "hell of a good time" he had doing it was really, more than any ideas about Cortes and the Aztecs, bloodshed or history, what he cared about conveying. It is, we may suppose, like the feeling he experienced when his high school teacher began to write William Collins's "How Sleep the Brave" on the blackboard:

> How sleep the brave, who sink to rest
> By all their country's wishes blest!

Collins doesn't want to know *how* they sleep, but is exclaiming how they *do* sleep, giving them voice and celebration in his elegiac song. Marvelously enough, the young student reading it—and who knows, even poor Collins himself writing it—felt more exhilarated than depressed, had something even that might be termed "a hell of a good time" doing it.

---

His experience as a wage-earner was at least as varied as his reading. No poet in this century has written more poems involving more different kinds of work than Frost, and a glance at some of the jobs he held between his first summer in New England in 1885 (when he picked berries at his uncle's New Hampshire farm) and the fall of 1892 (when he left for his brief academic stay at Dartmouth) shows their variety. He was a shoe-worker in a Salem factory and a leatherworker in the backyard establishment of a man with whom the Frosts were boarding; he did farm work, particularly mowing and haying; he was employed as a hired man on a farm and as general errand and messenger boy at a Maine coastal resort hotel; he worked as a bobbin boy in a woollen mill near Lawrence (hours seven to six, half an hour for lunch, six days a week). Later on there would be journalism, and for more sustained periods chicken-farming and school-teaching. In his words about *A Boy's Will,* this was the life he was "forced" to live, and its "unforced expression" found itself in many of the poems' intimate treatment of concrete physical activities. Perhaps only a man who tried his hand at one job after another, with varying degrees of enthusiasm and success, could have wanted to idealize or refine such activities into large formulations like the key one in "Mowing"—"The fact is the sweetest dream that labor knows"—or the one which ends "Two Tramps in Mud Time":

> Only where love and need are one,
> And the work is play for mortal stakes,
> Is the deed ever really done
> For heaven and the future's sakes.

Only in a poem whose words have the absolute yet elusive character of an "only" or a "really," can work be play-for-mortal-stakes (Frost once said that he wanted to add hyphens between those words, the better to emphasize their connection) rather than the flawed, imperfect series of jobs he struggled along with from one season to the next.

But love and need did become one when he met Elinor Miriam White in the fall of 1891 during his final year at Lawrence High School. Previous to this meeting there is not overmuch evidence in his life of contact with women, aside from his mother. To be sure he wrote at age twelve an engaging sequence of letters to a girl named Sabra Peabody in one of which he professed not to be the captive of one "Lida" ("because I like you twice as much as I do her") and assured Sabra he was no person for halfway measures: "There are not many girls I like but when I like them I fall dead in love with them." There is also a more shadowy encounter (recounted by Thompson in full detail, as if he were there looking on) which occurred during the summer of 1891 when Frost was working on a farm in Windham, New Hampshire, near Canobie Lake, and bunking with some other young men whose general air of sexual knowingness was pronounced. One of them boasted of his romantic successes with a young stenographer who was a guest at the place. Frost disliked these insinuations and defended what seemed to him the girl's high moral character, so he was dared by the other to take the stenographer for a row down the lake and see what would happen. This he did, was pleased with her lively conversation, then dismayed when she suggested they go ashore at a covert and pause awhile. He declined, rowed her back home, then lay in his bunk fearing he had been marked for a scapegoat, that perhaps the girl was pregnant. Eventually he quit the job.

If we imagine the tone in which Frost recounted this story many years later, it is hard to believe that he didn't regard it with a shade more humorous understanding than comes through in the anecdote as written up by Thompson. To understand it as an instance of his idealistic notions about female purity being severely put to the test is certainly reasonable, but does not invite excessive surprise or headshaking at the spectacle of a young man of seventeen, in 1891, being nervous or bewildered about sexual matters, or being offended by the bluntness of his less sensitive peers. At any rate, his meeting with Elinor White and their subsequent courtship was conducted on a more poetic plane, indeed was conducted largely *through* poetry. They met fortuitously, having been thrown together by a class seating arrangement, and when Elinor submitted poems to the school *Bulletin,* of which Frost was the editor, he published two of them under the name "Orlinn." Later on in life, Elinor Frost was eager to avoid any reference to those poems (one was titled "An Infinite Longing") either out of the wish to avoid competing with her fiercely competitive husband or simply out of embarrassment at the poetical efforts of youth. Frost's first gift to her was a copy of the poems of Edward Rowland Sill, whom he had recently discovered and whose work gave expression to the moral idealism he and Elinor found compelling. And they also discovered and admired Emily Dickinson, a poet who—perhaps because they were both associated with Amherst—Frost grew less fond of in later life.

A young man with a strong mother who has loved him is likely to respond to similar qualities in the woman with whom he falls in love; at least one is impressed by similarities of moral principle between Isabelle Frost and Elinor White. Remembering the former's passion for tales of romance, a literature in which nature was touched or transfigured by myth and legend, it seems fitting that Elinor should have published an essay in the *Bulletin* titled "A Phase in Novel Writing" which was in fact a defense of idealism in fiction, as opposed to realism. (She would have approved of Hawthorne's preface to *The*

*Blithedale Romance* where he pleads for "license" for the romance writer.) Having recently read *The Rise of Silas Lapham,* she compared Howells unfavorably with Walter Scott in respect to how deeply their heroines touch us, and made the following defense of the art which meant most to her:

> Whatever may be the resources of the various forms of art, the end is the same, they stir the heart and mind, to idealize the commonplace events of our life, and to subordinate the literal to some high conception of the imagination.

This idealization should happen in fiction as well as in poetry, she argued. Surely Isabelle Frost would have approved of these sentiments, and though they were probably conventional enough, especially among female readers a hundred years ago, Elinor White's sentences carry conviction, but also—in the comparison she makes between *Ivanhoe* and Howells's novel—a spirited literary intelligence.

Not surprisingly, Frost and Elinor were the two graduates with the highest averages, and though Elinor had taken the "English" program, which was presumably somewhat easier than the Classical-Preparatory one, they shared the office of co-valedictorian, with Frost giving the valedictory speech. Its striking title, "A Monument to After-thought Unveiled," suggests the intense, unembarrassed expressiveness with which he attempted to persuade his listeners to take a poetic view of things. Two sentences ring out with particular strength: "Not in the strife of action, is the leader made, nor in the face of crisis, but when all is over, when the mind is swift with keen regret, in the long after-thought. The after-thought of one action is the forethought of the next." What makes the sentences revealing of the young valedictorian's spirit is the characterization of a spiritual state after the battle, after the crisis, "when the mind is swift with keen regret." Regret for what might have been, but was not done? Inevitable sadness at the passing of any great moment in human life? In any case, it was the sort of "pang" which for Frost, then and later on, made poetry.

The long afterthought which occupied Frost and Elinor White during their post-graduation summer concerned the nature of their relationship, the kind of "forethought" of the next moment they were to take. She was about to enroll in St. Lawrence University; he, after being convinced by a teacher at Lawrence High School that scholarship help would be available, had decided to go to Dartmouth, a deci-

Robert Lee Frost, 1892.          Elinor Miriam White, 1892.

sion also encouraged by his grandmother Frost whose own son, she
thought, had fallen into bad habits at Harvard. In that summer of
1892, the lovers exchanged gold rings in a secret ceremony which took
on force from their mutual reading of Shelley's poetry, particularly of
"Epipsychidion." Thompson argues that the doctrines of liberty, openness, unconstraint, and disregard for institutions—marital or otherwise—which Shelley inculcated were important in overcoming what
he calls a "serious flaw" in their courtship "caused by Rob's impor-
tunate love-making," to which Elinor responded with shyness and reticence until released by Shelley. This attempt to explain or rationalize
intimate matters between the two leads Thompson also, in a footnote,
to invoke a poem Frost did not publish until 1942, after Elinor's death,
although it was written early enough to have been included in *A Boy's
Will.* "The Subverted Flower" is about an encounter between a young
man and a "girl" which ends in shame, sexual disgust and fear as she
flees from "the dog or what it was" her lover has been turned into
through her eyes. The man has attributed the power of sexual passion
to the flower—"And he lashed his open palm / With the tender-

headed flower"—and in an extraordinarily directly presented scene, the narrator looks with a wisdom unavailable to the participants:

> A girl could only see
> That a flower had marred a man,
> But what she could not see
> Was that the flower might be
> Other than base and fetid:
> That the flower had done but part,
> And what the flower began
> Her own too meager heart
> Had terribly completed.

This shocking poem (a "nightmare" version of the Frost–Elinor relationship suggests Richard Poirier) probably offers about as many "doors" as any poem Frost ever wrote. He himself made gestures toward opening them, when he would speak at public readings, rather coyly, about how its subject was "coldness" or "frigidity" in women. He did not read the poem aloud. Yet by its bizarre nature, part nightmare, part fairy tale, part dream-vision or fabulous imagining, "The Subverted Flower" proves resistant to any attempt simply to impose it as "proof" of the true relation between the young lovers back there in New England in 1892. To so impose it is to indulge in a procedure which, in the poem's language, too "terribly"—that is too easily— completes things by explaining too much, by simplifying the living individualities of two people whose privacy should be honored:

> And oh, for one so young
> The bitter words she spit
> Like some tenacious bit
> That will not leave the tongue.
> She plucked her lips for it,
> And still the horror clung.
> Her mother wiped the foam
> From her chin, picked up her comb,
> And drew her backward home.

The poem's world is both more terrible, and more simplified, than was the only partially composed life, the life outside poetry, which Frost and Elinor White found themselves making up as they went along.

The intensity of Frost's feelings about Elinor, the bad grace with which he "accepted" her going off to St. Lawrence rather than marrying him, or at least staying at home and waiting for him, throws into contrasting relief his extremely short term as a freshman at Dartmouth. In a letter written in 1915, he responded to a query put him by the then librarian of the college about his stay there twenty-two years previously. The nub of Frost's response is contained in his admission that by 1892 he was "getting past the point where I could show any great interest in any task not self-imposed." He told his correspondent that at Dartmouth he wrote a good deal, walked in the surrounding country, and participated with some pleasure in those odd rituals college boys participated in. "Much of what I enjoyed at Dartmouth was acting like an Indian in a college founded for Indians," he confessed, and went on to describe class rushes and how convenient it was to live in a room whose door opened outward, thus making it difficult for "marauding sophomore to force from the outside" (though he adds, "I had to force it once myself from the inside when I was nailed and screwed in"). This is a parody of high adventure, a mock-heroic version of college days, of which the other side was his loneliness and bitterness at being separated from the woman he loved who was living a life independent of his.

He seems to have had no significant experience of either a teacher or a course at Dartmouth, but the literary influence encountered there which lasted him all his life was Francis Turner Palgrave's famous anthology of English lyric poems, *The Golden Treasury*. Palgrave's anthology helped to extend his taste back from the nineteenth century into earlier English poetry, while the anthologist's tone toward the function and purpose of poetry was high enough to satisfy Frost's own exalted beliefs: "Like the fabled fountain of the Azores, but with a more various power, the magic of this Art can confer on each period of life its appropriate blessing: on early years Experience, on maturity Calm, on age, Youthfulness." Palgrave also hazarded a definition of "lyrical" poetry (his subtitle was "Of the Best Songs & Lyrical Poems in the English Language") as "turn[ing] on some single thought, feeling, or situation." Narrative and descriptive poems were excluded from *The Golden Treasury*, while "humorous" poetry was considered as foreign to the anthology's nature—as were forms like blank verse and the heroic couplet. One can see, then, the influence of Palgrave's principles on *A Boy's Will* which contains scarcely any of blank verse, few heroic couplets, and no "humorous" poetry—although the five-line "In Neglect," at which Pound is supposed to have chuckled, might possibly be excepted. But beyond its influence on *A Boy's Will,* Palgrave's anthology was to figure for Frost throughout his life as something magically synonymous with the very idea of Poetry. As mentioned earlier, one of his ways of "guessing" at why he went to England was that he went because it was the land of *The Golden Treasury*—the book thus taking on a symbolic importance even greater than his original pleasure and excitement in it.

His abrupt departure from Dartmouth was also to take on symbolic importance as another instance of impulsive "running away" from oppressive institutions—of his growing lack of interest in "any task not self-imposed." As a motive for flight, it seems as good as other ones which have been suggested: such as that his absence from Elinor was intolerable (but he would also be absent from her back in Lawrence); that his mother was facing extreme disciplinary difficulties at the district school in Methuen where she was currently teaching and where he aimed to take over and restore order; that he was just plain homesick, unhappy at being away from his mother for the first time. His leave-taking of Dartmouth possesses a quaint air of unreality verging on the comic; he and one of his friends holed up in the room with its famous outward-opening door, then proceeded to make merry by eating quantities of Turkish fig paste, while letting off periodic insults at the sophomores. Next morning he left town.

The time between his departure from Dartmouth in the fall of 1892 and his flight to the Dismal Swamp two years later was as erratically spent as at any period in Frost's life. For a few months he taught his mother's class at the Methuen school; more accurately, he subdued the students by engaging whatever corporal means semed effective, once even facing down a boy who pulled a knife on him. Then he lived with Elinor's ailing sister and mother, later to be joined by another married, pregnant sister and by Elinor herself (who was prevailed upon to take time off from college) at a rented homestead in Salem. His efforts to convince her to marry him rather than return to St. Lawrence were unsuccessful. He took a job as a light-trimmer (replacing burnt-out filaments in the arc lamps) in the Arlington Woolen Mill in Lawrence. Here, as at Dartmouth, where he discovered Palgrave's anthology, the experience had an unforeseen benefit. Frost used his non-working moments, which were evidently numerous, to read Shakespeare. The effect of his Shakespearean reading can be seen in the poem "To a Moth Seen in Winter," which when eventually published in 1942 bore the afterthought "Circa 1900" and which, in a somewhat different version, he included in an important Christmas packet of poems he sent to his admirer, Susan Hayes Ward, in 1911. In this poem the man speaks to the plight of a moth:

> And what I pity in you is something human,
> The old incurable untimeliness,
> Only begetter of all ills that are . . .

and bids goodbye to it with the reflection that

> You must be made more simply wise than I
> To know the hand I stretch impulsively
> Across the gulf of well-nigh everything
> May reach to you, but cannot touch your fate.

The strongly enjambed character of this blank verse and its sinewy syntactical flexibility—not to mention the humorous attaching of "Only begetter" to the moth—suggests how much the Shakespearean example was on the mind of the young poet, and foreshadows the wonderfully varied blank-verse cadence he would achieve in such poems as "An Old Man's Winter Night," "Mending Wall," and "Range-Finding."

Finally, in 1894, he quit his job at the Arlington Mill, the last factory employment he was ever to take, and obtained a grade-school teaching position in Salem Depot. He was also bold enough to send a completed poem, "My Butterfly," to the *Independent,* a New York magazine of some reputation, where it was accepted in March, payment fifteen dollars. Invited by Susan Hayes Ward to say something about himself, Frost replied in a touching document, not without misspellings and stiffness of expression ("I read novels in the hope of strengthening my executive faculties") but with a spirit of passionate and artful self-assurance that makes us aware of a formidable character in the making. He told Susan Ward that he had been awaiting such a letter as hers for two years, and had thus far received no useful criticism or intelligent praise. So he owed her thanks unlimited:

> Yet the consideration is hardly due me. Take my word for it that poem exaggerates my ability. You must spare my feelings when you come to read these others, for I haven't the courage to be a disappointment to anyone. Do not think this artifice or excess of modesty, though, for to betray myself utterly, such an one am I that even in my failures I find all the promise I require to justify the astonishing magnitude of my ambition.

These sentences need to be read more than once. What can he mean by claiming that the poem "exaggerates" his ability? That he's really not as good as it suggests? More likely, it is a graceful way of ruefully sending along the other poems—which doubtless won't be up to the mark—while asking her to be gentle, not so as not to hurt his feelings but because he hasn't the courage to be a disappointment to her. Did Miss Ward wonder momentarily whether the young poet was pulling her leg, as he went on to disclaim artifice, then promised to "betray himself utterly" and finally proceeded to reclaim even his poetic "failures"—since they contained enough promise to "justify the astonishing magnitude of my ambition"? When she came to that final phrase she must have felt Frost's claim to be in deep earnest; all the ducking, the tonal elaborateness and complicated gesturing, were really in the service of the powerful naming effected by those last five words.

Ironically enough, Susan Ward and her brother may have liked the poem for reasons or on principles quite different from those Frost would later commit himself to, like the "sound of sense" or the conversational thrust of a voice-tune playing itself against the regular meter of a line. For it would be difficult to find anything more unFrostian in their lush diction and rhyming than the *Collected Poems* of Sidney Lanier, which Susan Ward proceeded to send him. She had probably detected impulses similar to Lanier's in "My Butterfly," and it is possible to see why, if we remember how the poem begins:

> Thine emulous fond flowers are dead, too,
> And the daft sun-assaulter, he
> That frighted thee so oft, is fled or dead:
> Save only me
> (Nor is it sad to thee!)—
> Save only me
> There is none left to mourn thee in the fields.

This is stylistically more contorted and labored than the easeful Frost of the poems to come, and even its next section (which he would later point to as an early revelation of his distinctive quality) lacks ease and sounds highfalutin when the butterfly is described as

> In airy dalliance,
> Precipitate in love,
> Tossed, tangled, whirled and whirled above,
> Like a limp rose-wreath in a fairy dance.

In short, "My Butterfly" has a "poetical" ring about it; one is not surprised that the Congregational minister from Lawrence to whom Susan Ward wrote, urging him to do what he could for the poet, should have liked this poem but seen little in the other ones Frost would show him. Those others sounded too much like talk, rather than of "airy dalliance." And when a poem of his was accepted two years later by the *Independent* ("The Birds Do Thus," not included in his complete poems), it was markedly simpler and more direct than "My Butterfly." If the latter poem reads today like the tour de force of a young man trying perhaps too hard, the important thing was that Frost had made a start, and the solicitude of Susan Hayes Ward deserves gratitude.

The "astonishing magnitude" of Frost's ambition most would see as a healthy, even necessary condition for the aspiring poet to manifest: it is the boy's will at its fiercest. But when the ambition is to impose that will on another person, we draw back in disapproval or regret at such selfish disregard. Elinor White wanted a college education and wanted it enough to hold off from marrying until she completed it. Even at that she was impressively willing to compromise, arranging (by taking extra courses) to complete the four-year course in three years, surely at least in part for the sake of her impatient suitor. But he remained dissatisfied, and his very susceptibility to the pang which makes poetry made him all the more vulnerable to imagining the worst about Elinor's "social life" at St. Lawrence (it appears to have been innocuous enough). As noted previously, things came to a head in the fall of 1894 when he had printed up the small volume of poems, *Twilight,* and carried it all the way to Canton, New York, in order to present it to the woman he loved. Poetry could do anything; it might even transform the ambitions of another into a condition which would exactly mirror one's own. But Elinor did not see it that way; so the only place to go after that, poetically, was somewhere as symbolical of everything lost and final as the Dismal Swamp.

A little more than a year after he returned home to Lawrence from what he described to Susan Ward as wanderings about "Virginia, North Carolina, and Maryland, very liberally and without address"— which had been "desperately absorbing," he and Elinor married. Previous to that event there was at least one further blow-up, with Frost tossing his ring into the fireplace ashes and stalking out of the house, uttering threats of what he might do to himself. This time he got only as far as Boston and Cambridge, looked up a couple of friends, had a drink or so, and purchased a copy of Francis Thompson's melodramatic pursuit poem, "The Hound of Heaven" ("I fled Him, down the nights and down the days; / I fled Him, down the arches of the years; / I fled Him, down the labyrinthine ways / Of my own mind") which although it is about the sinner's attempt to evade the relentless God, could easily enough be converted into a more general sense of hopeless flight. But Elinor relented; by then she had graduated from college and was teaching in a private school—a recent creation of Isabelle Frost's—while Frost himself was also teaching, his brief flings at journalism with some Lawrence newspapers having proven no more lasting than factory work. Prospects for a marriage founded on some sort of financial base looked reasonable.

By then her defenses against the determined persistence of his suit must have been worn down. Much later in his life, after Elinor's death and in talking to his official biographer, Frost would portray himself as ruthless in his dealings with her, as bending her to his will. These accounts of his behavior were doubtless prompted by his despair and guilt after her sudden death in 1938, and they may well have been exaggerated. But his insistence that they marry can be seen also as an analogous instance in his private life, of the determination to be a poet, and not just any minor poet but one who would make a difference, whose early failures even (as he told Susan Ward) were enough to justify in his eyes the magnitude of his ambition.

As the ambition was large, so were the confusions and uncertainties of a young poet, now a young husband with no very fixed income and prospects. But his decision to attend Harvard College as a special student (he was now a young father as well, his son Elliott having been born in 1896) was at the very least a stabilizing move: an acceptance of the university from which his father had graduated; a provisional entertaining of the possibility that an educational institution was not simply something to avoid or run away from; an aspiration to a wider, more intellectual life than a purely homemade one. All these impulses, along with the more practical notion that further study of Greek and Latin would permit him to teach them in high school, made the Harvard special student program attractive. He wrote a letter to the dean of students as late as September of the year (1897) he proposed to enter, pointed out that he had passed the Harvard admissions examination five years previously, that he had been teaching school and tutoring but had neglected his Greek and was unsure whether he could pass a qualifying exam in it. He alluded briefly but wittily to the Dartmouth adventure and why he had received no honorable discharge: "I stood not upon the order of my going but went incontinently." And he winningly forced the issue by telling the Dean that "if I enter college it must be this year or never. It will be hard if a fellow of my age and general intelligence (!) must be debarred from an education for want of technical knowledge representing less than two months work. All I ask is to be admitted." He asked and it was given him; he borrowed tuition money from his grandfather, landed a three-nights-a-week job in North Cambridge as principal of an evening school, and became a student once more.

Twenty years after he entered Harvard, his eldest daughter Lesley began her first and only year at Wellesley College and wrote her father about some difficulties she was having with a Latin teacher whose attitudes toward grades and toward rules were on the monolithic side. Frost wrote back a fierce letter of support (one sentence of which began, referring to the female instructor, "And you tell the Latin bitch . . .") in which he defended the importance of taking what he called a "high" view of literature:

> Never be brought to take a low school view of literature, English French Spanish or Latin. English has come up out of that Egypt that Latin is still in within the years since I studied it (a very little) in college. A great many teachers would be ashamed to teach English now as you say Sheffield was mauling that poem. [Sheffield is a clever cut-and-dried-mind, but he is a survival. Remember he drove me out of Harvard.] English has come to realize that it has a soul to take into consideration . . . I think I should want to take you away from a bad English teacher whether you wanted to stay in college or not. What you suffer in Latin after all is not right at the center of your being.

The reference to having been driven out of Harvard by "Sheffield" (now Lesley's teacher at Wellesley) was a reckless simplification since although he suffered under Alfred Dwight Sheffield's hands as the instructor who did not like "The Tuft of Flowers" and other poems Frost submitted to him, he stayed on at Harvard until the spring of his second year. It is true though that his courses in Latin and English, taken that first year at Harvard, were unmarked by any significant encounter with a teacher (his Greek courses in the *Iliad* and the *Odys-*

*sey* were more congenially taught), but this may have had less to do with the uninspiring character of the Harvard faculty than with his own high and original standards for how literature—Latin or English—should be dealt with in a classroom. "Do it on the highminded," he wrote Lesley, and that "highminded" quality was lacking in the conventional presentations encountered at Harvard. Whether or not he knew it in 1897, he was following in steps Emerson had taken in "The American Scholar," an essay which says nothing about the importance of teachers in conveying "the Mind of the Past," but speaks rather of books: "They are meant for nothing but to inspire." It is not likely that Frost, any more than Emerson, could be satisfied with the earthly vessels and voices through which the books and their inspiration were dampened, rather than the opposite.

So in this same vein it is fitting that the most important influence on him, as he was often later to acknowledge, came from a teacher with whom he never took a course, in whose class he never sat, and whom he may never have laid eyes on: William James. He had planned to study with James in his second year at Harvard, but James, ill, had taken a year's leave. Could it not have been that his absence from the classroom made the sound of his voice, as it emerged from the printed pages of *The Principles of Psychology,* all the more powerful to Frost? The Emersonian "inspiration" of "books" might thus come through unimpeded, and surely inspiration was the word for the effect the *Psychology,* or essays of James's like "The Will to Believe" and "Is Life Worth Living?" had on him.

Consider a moment such as this one from "The Will to Believe" in which James is defending, even insisting upon our right to believe in advance of any demonstrable scientific proof and in the case of a certain class of questions of fact—"questions concerning personal relations, states of mind between one man and another." What about, for example, the whole matter of one person "liking" another?

> Whether you do or not depends, in countless instances, on whether I meet you half-way, am willing to assume that you must like me, and show you trust and expectation. The previous faith on my part in your liking's existence is in such cases what makes your liking come.... How many women's hearts are vanquished by the mere sanguine insistence of some man that they *must* love him! he will not consent to the hypothesis that they cannot. The desire for a certain kind of truth here brings about that special truth's existence ...

It is unnecessary to underline the "kind of truth" that, when he thought about his courtship of Elinor White, this passage would have had for Frost. But more central than anything James told him about heroism or active persistence or the vigorous energy it takes to face the question Is Life Worth Living? was the sound of a living voice so unmistakably heard in sentences from James's essay of that title:

> If this life be not a real fight, in which something is eternally gained for the universe by success, it is not better than a game of private theatricals from which one may withdraw at will. But it *feels* like a real fight,—as if there were something really wild in the universe which we, with all our idealities and faithfulnesses, are needed to redeem; and first of all to redeem our own hearts from atheisms and fears. For such a half-wild, half-saved universe our nature is adapted.

When James collected some of his essays he called them "Essays in Popular Philosophy," and one notes here the urgency and "popular" ring of "But it *feels* like a real fight," with its italicizing of the all-purpose word as added testimony to how strongly James wants us to feel he feels about it. Or there is the reference to a "half-wild, half-saved" universe, a formulation as witty as it is seriously meant. Years later in his short essay "The Figure a Poem Makes," Frost referred to what he called "the second mystery" of "how a poem can have wildness and at the same time a subject that shall be fulfilled." It had to be a "wildness of logic," and it is equivalent to what James is talking about here in "redeeming" the something "really wild" in the universe and in our own hearts. Frost's way of putting it was "Theme alone can steady it down."

Although he never studied with James, he did read the *Principles of Psychology* under the guidance of James's friend and colleague, Hugo Münsterberg. He also took a course with George Santayana, to whose elegantly ironic scepticism he responded with discomfort. In later life when the name was mentioned in his presence, Frost invariably told a story about how Santayana taught that everything was illusion, and that there were two kinds of illusion, true and false. Frost did not seem charmed by such disenchanted distinction-making, and he would doubtless have agreed with James's characterization of Santayana's philosophy as "the perfection of rottenness." It is arguable how much his recoil from Santayana was purely a matter of disagreement with the philosopher's ideas, and how much it was a personal distaste for the manner and tone of voice with which that suave lecturer performed his feats of analysis. Few students at Harvard could have resembled Frost less than Van Wyck Brooks, who entered there in 1904, and has written of how he roamed about Boston with Max Perkins, dining at old-fashioned hotels and attending burlesque houses in Scollay Square. After having fallen under the charm of Santayana's style, Brooks had this to say about the "feline" manner in which he made everything of "the esthetic principle":

> It was only later that I found so much that was unsympathetic in the "cynic and Tory in philosophy," his phrase for himself. This was after I had come to feel the magnanimity of William James, at whom Santayana always looked down his nose, as if in the nature of things the post-Catholic reactionary was better than the post-Protestant believer in mankind. Everything Santayana wrote contained an assumption of superiority when he was merely different, thrown on the defensive because he had been hatched from a Spanish duck's egg in a Yankee barn-fowl's nest.

Though Frost would have put it differently, he shared the sentiment.

It would be difficult to overstate how very special such a very "special student" must have felt during his less than two years at Harvard. Not just when compared with the mobile and sophisticiated Van Wyck Brooks, but with other special students who also became poets—like Edwin Arlington Robinson, who entered in 1891, and Wallace Stevens, who was there at the same time Frost was. For all his "loner" tendencies, Robinson belonged to a literary circle of friends, and Stevens published poems in the *Advocate* while having enough social instincts to join Signet, the undergraduate literary club. By contrast, Frost lived alone during his second year at Harvard, since Elinor, pregnant with their second child, had stayed on in Lawrence. There is no indication that a social life outside the classroom existed for him. As with his stay at Dartmouth, the presence of Isabelle Frost, whether mainly through her own or her son's insistence, asserted itself when Frost commuted to Lawrence one night a week to assist her in private school classes. Eventually, as Elinor's term of pregnancy drew to its close, he decided to withdraw from Harvard without completing his second year courses. At the end of March he announced his intention of so doing to Dean Briggs, who replied with a letter testifying that his dismissal was not only "honorable" but that he had done excellent work and that his loss would be regretted.

Out of his incomplete ventures at Dartmouth and Harvard, Frost later made up a myth about what college or education was, or should be. College was a place where you hung around until you "caught on," or—in another phrase of his—were "toned up." The implication was that once you caught on there was no further need to hang around for purposes of obtaining the degree, or finishing what you started, or justifying the financial investment of whoever sent you there. In the 1950s he often repeated a story about how a student had come to him in distress, dissatisfied with college and wondering what he should do. Frost suggested that he "head out for somewhere" and when the student asked where, Frost—only momentarily at a loss—replied, "Oh . . . Brazil." When the State Department invited him to go to Brazil in 1954 on a cultural mission, there (Frost delightedly claimed) was the young man, having taken the poet at his word! This is a joke about the power of suggestion as wielded by someone who could do anything with words; it is also an example of Frost talking as though really the thing to do, when one is dissatisfied with life at an institution, within a system—academic or otherwise—is to remove oneself from it and go in search of a world elsewhere. It might be argued that he simplified things recklessly ("Go to Brazil") by giving the authority of truth or myth to events in his own life which were in fact fugitive and uncertain. Could he have ever said, as he departed Harvard in March of 1899, that he had now "caught on," and was sufficiently "toned up" to have no further need of the place? But there is no reason to estimate at less than its high value the idea about education—or at least about going to college—which he came to believe. He took the imperfect materials of his own tenure at two places of higher learning, then converted them into a gesture of force and originality. Make of it what you will, he said—look what I did. The example has its point.

Hanging around at college until you catch on is, like going to England so as to live under thatch, a poetic and humorous way of understanding things ("The way of understanding is partly mirth," he wrote in "Not Quite Social"). But the physical facts of the matter were that Frost was suffering a variety of complaints which had manifested themselves the previous summer, when from time to time he had been plagued by pains in his chest and stomach and threatened with the possibility of tuberculosis by a doctor he consulted. During his second year at Harvard the pains recurred, along with general fatigue, and contributed to his decision not to complete the year's work but to return instead to Lawrence. When upon so returning he consulted the doctor again, the diagnosis remained uncertain but the prescription was for outdoor rather than academic work. Farming was an obvious possibility, and Frost who throughout his life was to preserve about farming a wary doubleness, refusing to label himself a serious farmer but insisting that he always had a farm in his backyard, decided that chicken farming might suit the less than absolute nature of his commitment. After consulting a local poultryman who claimed to have had success in the operation and who promised to help the beginner find places to sell his eggs and hens, he located a house and barn in Methuen, constructed his hen coops and went to work. Somewhat over a year later, and with his grandfather's financial assistance, he purchased the farm at Derry where he was to live for the next nine years.

For a time he was assisted on the farm by Carl Burell, hired man and botanizing friend who saw to the milking, gardening, and various other chores. The added presence was useful (though Frost also found it irksome) because of the farmer-poet's irregular habits. Kathleen Morrison has written entertainingly about his lack of affection for cows, his disinclination to milk them when they were supposed to be milked, his lack of finesse in the actual task itself. How many hours a day he put into farming during the Derry years, and how many he saved for writing poems, is unknown. But from the time in 1901 when he sent some poems to Susan Hayes Ward, one of which she accepted ("The Quest of the Orchis," published much later in a volume as "The Quest of the Purple-Fringed") there was a moratorium on further attempts at publishing until 1906, when he sent out and had accepted for publication three poems including "The Tuft of Flowers" and "The Trial by Existence." This moratorium looks to have been a deliberate attempt on his part to husband up some riches, to work over poems and not let them get too far away from him in case he wanted to work on them more. If, as he told his biographer Elizabeth Sergeant, "Mowing" was his first "talk song," it probably was written early in the Derry period (as Thompson suggests) but kept around, since its first published appearance was not until *A Boy's Will.* And if, as he also mentioned to Miss Sergeant, "My November Guest" was written *after* "Mowing," then it is precarious to claim that Frost's early poetry "developed" during the first decade of this century, since for all its wistful and melodic charm, "My November Guest" is much less prosodically and emotionally daring than "Mowing," (the poem in which Frost came so close to what he wanted to get that it almost made him despair of coming closer).

The move to the farm at Derry may have been given further impetus by the sudden death from cholera of the Frosts' three-year-old first child, Elliott. Frost blamed himself for the tragedy, since he had neglected to call the family doctor, mistakenly relying instead on the advice of his mother's doctor who misdiagnosed the disease. The guilt, anger, sadness, and recriminations ensuing from Elliott's death are felt most painfully in "Home Burial," the great poem he was to publish in *North of Boston.* Later that year (in the fall of 1900) Isabelle Frost died of cancer in the sanatorium where, after living for a time with the family, she had been placed. If, as in Wordsworth's line, "Nature never did betray / The heart that loved her," it was finding cruel tests for Frost's heart to undergo. And it was as lavish with its creations as with its destructions: in whatever spirit it may have been of submission or determination or resignation or hopefulness, Elinor Frost proceeded to bear three more children in the years 1902–1905 (Lesley had been born in 1899, just after Frost returned from Harvard). So his talk about "isolation" during the Derry years (of going into the "wilderness," as he said to Flint he had done) neglects to add that there were lots of infants around. Still, isolation in the midst of family turbulence is surely possible; Elliott's death and the successive births of more children ministered to moods of self-exploration in the father, from self-congratulating to self-castigating, fervid to pathological. The prime example of this latter mood is a wild occurrence which has behind it a childhood memory of Lesley's. About age six at the time, she was awakened one winter night by her father and led downstairs where her mother lay weeping at the kitchen table, hands over her face. The child then noticed that the father was brandishing a revolver, pointing it first at Elinor, then at himself, while announcing that Lesley was to take her choice since before morning one of her parents would be dead. Heady stuff for a child at any age, especially in the middle of the night, but what, more than testifying again to the erratic, impulsive, potentially violent character of her father, does it testify to? It is something like the Dismal Swamp revisited; that is, Frost did not pull the trigger, just as he did not succeed in obliterating himself in the ooze and slime. Lesley declined to make the choice and was led back to bed by her mother. The father's gesture had been a melodramatic one of a most terrifying sort. But without seeming to take the event lightly, whose traumatic disruptions were not likely to be forgotten quickly by those involved, it can also be called a very bad piece of theatricality, unworthy, to say the least, of the Frost who prided himself, at least in his written poetry, on making the worthily "reckless choice."

Brandishing a gun in the presence of wife and child is some sort of ultimate playing at a bad game. On the coin's other side, was Frost's most ambitious attempt during the Derry years to write a poem addressed to ultimate moral and religious concerns. Not recognizably "Frostian" (as is, say, "The Tuft of Flowers," also published in 1906), "The Trial by Existence" when it appeared in *A Boy's Will* would be the longest poem in that volume, nine stanzas of double quatrains in octosyllabics and bearing a gloss in which the youth resolves "to know definitely what he thinks about the soul." There is surely some irony in this use of "definitely," but the poem itself conducts matters in a very grand manner, speaking from a vantage point above or beyond mankind, the angels, heaven, even God himself. It is an existentialist poem before the word became fashionable, and it has been read and understood as the culminating early expression of what Frost believed about things. But however ringing and confident he may have tried to sound, the poem ends up rather less "definitely" than is promised by the gloss.

The fable in "The Trial by Existence" is that death is not the end of life but the beginning of another life in which the same struggle will go on. Having served honorably in the last struggle, man is transported to a paradise of "wide fields of asphodel fore'er," where it turns out that a "valor" similar to earthly valor also prevails. Man finds "that the utmost reward / Of daring should be still to dare," as the newly assembled souls are gathered together and instructed by God in the lineaments of the "trial" they are about to enter once more of their own free choice. But God saves the best part for last, which is that it would be comforting if one could retain "The memory that he chose the life":

> "But the pure fate to which you go
>   Admits no memory of choice,
> Or the woe were not earthly woe
>   To which you give the assenting voice."

In the final stanza the poet reflects on the fable to see what can be made of it:

> 'Tis of the essence of life here,
>   Though we choose greatly, still to lack

> The lasting memory at all clear,
>  That life has for us on the wrack
> Nothing but what we somehow chose;
>  Thus are we wholly stripped of pride
> In the pain that has but one close,
>  Bearing it crushed and mystified.

Although the tone in this final stanza has something of a boy scout "uplift" ring to it, the final quatrain's sense is not as loud and clear as that tone may suggest. In his conversations with Mertins, Frost later referred to the poems he wrote during the years at Derry as containing "lots of teasing," and although in its high-minded, aspiring way, "The Trial by Existence" looks as far removed from "teasing" as poetry could be, still the poem's large truth is made difficult to extract and write on the wall. Its final stanza begins with a bold gesture confiding to us what "the essence of life" is, yet it turns out to be an absence rather, since we can't remember "at all clear" that whatever happens to us in the "wrack" of life is "Nothing but what we somehow chose." In the fogginess of that "somehow" lies a real lack of any explanation. In "somehow" choosing any life, we become fatally doomed to it, and the difference between choice and fate seems more verbal than substantive. So the reminder that we somehow chose life has the effect of putting us into a most un-confident situation about ourselves: "stripped of pride," "crushed and mystified," we are the bearers of a pain which will end only in death and then begin all over again.

In other words, rather than making some heartening sense of life, of the soul, of the "obscuration upon earth" that is human experience, "The Trial by Existence" offers pretty cold comfort. The reason for singling it out, biographically speaking, is that it shows the ambiguous use Frost made of William James, the teacher he never had and who was nevertheless a great influence upon him. It is certainly true, as Thompson asserts, that in writing "The Trial by Existence" Frost tried to build into it some of the attitudes and recommendations he had encountered in James's "Will to Believe" essay. Yet compared to Frost's poem, how buoyant and enthusiastic and earnest James sounds, how confident that, finally, it is all worth making a fight for. By contrast, whatever affirmation Frost's poem achieves is darkened and made regretful by the odd sort of consolation offered. Moving from the poem to Frost's life we can read its advice as follows: if life has for you "on the wrack" such things as the death of a first child at an early age, just remember that you "somehow chose" it by committing yourself to the trial by existence. But such knowledge of your "choice" probably won't allow you to sleep any easier. At least with Wallace Stevens's "Sunday Morning" we can console ourselves with the idea that "Death is the mother of beauty," and that recognition of this human fate brings out, as only it can, the perishing loveliness of our surroundings. For Frost, "existence," even after he tells us in this poem that we somehow chose it, is and continues to be a trial, with no incidental pleasures and benefits emphasized.

Of course it is a poem we are speaking of: words about "life," a part of it but also apart from it. In his report of conversations with Frost, Mertins has him saying this about how his Derry neighbors responded to the sort of farmer they took him to be:

> They would see me starting out to work at all hours of the morning—approaching noon, to be more explicit. I always liked to sit up all hours of the night planning some inarticulate crime, going out to work when the spirit moved me, something they shook their heads ominously at, with proper prejudice. They would talk among themselves about my lack of energy ... I was a failure in their eyes from the start—very start.

If the poems contained "lots of teasing," so was this improper behavior a provocation to the honest farmers who looked on, and Frost needed to imagine them looking on in disapproval, having conversations about his lack of energy, pronouncing him a failure. (Who knows what they really *were* doing?) Only in this way, evidently, could the stolen sweets of poetic success, the "planning some inarticulate crime" as he extravagantly put it, be fully savored. Meanwhile, as he was imagining what they said about him, he was also taking in the sound of their voices and beginning to put them in the poems which would later be published in *North of Boston*.

After he returned from England in 1915, Frost briefly cultivated William Stanley Braithwaite, an anthologist and writer for the Boston *Evening Transcript*. At one point he wrote Braithwaite a long letter about his poetic career, speaking of *A Boy's Will* as "an expression of my life for the ten years from eighteen on when I thought I greatly preferred stocks and stones to people." Chronologically this remark would refer to the years 1892–1901, years of varied employment, unfinished educational ventures, courtship and marriage ending more or less with the death of his mother and of his first child. A further paragraph broadens and heightens this account into the mythical:

> I kept farm, so to speak, for nearly ten years, but less as a farmer than as a fugitive from the world that seemed to me to "disallow" me. It was

all instinctive, but I can see now that I went away to save myself and fix myself before I measured my strength against all creation. I was never really out of the world for good and all. I liked people even when I believed I detested them.

However much or little Frost "really" liked people, he went on in this letter, apropos of *North of Boston,* to tell Braithwaite that about ten years previously (which would be in 1905, in the middle of his Derry years—though the chronology is casual and confusing) he made the discovery "in doing The Death of the Hired Man that I was interested in neighbors for more than merely their tones of speech—and always had been. I remember about when I began to suspect myself of liking gossip for its own sake." Listening to the tones of speech of your neighbors, and liking their gossip for its own sake, seem hardly separable activities, but the import of his account suggests that during the years at Derry he ceased to be a "pure" poet and began to get outside himself, into the voices and the lives of others.

His undertaking of teaching at Pinkerton Academy in 1906 asks to be understood in similar terms. Five years of chicken farming, done with a "lack of energy" (as the "real" farmers perceived it) was enough. At about the time he sent "The Trial by Existence" to Susan Hayes Ward, he allowed "The Tuft of Flowers" to be read aloud at the Derry Men's League meeting—an act of reaching out, however uncomfortable it made the author. That poem was subsequently published in the town newspaper, in a possible gesture of the "fellowship" which later, in *A Boy's Will,* the youth supposedly learned about in the poem. "The Trial by Existence" insists, no matter how desperately and woefully, on the necessity of daring, of persistence, of "somehow" choosing and thus being responsible for the life you lead. "The Tuft of Flowers" celebrates the dignity of imaginative labor, a condition which can be fulfilled only when there is the attempt to imagine another person, separate from one but acting in ways recognizable as humanly generous and free-spirited—as doing something just for the pure pleasure of it. In a "Meet the Press" interview from the 1950s, Frost was asked by the fearless Lawrence Spivak whether poetry was an escape from life, and without hesitation came back with "No, it's a way of taking life by the throat." So, as these two published poems in their very different ways presumed to take life by the throat, Frost's decision to commit himself to the routine of regular teaching (he became part-time that spring, full-time in the fall of 1906) was similarly a forcible engagement with life. And the presence of students in

Pinkerton Academy, 1911. Frost as umpire, top right.

the classroom, to whom he had to show that "English" was something
that mattered, never to be taken a "low view" of, was further invitation to the social contract. Someone begins alone with a book in hand,
a poem in the head, and what is heard and seen stimulates that person
to talk to somebody else about it.

Or so it appeared to him in retrospect at a Ford Hall Forum in
1960. Beginning in 1957 Frost appeared yearly at this Boston event,
usually late in the fall, and gave some of his finest performances, elab-
orating a general theme for the evening, reading poems, rambling and
digressing, then circling back to his theme, finally throwing the whole
thing open to questions of any sort. He began the 1960 appearance by
posing himself the question whether he had ever taught anybody anything. He seemed doubtful that he had, but was really interested in
the motive out of which he entered the classroom as a teacher. It was
not, he said, to teach them something, but because he was "seeking
kindred spirits—to comfort them and comfort me." It was the same
motive out of which poetry got written—not to convert anybody, but
to seek companionship. All the great things, he went on to say, are
done for their own sake. It was the same way in teaching as in poetry,

in love as in war (even in war, which he says the generals at least must love for its own sake!). In lines he might have quoted from "The Tuft of Flowers," the mower had spared the flowers "Not for us, / Nor yet to draw one thought of ours to him, / But from sheer morning gladness at the brim." To look at teaching in this way would be, then, to take the imaginative view of it, the "high view."

Even though his teaching at Pinkerton was interrupted early in the spring of 1907 by a serious bout with pneumonia, we can see from the statement of the curriculum in English, which he eventually wrote and which appeared in the Pinkerton catalogue for 1910–11, how ambitious and large-minded was his attempt from the beginning to make something out of the four-year experience of "English." "The general aim of the course in English is twofold: to bring our students under the *influence* of great books, and to teach them the *satisfaction* of superior speech," the statement began. There was nothing particularly startling about these "great books" or their authors included under the "readings" section of each year's plan: Stevenson and Defoe and George Eliot and Hawthorne; Thoreau and Shakespeare and Wordsworth and Kipling—and others. But some of the further explanatory comment is revealing: "Expression in oral reading rather than intelligent comment is made the test of appreciation," runs the description of English I, the first of the four-year courses. In other words, the students would be coached—encouraged and corrected and judged—in the manner of their saying aloud lines from Arnold's "Sohrab and Rustum" or Macaulay's "Horatius at the Bridge." This was probably not the exclusive method of procedure, since under English II it is promised that "Discussion proceeds more and more without the goad of the direct question." But to begin the study of English in high school by reading aloud, by performing rather than commenting on a piece of imaginative writing, by reading aloud a paragraph of George Eliot's writing in *Silas Marner*—rather than being asked questions about Silas's character or the author's use of symbolism—this was and still is a most original way for an English course to be conducted. Decades later Frost's emphasis remains a radical one, honoring in its priority the notion of a speaking voice which in the years to come he would make the cornerstone of his poetics. But also notable is the emphasis put, in the last of the four courses, on rereading selections "remembered with pleasure from previous years." The idea that time could be made, in class, for rereading books and doing it out of nothing more than *pleasure* (a word not often found in course catalogues) is consonant with ideas within the poems he was writing. It is but another instance of doing a thing for its own sake, "from sheer morning gladness at the brim," without regard to its larger significance and without justifying it by saying that it contributes to learning or a disciplined character, or some such social value.

So to "fall under the *influence* of great books," as was the first general aim of this education in English, would be no drearily highminded regime of cultural self-improvement, but an activity that was undetermined in its nature, full of surprises and discoveries, with many confusions and here and there a clarity. As for the program's second aim, to teach students "the *satisfaction* of superior speech," it could, if interpreted narrowly, reduce English teaching to a species of elocution or instruction in correct usage, or at best an aesthetic satisfaction in some learned style, more or less artificial. But in fact, as one can see from the explanations supplied under three headings—Composition, Rhetoric, and Memorizing—it was designed to be much more, since "Composition" meant fifty assigned themes over the first two years, then thirty the last two, "given direction by assignment of subjects." Both subject matter and form would be up for criticism. And though "Rhetoric" is not much filled in (unlike the previous Pinkerton catalogue description in which four books on the subject were required reading), it is promised that there will be "Talks on the subject, what it is (with copious illustrations from the experience of the teacher)." Frost evidently felt confident about his own experience as the main supplier of material. Finally, "memorizing" involved learning twenty poems from Palgrave's anthology the first year, which poems would provide a base for subsequent literary study. Another year it was "twenty poems learned from dictation," or "Lines from Milton."

The satisfaction of superior speech, then, could be felt—and there is no reason to doubt that it was felt more than once—by a reader of Milton who had memorized Comus's speech to the Lady, had managed (in an oral or written rendering) to "get it right," and whose practice in oral reading may have assisted him or her in getting it right, not just as something memorized but as something heard, then sounded correctly. This idea was of a piece with the insistence on reading for pleasure, or (as Frost also emphasized in the 1960 Ford Forum) on the satisfaction that comes merely and purely from repeating a line from a poem correctly: the doing it for its own sake, not even for purposes of training and improving the memory. Surprised as Frost might have been at the time to hear it said, his procedures were in the spirit of education as John Henry Newman had memorably defined it: liberal knowledge was knowledge which has its end in itself, which need not issue in practical or moral fruit. To know the speech from *Comus* for its own sake was to know it liberally.

We can imagine the mixture of respect and animosity with which Frost's fellow teachers at Pinkerton Academy regarded him. Here was a published poet, of as yet undetermined worth, who had moved rapidly from part-time teaching to a position in which he was taking charge of things like the English curriculum, or the student literary paper (for which he acted as an advisor), or the dramatic productions put on by students. These last had, previous to his time, taken the form of a Shakespearean play produced each year. Ingeniously Frost upset the routine by selecting plays from four authors who would illustrate something of the variety of English dramatic composition, and, after the plays were pared down by his own editorial cutting, would provide especially vivid and immediate instances of the "satisfaction of superior speech." Marlowe's *Faustus,* Milton's *Comus,* Sheridan's *The Rivals* (which was advertised rather grandly as the best comedy written since Shakespeare) and two of Yeats's early plays, were those selected. With minimal scenery in use, the actors had to depend on their abilities to put across those dramatic tones of meaning in which Frost was interested.

As is hardly surprising, he invested some of his ego in different sorts of theatrical operations. For example, when "The Trial by Existence" was published near the beginning of his term at Pinkerton, some misprints occurred, one of which was the identification of his place of residence as "Derby" rather than Derry. In a letter to Susan Hayes Ward he joked about the response his colleagues made when his poem "turned up in the school library":

> Its effect was startling. From the moment of its appearance, all the teachers abruptly broke off all but the most diplomatic relations with me. Put to it for a reason, I thought at first that my poem had led them to question my orthodoxy (if not my sanity). Then I thought that a flock of teachers would be more apt to loathe me for misspelling Derry than for grafting Schopenhauer upon Christianity.

But, the Congregational minister had informed him, he was wrong in both cases:

> I had made myself unpopular by the simple act of neglecting to give Pinkerton the credit for harboring the poet that wrote the poem. It was

too funny. But while it lasted and I was still guessing, I was rather miserable.

Lying not very far behind this theatrical foolery is somebody who has, he thinks, been seriously snubbed. As with his farm neighbors in Derry who regarded his activities in that direction, so he imagined, with amusement and derision, the Pinkerton "flock of teachers" who wouldn't be offended by anything the poem really *said* about theology (they weren't oversensitive on such an intellectual level), would very much resent, in their parochialism, the absence of the school's name in the author's credits. It is unlikely that given this beginning to relations with colleagues, the attitude of mutual uneasiness would be eradicated as Frost accomplished further things. And indeed the dramatic productions were broken off abruptly when his attempt to have circulated his reduced version of Ben Jonson's *The Silent Woman* met resistance on the part of another faculty member.

The years spent teaching at Pinkerton were ones in which Frost was on the move in a number of ways. There was first the movement of poems out toward various magazines: local ones like the Derry *News* and Pinkerton *Critic;* ones of larger range like the *Independent,* the *Youth's Companion* and the *New England Magazine.* There was a movement away from the rooted sufficiency of his Derry farm out into more temporary places to live, especially during hay fever season (Frost was a serious sufferer) at farm houses in New Hampshire or camping near Lake Willoughby in Vermont. In 1909 he and his family moved into an apartment in Derry Village. There was also movement within the profession of teaching. Frost was asked by the superintendent of schools for New Hampshire to speak at a convention of English teachers about his methods at Pinkerton; he did so with success, and further talks were scheduled. There was, in 1911, the move beyond Pinkerton, out of Derry and into a one-year teaching position at the Normal School in Plymouth, New Hampshire. This move was instigated by Ernest Silver who had just recently become president of Pinkerton Academy and under whose auspices Frost had written the catalogue statement about English teaching. Silver accepted a job as principal of the New Hampshire State Normal School at Plymouth, a school for young women who planned to be teachers. There was no opening in English, but Silver was sufficiently committed to Frost's power and presence as a teacher to write him, in effect, a blank check. Since the only openings were in psychology and the history of education, he was invited to teach these subjects; the whole question of qualifications was avoided, and the recent farmer now became, if briefly, a participant in the vexed problem of how to educate at a state teacher's college.

Frost's solution was, as it had been at Pinkerton, to trust books, believing that if he could put some of the right ones into the hands of students, they would find themselves responding to sentences with pleasure, as issuing from an identifiable writer's voice. To this end they would read parts of James's *Principles of Psychology* or Rousseau's *Emile,* rather than take notes on and learn the principal points from this or that history of educational psychology. If our present impulse is, rightly, to groan at the idea of courses in theories of education as traditionally taught, and therefore to applaud Frost's innovative approach, we should remind ourselves that nothing is easier, especially at the remove of decades, than to disdain old-fashioned systematic methods as unimaginative and repressive. Thus the rebel outsider, operating on his impulses instead of wielding a textbook, claims our sympathies. When Sidney Cox, a younger fellow-teacher at Plymouth, met Frost and fell under his influence for life, Cox felt in his speech and attitudes "an absence of conformity," found "something earthy and imperfectly tamed about him" which drew the younger man. And when during an early meeting between the two, Cox moved to break away on the grounds that he had English themes to correct, Frost's response was something like, "Tear 'em up, throw 'em out the window." No doubt Cox was being teased, and no doubt it was fun for Frost's students when instead of drilling them in a textbook their teacher read parts of a novel aloud to them (his favorite novel for that purpose seems to have been Twain's *A Connecticut Yankee in King Arthur's Court*). His first biographer, Newdick, received an account of his classroom procedures as recalled by one of his students at the school that year, which Newdick summed up partly as follows:

She recalled [him] as conducting in his classes an open forum, covering a wide range of subjects, speaking in a low voice. He gave examinations occasionally, she thought, to meet school requirements but thought he never graded them. Being convinced he probably put the papers into his stove, she wrote, on one occasion, instead of the answers to his questions a flippant and irrelevant discourse. After several days, receiving no grade, she stopped after class to ask how she had done on the paper. After a moment's puzzlement, he assured her that she had done quite acceptably.

Another incitement for giving examinations may well have been that it allowed the instructor more time to read on his own, especially if he did not grade the examinations.

Important here is the pattern that was established during Frost's years at Pinkerton, but shows itself more flagrantly during the Plymouth year and was to continue with no significant variation over the course of his teaching at Amherst College and elsewhere. A way of putting it would be to call him an academic who held in not much regard, sometimes in contempt, the ordinary tools and materials of educational procedure—a "symbolic teacher," as he once called himself, who thought most teaching and probably most teachers were less than glorious and surely not to be emulated. As against these he held up books—the ones by men and women who were *writers*—and his own voice, drawing upon resources of wit and experience which by his thirty-eighth year he could depend on. There is little doubt that, as in the young woman's account of his classes, Frost's students remembered him.

---

The Derry farm was sold in November of 1911, and with the increased annuity from his grandfather's will added to the proceeds, Frost could count on enough material support to ballast his plans for making the reckless choice and setting out for somewhere. At Christmas time he put together the collection of seventeen poems, referred to earlier, to send to Susan Ward as an appreciative token of what she had done for him. Some of these poems would appear, with changes of minor sorts, in *A Boy's Will* ("Reluctance," "Wind and Window Flower"). Others would appear in that volume under different titles: "To the Loud Southwester" as "To the Thawing Wind"; "Determined," as "October"; "Unchastened," as "In Neglect"; "Pan Desponds," as "Pan with Us." Still others he would keep around for short or longer periods of time before they saw print: "The Little Things of War" eventually became "Range-Finding" in *Mountain Interval* (1916); "Death" metamorphosed many years later into part of "The Rabbit Hunter"; while "To a Moth Seen in Winter" had to wait three decades before it was published, with the afternote "Circa 1900." Others were never published at all, even though they are charming, slight accomplishments such as the little poem called "On the Sale of my Farm" whose closing lines insist that—even though he is willing to give it up—"It shall be no trespassing, / If I come again some spring / In the grey disguise of years, / Seeking ache of memory here." The letter to Susan Ward which accompanied this group of poems was a typically adroit dance of humor and seriousness, as Frost pleaded ignorance of how at the moment she was "disposed toward minor poets," and apologized for the manuscript which represented "not the long deferred forward movement you are living in wait for, but only the grim stand it was necessary for me to make until I should gather myself together." Though the word is still, he says, "manâna" he warns her not to laugh at his boast as she may have at the boasts of other poets, since "In my case you would find yourself mistaken."

This note of strong, even threateningly aggressive self-confidence is one we have heard before and will hear again in much louder tones. An easy way of psychologizing would note it as a manner of cheering oneself up, of trying to bring the future into being by insisting that it must be the way one wants it. My sense is that though such an explanation may do to take the measure of lesser talents, it cannot take Frost's, because his conviction of being marked out for a triumph in poetry ran so deep, as deeply at the age of thirty-eight as it had ever done. The conviction, furthermore, that he was in touch with a larger purpose or purposes in the universe to which it was his duty to be true, emerged in another letter to Miss Ward from that same period, just after he had paid her a visit in New York:

Two lonely cross-roads that themselves cross each other I have walked several times this winter without meeting or overtaking so much as a single person on foot or on runners. The practically unbroken condition of both for several days after a snow or a blow proves that neither is much travelled. Judge then how surprised I was the other evening as I came down to see a man, who to my own unfamiliar eyes and in the dusk looked for all the world like myself, coming down the other, his approach to the point where our paths must intersect being so timed that unless one of us pulled up we must inevitably collide. I felt as if I was going to meet my own image in a slanting mirror. Or say I felt as we slowly converged at the same point with the same noiseless yet laborious strides as if we were two images about to float together with the uncrossing of someone's eyes. I verily expected to take up or absorb this other self and feel the stronger by the addition for the three-mile journey home. But I didn't go forward to the touch. I stood still in wonderment and let him pass by.

The incident revealed "Some purpose I doubt not, if we could have made it all out."

An utterance like this is just the sort of thing which at first glance cries out for interpretive attention, since it contains the literary-psychological figure of "the Double," always fair game for speculative analysis. Or it could be read as interestingly predictive of poems Frost was soon to write; notably "The Road Not Taken," with its insistence that the two roads were worn just about the same; or "Meeting and Passing," in which the lovers meet but then move on without further uniting ("as if we drew / The figure of our being less than two / But more than one as yet"). But the most important fact about this account from a letter, is its impressiveness as a piece of writing. In the combined daring and assurance of its sentences, it is as large an utterance—also as "poetic" a one—as anything Frost had made up to that point in his life, either in prose or verse. We can guess how "surprised" he was by the way the sentences unfold themselves in unexpectedly satisfying ways: how the approaching man looked in the dusk "for all the world like myself"; how the slow convergence to the "inevitable" collision works itself out in other words, "Noiseless yet laborious" (a wonderful combination of adjectives); how the images float together "with the uncrossing of someone's eyes" to create a strangely visionary turn (whose eyes? "Someone's"). And then the decision—on impulse? on reflection?—not to "go forward to the touch" (but did they at least speak, or nod hello, or just grunt at each other the barest breath of acknowledgment?). Perhaps it is that once you expect yourself to "take up and absorb" another self, there is no need to put it to the test of touch; indeed that might be an all too literal way to behave about imaginative matters. The strengthening, the absorption, has already occurred, and we can only attest to how "verily" he felt it by the power of the writing. The man stands still in wonderment, but the writing is an expression of someone who feels purposive, marked out for something even though he can't "make it all out."

I dwell on this dreamlike piece of evocation as a way of concluding these pages about Frost's earlier years, because it is such a striking embodiment of the poet on the threshold, gathering strength into himself as he prepares to measure that strength against all creation, sail away to England, publish a book, and see what happens in the "trial by market everything must come to" that he wrote about later on. It is a moment of poise which has the effect, so we feel, of imparting some of its strength even as it floats together with us. More than two years previously he had published, in the *New England Magazine,* a poem called "Into Mine Own," which was to become the first poem in *A Boy's Will* ("Into My Own"). But reading the rather sweetly hopeful conclusion to that poem—"They would not find me changed from him they knew— / Only more sure of all I thought was true"— and comparing it with the experience rendered in this letter to Susan Hayes Ward, one sees how safely controlled is the poem about stealing away, and how little it can be taken as an adequate way of understanding the real coming-into-his-own Frost was about to enact.

# III

## *Not Undesigning*

In the summer of 1912, the Frosts sailed from Boston to Glasgow on a steamer, the *S. S. Parisian,* then traveled to London where they spent a week in a hotel, attended the theater (they saw a play by Shaw), and generally seem to have made the transition from New Hampshire to the great metropolis with a minimum of turbulence. After settling in the small house in Beaconsfield called "The Bungalow," Frost converted it, in his letters, to "The Bung-Hole" ("It is only The Bung for short and Hole by discourtesy"), then converted the manuscript at the bottom of his trunk into *A Boy's Will,* published by David Nutt in April of 1913. At that time he wrote to John Bartlett about his "dazzling friend" Ezra Pound, and how through Pound he had met Yeats who praised his book, and how Pound was going to review it in *Poetry,* and how—all this having transpired in six months—he should by rights be satisfied. But no, he said, "The boom is not started yet." Nor was Elinor overwhelmed by her husband's success. She wrote to Bartlett three months after the book was published, expressing her disappointment that reviewers hadn't been more enthusiastic; yet it is difficult to see why she should have been disappointed. For although the anonymous praise in the *Academy* was still to come in September ("One feels that this man has *seen* and *felt:* seen with a revelatory, a creative vision; felt personally and intensely"), the book had received good, if brief, notices in the *TLS* and *Athenaeum,* as well as fuller praise from Flint and from Pound. There is no disappointment in the tone of Frost's own letters at the time; on the contrary, they are filled with energetic schemes for making sure that the modest success of his first book would be but a mild prelude to the next one. Referring to Pound's review in *Poetry,* he wrote to Thomas Mosher, the Maine book collector and publisher who had shown interest in his work, that he, Mosher, could be counted on to know what he, Frost, was about: "You are not going to make the mistake that Pound makes of assuming that my simplicity is that of the untutored child. I am not undesigning."

His designingness can be observed in a number of directions and might be regretted only if one thinks poets should be above such worldly concerns, should simply loose their books on the world and hope that the world—or at least a reviewer or two—will approve. Needless to say, this was not Frost's way. Close on to forty years old, he had too much intention and motive invested in his enterprise to let it run the risk of languishing. When he wrote Bartlett later in the year that "I want to reach out, and would if it were a thing I could do by taking thought," he had already begun reaching out by taking not only thought, but action. The energy and agility with which he carried out this action is of more interest than the question of whether he was not overly competitive or manipulative or self-promoting in his efforts: after all, where are the rules for correct behavior in such matters to be found? Frost's designs showed themselves in ways which may be roughly named as follows: his attempt to publicize the forthcoming book by spelling out, to his friends and to himself, what amounted to a theory of poetry; his detaching himself from Pound and attaching himself instead to some of the Georgian poets, while making clear to his American friends that he had reservations about their individual work and about the work of other contemporary British poets; his taking a long look back at America and anticipating his reception there upon return.

Frost's attempt, generally, was to make the nature of "reaching out" so inclusive as not to exclude any possible reader anywhere from membership in his audience. In a local and rather trivial way, this involved keeping after John Bartlett to publish, in newspapers, an account of his success thus far. With Bartlett's assistance, an article could be written to stun the folks back in Derry, particularly a couple of old "enemies" at Pinkerton Academy whom he thought news of his fortune would discomfit. This "Bouillabais[s]e" (Frost's word for it) consisted of bits and pieces from Pound's and Flint's and Norman Douglas's reviews of *A Boy's Will,* mixed together in an effective way. Derry readers were to be told that the *English Review* (where Douglas's anonymous notice had appeared) was a leading English monthly; however, they were not to be told of Pound's unfriendly cracks at

Frost, in England, 1913.

American editors who couldn't recognize a good native product. "We may want to use them some time," was his designing reason for not possibly offending those in power. Nor was Bartlett to cook up the stew with only "favorable" ingredients: "Leave in any derogatory remarks," Frost said with reference to Pound's review—"We like those." "We" liked them, presumably, not just because they created a more believable picture of the poetry described, but also because— a bit deeper down—Frost knew that *A Boy's Will* had its faults and didn't mind (he told Bartlett) that Pound or Flint had identified some of them. "A little of that won't hurt us," he sanely remarked, referring to certain criticisms made by Flint.

So Bartlett pieced together a long composite review, using the sources already mentioned plus another, glowing one from the *Academy*. It was accordingly published in the Derry *News* and reprinted in the *Plymouth Normal School Prospect* with a few words of introduction Frost guessed were written by Ernest Silver, the principal at Plymouth who disapproved of his English venture. But Silver's words of introduction were warm ones, and in writing to thank him for them Frost indulged in one final twist of improvisation, saying he had come to the conclusion that "a man can stand being overpraised better than underpraised" and that "If John [Bartlett] lays it on a little thick anywhere, you have to remember John was a favorite pupil and never disliked anything I said or did." The whole incident is representative of Frost's dealings with other people where his own work is concerned. Having coaxed and coached Bartlett into a "review," which except for a couple of introductory paragraphs by him consisted wholly of the published words of others, Frost plays the role, for Silver, of the modest poet who is naturally a bit embarrassed by all the publicity ("Laying it on a little thick") but willing to tolerate it, since after all "John" is one of those adoring pupils whose judgment takes second place to their affection. One may choose to deplore the manipulation, but it is really better perceived for its ingenuity and expertness. Nobody was hurt by it, no serious lies were told; the folks back home in Derry and Plymouth got to read about their neighbor or teacher or colleague in a way they would not otherwise have, unless in the unlikely event they subscribed to English literary reviews. Glory was reflected on Pinkerton Academy (Bartlett mentioned that some of the poems had been written while Frost taught there) and on the Derry and Windham district generally. But it took persistence and a willingness to self-advertise for the thing to be achieved.

As for Pound, Frost's nervousness about having been reviewed by him had mainly to do with Pound's aggressive manner, his use of Frost as a stick with which to beat American editors. Frost was convinced, as he wrote to Bartlett in August 1913, that he was "one of the few artists writing," in the sense that he was one of the few with a "theory" upon which all their work was founded: "I expect to do something to the present state of literature in America. That is why I don't want any slaps at my friends at home." This statement of high literary expectation is made in the boldest terms, which turned out to be accurate ones. But to make it happen he had to create "friends at home" where at present they didn't exist. So Pound had to be rejected, with his "slaps" at the country in which Frost was to flourish. If he was a "dazzling friend," he was also (in the letter to Bartlett written just after *A Boy's Will* was published) a "stormy petrel" whose review "over did" it in its reference to American editors. By that summer he was chafing under Pound's patronage, calling it "bullying" and remarking sardonically to Mosher that "The fact that he discovered me gives him the right to see that I live up to his good opinion of me."

It may have been, as he insisted to Mosher, that Pound advised or ordered him to write "something much more like *vers libre* or face the consequences of neglect." At a later date Frost told Sidney Cox that the quarrel began after Pound had tried to peddle "Death of the Hired Man" to the *Smart Set,* a New York magazine whose title Frost disliked. But it seems unlikely that the break with Pound came about because of a formal disagreement over the proper technique of poetic composition, or over the issue of a poem in a particular magazine. And although Frost expressed his prideful independence of Pound in a lengthy piece of free verse parody he sent to Flint (who advised him not to send it to Pound), there is also in that poem a sense of woundedness, as if Pound had somehow betrayed the innocent illusions of his compatriot by trying too hard to organize his career:

> I suspected though that in praising me
> You were not concerned so much with my desert
> As with your power
> That you praised me arbitrarily
> And took credit to yourself
> In demonstrating that you could thrust anything
>     upon the world
> Were it never so humble
> And bid your will avouch it.

These quite serious lines provide a partial truth about Pound's patronage of other artists (Wyndham Lewis's angry response to it in the 1920s was a later example of biting back at the hand trying to feed you), though Frost's motive for breaking away had other reasons behind it.

All in all, the quarrel was a good one, showing strong literary egos of an invigorating order. Here were two extremely ambitious men, their wits and critical intelligences a match for one another, their styles too dissimilar to live together peaceably for long. A presentation copy to Frost of one of Pound's earlier books of poetry, *Ripostes* (1912), contains "Portrait d'une Femme" in the margin next to which Frost wrote a number of less than flattering comments. The poem is about a woman whom Pound compares to the Sargasso Sea and from whom rich treasures can be fished up; at one point in the poem it is noted that one comes away from this woman with "a tale or two, / Pregnant with mandrakes." Frost wrote in the margin, "Bosh," in response to Pound's exotic, indiscreet literariness. Just before returning to America, he toyed with but rejected the idea of publicly dissociating himself from Pound so that American editors might take note. But he admitted (in the letter to Cox where this occurred) that Pound was "a generous person." For Pound on the other hand, Frost was a little "raw" and eventually (as he wrote H. L. Mencken) "dull perhaps"—though he added, "But has something in him." And he wrote genially to Frost in December of 1915, after the latter's return to America: "You seem to be having things pretty much your own way. My congratulations for what they can add to it."

There were of course to be no mandrakes in the tales Frost was gathering together and currently writing for a second volume first advertised as "Farm Servants and Other People" in the David Nutt catalogue. "I am looked on as someone who has got the poetry of the farm," he wrote to Bartlett in May of 1913 and advised him, in a mock-sensational tone, to advertise *A Boy's Will* in Vancouver as "hot stuff." "A few choice copies left. Call it a farm product without fear of contradiction," he instructed. These two references may suggest the quite complicated reservations with which he regarded himself and his poetry as a "farm product." He knew, he must have known, how private and inner was the landscape in much of his first book, filled with dreams and wistfulness and a delicate, musical treatment of "life." Still, there were trees and weather and scythes and flowers, and if this meant to the English reviewers and other readers that here was an American rural poet specializing in "farm" materials, then that supposition was a place on which to build. But the subjectivity of *A Boy's Will* must now be avoided; indeed by 1913 Frost probably felt remote from many of the poems in it, composed as most of them were years before. He told Wilbur Rowell, his lawyer in America, that he was glad to send him a copy of *A Boy's Will* but wasn't sure he would like it—"so very personal in this first book"—and assured Rowell that "The next book, if it comes off, should be more objective and so perhaps more generally interesting."

Along with the stress on objectivity, he sensed that another book of lyrics might not be desirable at this point, even though (as is evident from the Christmas batch he sent Susan Hayes Ward in 1911) he had some on hand. In an interesting account written to the publisher Mosher on the same day as the letter to Rowell, he made the following analysis of his design as it was to realize itself:

> I am made too self-conscious by the comment on my first book to think of showing another like it for some time. If I write more lyrics it must

be with no thought of publication. What I *can* do next is bring out a volume of blank verse that I have already well in hand and won't have to feel that I am writing to order. I had some character strokes I had to get in somewhere and I chose a sort of eclogue form for them. Rather I dropped into that form. And I dropped to an everyday level of diction that even Wordsworth kept above.

The claim about diction in what was to be *North of Boston* will be taken up presently; relevant here is the apt play on "self-conscious" with regard to the display of personal lyric he had just made in his first book. It was the move from consciousness of self to consciousness of others that he hoped to accomplish in the more "objective" second volume, which, he went on to imagine, would therefore be of *general* interest. Similarly, in the letter to Bartlett mentioned earlier about "reaching out," he spoke of the "general reader" he was determined to make his own. In a homely phrase he told Bartlett that there was a "kind of success called 'of esteem' and it butters no parsnips." He did not want to be "caviare to the crowd the way my quasi-friend Pound does"—thus another way of understanding the separation from his compatriot. Frost's desire was to make himself available to the "general reader who buys books in their thousands." He admits that he may not be able to do it, but he believes in doing it; his design stretched at least as far as making the attempt.

His reach was boldest, his designing most extreme and audacious, in the realm of poetics, where he attempted to propose a theory of verse composition which could rationalize the poems—particularly in *North of Boston,* but to some extent in *A Boy's Will* also—that he had written and was writing. The theory would distinguish his practice not only from that of his Victorian and post-Victorian forbears in England and America, but also from the radical aesthetic Pound was insisting upon in his Imagist pronouncements, and even—for all his friendly affiliations with them in the latter half of his stay in England—from the Georgians: Wilfred Gibson, Lascelles Abercrombie, W. H. Davies. And it would serve as a standard by which his great friend to be, the just-budding poet Edward Thomas, could measure his own experimental work. Of course these are relatively objective ways of understanding Frost's reach into theory; a more human way to think of it is as a dramatic, even theatrical self-advertisement, not just to promote the poet's work in the eyes of others but to convince himself he was engaged in something original and significant. In other words, one should be advised in considering Frost's poetic manifesto, as we may call the declarations he sent back home in letters, to take it as a vigorous performance (an "extravagance" as he later liked to say) whose value cannot be estimated merely by deciding whether it is true or false. As with the phrase from James's "The Will to Believe," it was a way of believing the future into existence.

The extravagance of believing the future into existence was immediately apparent in a Fourth of July 1913 letter to Bartlett: "To be perfectly frank with you I am one of the most notable craftsmen of my time. That will transpire presently." Frost's declaration of poetic independence began here. Its extravagance lay, as is usually the case in his prose, in the tilt of the tone away from mere boasting to an incorporated awareness of the boasting as something indulged in like a game. First he introduces himself as one of the most notable craftsmen of his time, but in the very act of so doing winks at the boast by prefacing it with the *faux-sincère* (to a good friend like Bartlett) "To be perfectly frank with you." Next, while admitting that there is as yet little public evidence of this notable craftmanship, he assures Bartlett that it is all to come, all lying ahead—"That will transpire presently," as if the process were as simple and inevitable and easeful as breathing. What transpires in the following sentences, however, is almost as interesting:

> I am possibly the only person going who works on any but a worn out theory (principle I had better say) of versification. You see the great successes in recent poetry have been made on the assumption that the music of words was a matter of harmonised vowels and consonants. Both Swinburne and Tennyson arrived largely at effects in assonation. But they were on the wrong track or at any rate on a short track. They went the length of it. Any one else who goes that way must go after them. And that's where most are going. I alone of English writers have consciously set out to make music out of what I may call the sound of sense.

Never mind that the claim to be the only English writer to turn away from those "effects in assonation" which Swinburne, Tennyson, and other late nineteenth-century poets had "largely arrived at," was an extravagance that declined to consider the more recent examples of Yeats, of Hardy, or of the Georgian poets with whom he was becoming friendly at the time. The important thing for Frost was that he not conceive himself as going "after them"—any more than he wished to go after Swinburne or Tennyson—in the sense of imitating their styles.

To make a new sort of "music"—or at least one not recently heard in English poetry—was the aim, and its elements added up to what Frost calls, in a phrase surely original to him, "the sound of sense." The phrase may accommodate either an underlining of "sound" or of "sense," thereby setting up a playful shuttling between the poem as communicating something, some grain of wisdom or truth about the world (the sound of *sense*) and the poem as wholly embodying that truth through its particular music, so that one is mainly aware of something heard (the *sound* of sense). It is like the mower asking himself what the scythe whispered, and finding out over the course of his inquiry in the poem that "The fact is the sweetest dream that labor knows," which "message" is not a whispered confidence from a wise farm implement, but the climax in a development which is the poem itself. The line "says" something, but the more one listens to it the harder it becomes to define the "something" it says. For all the seemingly confident advertising of his new program to Bartlett, Frost was really seeking a more elusive, less down-to-earth effect than might at first be thought.

He continues to explain himself in the letter by remarking that the best place to hear "the abstract sound of sense is from voices behind a door that cuts off the words," and he invites Bartlett to imagine how sentences like the following would sound "without the words in which they are embodied":

> You mean to tell me you can't read?
> I said no such thing.
> Well read then.
> You're not my teacher.

Frost says these are examples of strong sounds which "context" (always, of course, a vexed notion) must "unmistakably" indicate so that the reader can "give his voice the posture proper to the sentence." "Never if you can help it write down a sentence in which the voice will not know how to posture *specially*," he tells Bartlett, speaking to himself as well. A poet must learn to "get cadences by skillfully breaking the sounds of sense with all their irregularity of accent across the regular beat of the metre." This insistence, which he would continue to make for the rest of his life, was not new to English poetry; the breaking of rhythm against meter can be found at least as far back as Donne, and was theorized about by Coleridge. But Frost goes further in speaking of the sound of sense as "the abstract vitality of our speech," and saying that "One who concerns himself with it more than the subject is an artist." Here he foretells the sort of poet he was to become. Previous to and taking precedence over any interest in "content," must be the artist's radical concern with "it," with the strong, unmistakable, yet elusive accents of the sound of sense. In an exchange between him and Wallace Stevens many years later, Stevens accused Frost of writing poems about "subjects," whereupon Frost retorted that Stevens's poems were about "bric-à-brac." But much as the poems he was writing for *North of Boston* have homely, ultimate "subjects" like the death of an old man or the presence of a dead child in the minds of its still living parents, their deeper concern is with something more "abstract" and even more vital.

A recent writer on Frost, Margery Sabin, has emphasized how far from a narrowly technical concern was his obsession, during the years in England, with speech rhythms, with the sound of sense:

> Frost in 1914 wanted to believe—and wrote poems out of the belief— that human vitality takes on a suprapersonal existence in the established intonations of speech, intonations which the individual may draw on for personal expression and, perhaps even more important, for the reassuring recognition that his single life is connected to other lives . . . What Frost calls "the abstract vitality of our speech" gives reassurance that the life within us is not eccentric or monstrous. It ceases to be monstrous once it participates in the verbal forms through which other people also enact their lives.

Here, surely, is an important way of understanding how Frost's poetics was intimately connected with his increasing responsiveness to other people, to the enlarging of the boy's will into more inclusive, more social and "objective" forms in the poems which would make up *North of Boston*. So the term "abstract" (in "the abstract vitality of our speech") means the opposite of diminished or attenuated, and is, instead, an indication of our solidarity with a life wider than our own.

In the months following the Fourth of July letter and preparatory to publication of the new book in May of 1914, Frost repeated his thoughts, in slightly different forms, to his American friends Bartlett and Cox. To the latter in January 1914, and provoked by the poet laureate Robert Bridges's rival theory of poetry in which English syllables had a fixed quantity, Frost insisted that "The living part of a poem is the intonation entangled somehow in the syntax idiom and meaning of a sentence. It is only there for those who have heard it previously in conversation." "Words exist in the mouth, not in books," he put it most succinctly in the same letter. Related to this insistence was the slogan he had used while teaching at Pinkerton Academy: "Common in experience; uncommon in writing." The distinctiveness of art should be felt in its expression, its "writing," rather than in the subject or material expressed. He had said as much to Bartlett in defining the artist as one who was more interested in "it"—the expression—than in the subject expressed. And in February 1914 he put it another way, speaking about the notion of "recognition": "In literature it is our business to give people the thing that will make them say, 'Oh yes I know what you mean'. It is never to tell them something they don't know, but something they know and hadn't thought of saying. It must be something they recognize."

To illustrate such a shock of recognition, Frost quotes a little poem, "A Patch of Old Snow," he had not yet published:

> There's a patch of old snow in a corner,
> That I should have guessed
> Was a blow-away paper the rain
> Had brought to rest.
>
> It is speckled with grime as if
> Small print overspread it,
> The news of a day I've forgotten—
> If I ever read it.

He paraphrases the poem's content, then says that content is of no interest ("no good") except for "certain points of recognition in it," blow-away papers and dirty old snow, and how ephemeral is yesterday's news. What interests him rather is the sentence sound—not the first stanza's (which he says is "merely ordinary and bookish")—but the second's, which has "the very special tone with which you must say—news of a day I have forgotten—if I ever read it. You must be able to say Oh yes one knows how that goes." I think it likely that Frost was especially drawn to that sentence sound because of the unmistakable way it changes pitch in its final "If I ever read it," that concluding line coming after the drawn-out pause made by the dash which follows "forgotten." Such an assurance that the speaking voice is alive and changeable, figures as an important part of his campaign to celebrate the abstract vitality of speech. It is variety of this sort for which he speaks most winningly in striking off a distinction between eye-readers and ear-readers:

> It is so and not otherwise that we get the variety that makes it fun to write and read. *The ear does it.* The ear is the only true writer and the only true reader. I have known people who could read without hearing

the sentence sounds and they were the fastest readers. Eye readers we call them. They can get the meaning by glances. But they are bad readers because they miss the best part of what a good writer puts into his work.

This promoting of ear over eye is in no way an overstatement or a merely corrective setting of the balance, but absolutely central to the kind of poetry Frost committed himself to writing. It is in fact a more radical notion of where the reader's interest should lie than can be found in Ezra Pound's poetics, for all the latter's loud pronouncing about "technique." In his review of *North of Boston,* after admiring the way Frost achieved sentence sounds in those poems, Pound draws back and assures us that, just as Jane Austen is less interesting than Stendhal, so Frost's poems suffer from their provincial subject matter: "A book about a dull, stupid, hemmed-in sort of life, by a person who has lived it, will never be as interesting as the work of some author who has comprehended many men's manners and seen many grades and conditions of existence." Exactly here lay the nub of contention between the two poets. Insofar as he committed himself to the priority of ear-reading to eye-reading, of listening to seeing (or thinking, or figuring out, or knowing), Frost refused to grant special privilege to any subject matter at the expense of another, even if it was the battle of Waterloo or the death of kings as compared to a patch of old snow. To speak in the review, as Pound did, of Frost having written "about" dull, stupid, hemmed-in lives north of Boston, indeed of the author having lived such a life himself (how intolerable this condescension must have been to Frost!) is to talk as if subjects were fixed in their natures, just sitting there waiting to be picked up and written about by the poet. But in Frost's more sophisticated principle, subjects are not made up in advance, any more than words are.

Or at least the true poet must resist the already made-up words, must avoid using or being used by a poetic diction which has separated itself from language as it is spoken. The true poet's pleasure, he wrote to Cox "must always be to make his own words as he goes and never to depend for effect on words already made even if they be his own." And, to bring this charting of Frost's theory to its close, he himself seemed to wrap it up by telling Cox that "We write of things we see and we write in accents we hear. Thus we gather both our material and our technique with the imagination from life; and our technique becomes as much material as material itself." This fine pronounce-

ment, interestingly enough, anticipates one of T. S. Eliot's in his introduction to the 1928 edition of *The Sacred Wood,* where he cautions
or reminds us that "we cannot say at what point 'technique' begins or
where it ends." It was an original thing for Frost to have said in 1914
and an appropriate response to the original poems in *North of Boston.*

---

Frost's practice of "making" the words as he went along rather than
using them as already made-up counters, was not confined merely to
the poems he wrote. He was as much a poet in his letters, even in the
most casual, unbuttoned conveyance of some gossip to Sidney Cox as
he describes a visit from W. H. Davies, whom Frost referred to as "the
unsophisticated nature poet of the day—absolutely uncritical
untechnical untheoretical." Such qualities hardly recommended Davies to him, nor did the nature poet's conceit:

> We have had a good deal of him at the house for the last week and the
> things he has said for us to remember him by! He entirely disgusted
> the Gibsons with whom he was visiting. His is the kind of egotism
> another man's egotism can't put up with. He was going from here to
> be with Conrad. He said that would be pleasant because Conrad knew
> his work *thoroughly*. After waiting long enough to obscure the point
> we asked him if he knew Conrad's work *thoroughly*. Oh no—was it
> good? We told him yes. He was glad we liked it.

The account begins in a fairly straightforward manner, like the first
sentence-stanza from "A Patch of Old Snow," and "disgusted" is an
already "made" word that we more or less understand in a general
sense. But with the third sentence—"His is the kind of egotism
another man's egotism can't put up with"—the attack on Davies's
crudities modulates into a wittier kind of reflexiveness. From there on
the play increases: as "thoroughly" is thoroughly worked on; as
"good" becomes, in Davies's oblivious mouth, something wholly inadequate to Conrad's art; as "He was glad we liked it" dances around
in contemptuous mirth. By now we have a context, as we did not have
earlier with "disgusted," and we can hear the unmistakable special
posture these sentence sounds make. As if to bear out the schoolroom
motto "Common in experience; uncommon in writing," there is nothing here in the individual words, or in the "subject" of the passage,
which is odd or striking, which causes the least stir. The stir is created

rather by the uncommon writing, the fluidly inventive, ever-changing voice, seizing the occasion, playing itself along from one verbal event to the next.

This letter about Davies's unacceptable behavior was written in May of 1914—just three days after *North of Boston* was published— from Little Iddens, Gloucestershire, where Frost had moved himself and family the previous month. Their plan was to live near the newly-made friends Abercrombie and Gibson and to experience an English spring in more rural surroundings than the Beaconsfield where the Frosts had been living. Just before the move, he arranged with Harold Monro to be paid for his contributions to Monro's *Poetry and Drama* ("The Fear" and "A Hundred Collars") by living rent-free with Elinor and the children for a week in some rooms of the Poetry Bookshop in Devonshire Street. Frost hardly qualified as a conventional sightseer of London, writing to Cox just before they moved that "There must be a great deal to see in London if one will look for it. There is The Tower and—well there simply must be something else." He guesses he had better get a guidebook, but confesses about his activities as a tourist generally ("straggling around Edinburgh Castle for a day") that "Places are more to me in thought than in reality. People are the other way about." Nevertheless the Frosts spent the week in London, where the father received more pleasure and excitement from his contacts with literary men of the moment than from the inspection of historic monuments. These men now included—through Gibson's offices—the poet Ralph Hodgson, and through Hodgson, Edward Thomas, who would visit and lodge near Frost in Gloucestershire that next summer, deepening and extending what was probably the most important friendship—certainly on a literary level—of each of their lives. But he also met the poet and translator Laurence Binyon, and through Binyon the just-made Poet Laureate Robert Bridges, as well as such minor lights as R. C. Trevelyan, Gordon Bottomley, and John Cournos. These poets were all outside what Frost now referred to as "the Pound clique," and he observed correctly, apropos of his move to Gloucestershire, that it was the manuscript poems soon to appear in *North of Boston* which had drawn them to him.

The beauty of Gloucestershire that spring and summer of 1914 was compellingly testified to by Elinor in a letter of June written to her sister:

I wish I could make you feel what a lovely country this is. When we first came, the meadows were covered with yellow daffodils and the cuckoo had just begun to sing . . . The pastures here are so rich that they are just as green as the mowing and wheat fields, and they are separated by dark green hedges and bordered by huge elms. Great flocks of sheep and herds of cows are everywhere. From a hill about four miles away, one can see the Severn river winding along, and the mountains of Wales in the distance. The cottage we are living in is very old—about 350 years old, and all the floors downstairs are brick tiled and the beams show above. We have five rooms and the rent is only $50 a year.

If it wasn't quite living under thatch, as the fancy had moved them (and which they did eventually when staying with the Abercrombies) it had comparable charms, even though the children became restless and homesick for America, so Mrs. Abercrombie was to recall. One of Frost's letters refers to how he is cooking some of the meals "in my wife's present state of health," the first of many such references to come. There was also the mounting anxiety of the war, which broke out in August and put an end to what he spoke of as "our game" of publishing books in England. So it must have been with pleasure and some relief that he received a letter from Mrs. Henry Holt, wife of the American publisher, telling of her interest and admiration for *North of Boston.* By September of that year, and after first demurring about publishing *North of Boston,* the Holt firm committed itself to publishing it as well as later books by the author. Frost's eagerness to return home was surely increased by this circumstance.

---

In later years he affected not to know or care what reviews or reviewers were saying about his books, but such was far from the case in the summer of 1914 when *North of Boston* was reviewed widely and favorably. "No book of verse has had as much space given it for a good while," he wrote Cox, providing him with the names of nine magazines which had dealt with it, even specifying how many columns it received. It has to be noted—though with no suggestion of a conspiracy of back-scratching such as poets (and other mortals) are not averse to—that two of the reviews were by Gibson and Abercrombie, his Gloucestershire neighbors; another was by Harold Monro; and the most perceptive of them all by Edward Thomas, who in fact reviewed the book three times. There is no reason to assume that Frost overstated the warmth of this reception, which he took as vindication of the predictions and prophecies made over the past year—often in a very loud way indeed—to his American friends. He had warned

Bartlett that he was one of the most "notable craftsmen" of his time, and promised that it would "transpire presently." Lo, within a year it was seen to have transpired, and the theory of sentence sounds on which he claimed the craftsmanship to rest had strikingly paid its way. He warned Cox that of course not everyone would like or feel easy with the book, but those people would be "simple souls, educated and uneducated" who would miss "the poeticisms by which they are accustomed to know poetry when they see it."

It is important to be clear about the course Frost was charting for himself. On one hand, as seen by the above remark about simple souls missing them in *North of Boston,* he was scornful of "poeticisms." These might be of various sorts, at one level as easy to spot as those of an Alfred Noyes ("Alfie No-Yes" as Frost contemptuously referred to him), author of "The Highwayman" whose selections in the *Oxford Book of Victorian Verse* Frost found to be characterized by "sing-songing" rather than "song-singing." Noyes could manage a pleasant enough lilt ("When Spring comes back to England / And crowns her brows with May, / Round the merry moonlit world / She goes her greenwood way") but there was nothing "stirring" about either his music or his thought: "Swinging is not stirring you know. Neither is swelling necessarily stirring. The poem in which he [Noyes] gets Francis Thompson 'purpureally enwound' ["On the Death of Francis Thompson"] swells, but who cares a pin." By contrast, he praises Yeats's poems (spelling it "Yates") in rather old-fashioned sounding terms ("They make the sense of beauty ache") but also singles out a prosaic sentence-sound from one of his plays—"The butter's at your elbow, Father Hart"—as potentially productive of "the Masefield and Gibson sort of thing." That "sort of thing" was a narrative realism which would not depend for its power on traditional poetic effects, on "poeticisms."

But the alternative to "swelling," to poeticisms, was not necessarily the way of the Georgians with whom he was keeping company. Although he insisted on how much Gibson and Abercrombie meant to him, indeed went back to visit them both when he returned to England in 1928 (he seems to have felt a good deal more warmly toward Abercrombie), one suspects that their poems did not touch him very deeply. Nor did he feel threatened by them, nor terribly competitive with them. Lascelles Abercrombie was scarcely known in America, and although Frost wrote home to Mosher, while he was staying with the Abercrombies at "The Gallows" in Gloucestershire, that Abercrombie "leaves them all behind in the sublime imaginative sort of thing," the praise is vague. One might apply the words "sublime" and "imaginative" to Abercrombie's long poem "The Sale of St. Thomas" which appeared in *Georgian Poetry* 1911–12, but read today it feels stiff and prolix, as Abercrombie's work often feels. And although his play *The End of the World* takes characters from a lower social order, employs a relatively "natural" diction, and manages at times to get something like the sentence sounds Frost was after, the piece's effect as a whole is diffuse and humorless. Toward Wilfred Gibson, Frost took a more critical tone. Gibson was to write effusively years later in his poem "The Golden Room," of Gloucestershire gatherings at the "Old Nail-shop" in July of 1914, with the Abercrombies, Rupert Brooke, and the Edward Thomases, at which occasions "Frost's rich and ripe philosophy / That had the body and tang of good draught-cider" especially delighted them, as did "the shrewd turns and racy quips, / And the rare twinkle of his grave blue eyes." As perhaps can be seen from this effusion, Gibson was a rather simple, "sincere" (indeed corny) poet who enjoyed some popularity in America; and while Frost was genuinely indebted to him for his kindness, that did not make up for certain personal and poetic deficiencies, the latter of which he addressed in some words to Cox written just prior to his departure from England:

> You and I wont believe that Gibsons is a better kind of poetry than mine. Solway Ford is one of his best. It is a good poem. But it is oh terribly made up ... And then look at the way the sentences run on. They are not sentences at all in my sense of the word.

Few readers today are familiar with Gibson's work generally or "Solway Ford" in particular. But Frost's criticism is worth pausing over as something more than a jealous or competitive one (though the competitive aspect was never absent from his judgments of contemporaries). In understanding why he was dissatisfied with Gibson's way of writing, even in a "good poem" like "Solway Ford," we may see by contrast what so interested him in the work of Edward Thomas, and we can then turn to *North of Boston* with a clearer sense of what Frost was after. Gibson's "Solway Ford" is a poem of eighty-four lines in which a man and his horse and wain are proceeding home, unaware of "the far off tide" of Solway Ford. Suddenly the man stumbles, the horse rears and the wain crushes the man, pinning him down as the sea advances. He dreams he has drowned, and though eventually saved is never the same afterwards, changed by his dream of death. Some lines early in the poem may suggest both the "sentences" it makes and the way, in Frost's term, it is "terribly made up":

> He lay and listened to the far-off sea
> And seemed to hear it surging overhead
> Already, though 'twas full an hour or more
> Until high-tide when Solway's shining flood
> Should sweep the shallow firth from shore to shore.
> He felt a salty tingle in his blood
> And seemed to stifle, drowning: then again
> He knew that he must lie a lingering while
> Before the sea might close upon his pain,
> Although the advancing waves had scarce a mile
> To travel, creeping nearer inch by inch
> With little runs and sallies over the sand.

The "made up" quality is apparent in the remoteness of the material chosen (it reminds one of a scene in Scott's *Redgauntlet*) from anything W. W. Gibson, Georgian poet of Gloucestershire, might have lived through. And it is possible, though Frost does not make the claim, that "the way the sentences run on"—which obviously he does not admire—has something to do with the "literary" melodramatics of the situation. It may be that the ease, even the headlong pace at which the sentences spill over the lines (while punctuated at regular intervals by rhymes) is a measure of Gibson's distance from the experience recorded: "He felt a salty tingle in his blood / And seemed to stifle, drowning: then again / He knew that . . ." The words seem arbitrarily forced into the metrical pattern. We are not moved to participate, in any very inward way, with their rhythms; rather we swing along with them in order to extract information, in order to get the "story" of the man's adventure. But there is no adventure, no sense of peril, in the untroubled verse itself, whose sentence sounds are artificial and external instead of emanating—as Frost would have them do—from within.

After Edward Thomas's death in the war, Frost wrote to Edward Garnett about their relationship, saying that he still could not understand how an American and an Englishman, meeting in middle life, could have grown to mean so much to each other: "I hadn't a plan for the future that didn't include him," said Frost. In late 1913 when they came together for the first time, Thomas, already the author of many prose works—biographies, travel and nature observations, critical

studies—was suffering from serious melancholia and entertaining profound doubts about both his professional and his marital life. Perhaps,
in retrospect, it is more natural than Frost thought that they should
have bound themselves to each other in deep friendship. Thomas
needed someone to tell him he was a significant writer, not just a
professional scribbler but—as Frost evidently convinced him he was—
a poet. And Frost, filled with himself, the poems he was writing and
the theory he had made to back them up, needed Thomas as someone
into whom he could pour his own enthusiasm—someone with whom
to share the confidence he had developed about himself and about
poetry. When Thomas's prose work *In Pursuit of Spring* was published in the spring of 1914, Frost found this "loveliest book on spring
in England" to contain ample evidence that Thomas was already a
poet, in that he had both the material and the ability to shape that
material into the sentence sounds of verse. The cadence was there, so
Frost perceived, and his perceiving it to be there helped make lines
possible like the following ones from the beginning of a poem Thomas
would write, along with a number of others, in the coming December:

> The rock-like mud unfroze a little and rills
> Ran and sparkled down each side of the road
> Under the catkins wagging in the hedge.
> But earth would have her sleep out, spite of the sun;
> Nor did I value that thin gilding beam
> More than a pretty February thing
> Till I came down to the old Manor Farm,
> And church and yew-tree opposite, in age
> Its equals and in size. Small church, great yew,
> And farmhouse slept in a Sunday silentness.

These lines from "The Manor Farm" are in no way surprising, indeed
might be said to represent a fairly ordinary patch of Thomas's poetry.
But they cannot be read without hearing, as well as seeing, something;
and if one tries the experiment of, in Frost's comparison, imagining
how the voice would sound if heard from behind a closed door, so not
the words but the sentence sounds only could penetrate, one is able to
identify the "special posture" each sentence demands. To consider, by
contrast, the lines from Gibson's poem, is to note how indistinct and
unvaried are its sentences, how little "sound" they make.

This is not to devalue Thomas's distinctive verse by calling it merely
an aping of the Frost style as it appears in a *North of Boston* poem

like "The Wood-Pile." Thomas is quieter, less interested in dramatizing an "I," generally less humorous and ironical. The movement of his verse is if anything more complicated—sometimes to the point of tortuousness—than Frost's, and the best place to observe it is in a poem he wrote a year or two after Frost returned to America. Its first three stanzas may suggest Thomas's ability to create the sound of sense within a rhymed stanza, not just in blank verse; while the subject celebrated was surely the friendship between him and Frost:

> The sun used to shine while we two walked
> Slowly together, paused and started
> Again, and sometimes mused, sometimes talked
> As either pleased, and cheerfully parted
>
> Each night. We never disagreed
> Which gate to rest on. The to be
> And the late past we gave small heed.
> We turned from men or poetry
>
> To rumours of the war remote
> Only till both stood disinclined
> For aught but the yellow flavorous coat
> Of an apple wasps had undermined . . .

That last sentence continues on through another stanza, even into the one following that, but this excerpt from "The Sun Used to Shine" may suggest the subtlety and irregularity of sentence-pacing, and the exquisitely nuanced voice whose rhythms can be heard even apart from the particular words in which they are embodied. It was the suppleness and delicacy of this voice which Frost helped bring into being through his encouragement of Thomas.

Thomas's death in France cast a heroic aura over what was already a romantically idealized relationship. Frost had previously formed friendships with men significantly younger than himself and to whom he was clearly the teacher. But Thomas was nearly his age (b. 1878) and possessed a literary gift, while his melancholy and driven temperament were a compelling confirmation of similar feelings in the older man. As Frost wrote to Garnett, Thomas was "the only brother I ever had," and he inspired the only poem Frost ever titled simply with the initials of the person for whom it was written. "To E. T." seems undistinguished by Frost's usual range of tone and wit, and has wrongly been called sentimental because of the unabashed directness with which it idealizes the dead Thomas. In fact it is spoken by an abashed presence who says he fell asleep while reading Thomas's poetry

> To see if in a dream they brought of you
>
> I might not have the chance I missed in life
> Through some delay, and call you to your face
> First soldier, and then poet, and then both,
> Who died a soldier-poet of your race.

There follows what must have been an extremely personal testimony which doubtless he thought twice about before publishing:

> I meant, you meant, that nothing should remain
> Unsaid between us, brother, and this remained—
> And one thing more that was not then to say:
> The Victory for what it lost and gained.

When Thomas met "the shell's embrace of fire / On Vimy ridge," "The war seemed over more for you than me, / But now for me than you—the other way." The poem plays, ruefully and sadly, with the sense in which something is "over"; and in calling out to Thomas as "brother," there is preserved the irony of what there "remained to say"—merely the poem, which could only be written when Thomas was no longer there to hear it:

> How over, though, for even me who knew
> The foe thrust back unsafe beyond the Rhine,
> If I was not to speak of it to you
> And see you pleased once more with words of mine?

Certainly the words Thomas wrote about *North of Boston* in his unsigned piece for the *English Review* in August 1914 must have pleased Frost immensely. It is hard to believe he could have been unaware of the reviewer's identity, since Thomas had visited him in Gloucestershire more than once, although he writes (in a letter of 15 August) of the *English Review* piece as "among the best I have had," without mentioning Thomas's name. In fact each of Thomas's reviews contained, and still contains, some of the most valuable criticism of Frost's poetry which exists. In an admirably compressed single paragraph (from the *English Review* notice ) he characterized the kind of poem found in *North of Boston:*

The result is a unique type of eclogue, homely, racy, and touched by a spirit that might, under other circumstances, have made pure lyric on the one hand or drama on the other. Within the space of a hundred lines or so of blank verse it would be hard to compress more rural character and relevant scenery; impossible, perhaps to do so with less sense of compression and more lightness, unity, and breadth. The language ranges from a never vulgar colloquialism to brief moments of heightened and intense simplicity.

And he called the best poems in the book—which he judged to be "The Death of the Hired Man," "Home Burial," "The Black Cottage," and "The Wood-Pile,"—"masterpieces of deep and mysterious tenderness."

In another review (*New Weekly*, 8 August) he took up the question of Frost's poetic forebears, singling out Wordsworth, Whitman, and Browning, and saying he had never met a living poet "with a less obvious or more complicated ancestry." In his judgment Frost had done something beautiful and unique:

> [He] has, in fact, gone back, as Whitman and Wordsworth went back, through the paraphernalia of poetry into poetry again. With a confidence like genius, he has trusted his conviction that a man will not easily write better than he speaks when some matter has touched him deeply, and he has turned it over until he has no doubt what it means to him, when he has no purpose to serve beyond expressing it, when he has no audience to be bullied or flattered, when he is free, and speech takes one form and no other. Whatever discipline further was necessary, he has got from the use of the good old English medium of blank verse.

Many years later, in "The Figure a Poem Makes," Frost was to write that the only "freedom" he cared about was "the freedom of my material—the condition of body and mind now and then to summons aptly from the vast chaos of all I have lived through." Thomas identified the freedom he found in *North of Boston* first by saying (in the *English Review* notice) that Frost "had got free from the habit of personal lyric," that is, from the more dreamily inward parts of *A Boy's Will*. But the freedom was also identified, in the second review, as a freedom from "audience," from the sense that there was a reader out there to be entertained or cajoled or perhaps even "bullied." The poems in the new book, at least the best of them, seemed to Thomas to have no motive beyond that of having been written out of something which touched the poet so deeply and clearly that "he has no purpose to serve beyond expressing it." This freedom is further extended by comparing

Frost to Wordsworth and Whitman who each, in their different ways, "went back, through the paraphernalia of poetry into poetry again." Such a way of talking is in one sense difficult to question, since it is elusive and vague: what is "poetry"—the real, the essential—as opposed to "paraphernalia"—the illusory, the trivial? But Thomas is brilliantly right to make the comparisons he does: the Wordsworth of *Lyrical Ballads,* the Whitman of *Song of Myself,* refuse to provide us with expected kinds of poetic diction or moral attitudes, and throw us back on ourselves in disconcerting ways—as the really new work of art is wont to do. So the "deep and mysterious tenderness"— in the phrase he found to describe the best poems in *North of Boston*—was Thomas's reach for ultimate words to describe poems that, on the one hand, were formally unsurprising ("the good old English medium of blank verse" being employed almost entirely throughout) but, on the other hand, very surprising indeed. How was one to account for the strange new way in which these poems achieved their effects?

From the vantage point of seventy years later, *North of Boston* remains not only the most individual of all Frost's collections of poetry, but the one which as a *book* stays most vividly in our minds. Partly this is because it contains fewer poems (fifteen, plus "Good Hours," originally printed as an epilogue in italics), no one of which could be confused with another one even though they are not all equally successful ("Blueberries" is trivial; "The Generations of Men" is prolix). But the poems are also arranged in such a way as to accentuate variations in their form and mood. At the beginning and end of the volume come two of the book's three "personal" monologues: "Mending Wall"—where the few words spoken by another character ("Good fences make good neighbors") are conveyed to us through the speaker's shifting terms—and "The Wood-Pile," where the voice comes wholly from within. The third monologue—the incomparable "After Apple-Picking"—comes just over halfway through the book and moves things briefly into a remote key seldom to be heard again, even in Frost's later work. The other twelve poems are longer excursions into the voices and situations of different chapters in this "book of people," as Frost originally designated *North of Boston* in an epigraph. They are pretty well evenly divided between those which, through the interplay of voices or through the utterance of a single voice, create an atmosphere tipped toward the tragic or pathetic, and those more relaxed, garrulous ones which work within the idiom of comedy—the tall tale, or the humorous dialogue. "Home Burial" and "A Servant to Servants" are prime examples of the first mode; "The Code," "A Hundred Collars," and "The Mountain" exemplify the second. Frost said later to Louis Untermeyer that seven poems out of the fifteen were "almost humorous," four of them "almost jokes." And humorous accents can be found in "serious" poems like "The Black Cottage" or "The Housekeeper" even as they engage with deeper matters.

If variety is felt in the different forms Frost used and in the different ways of tale-telling within these forms, it is also there in the poems' diction. Although he spoke as if the level of diction were uniform ("I have dropped to an everyday level of diction that even Wordsworth kept above"), a language "absolutely unliterary" he assured John Bartlett, his actual practice was not at all so uniform. This can be seen by comparing the "unliterary" parts of certain poems with other, heightened moments in them where the diction rises to express a passionate feeling which momentarily surfaces. Edward Thomas had seen as much when he pointed out how the language ranges from the colloquial to "brief moments of heightened and intense simplicity." This contrast between styles is felt most strongly in the deeper poems from the book, those whose drama consists especially in a character's, usually a woman's, successful attempt to say something she has never said before—to utter a secret long repressed.

Frost's later remarks about what he was doing in *North of Boston* are fascinating, especially those in the previously mentioned 1915 letter to W. S. Braithwaite who was writing about him for the Boston *Transcript*. Like many others he wrote, Frost's letter is looked upon by Lawrance Thompson, in his edition of the letters, with knowing disapproval. His "tactics," Thompson says, were "to fill a letter with tendentious confidences, facts, ideas, and theories which had the makings of good 'copy' for explanatory articles on RF, the poet and man." The word "tendentious" suggests that there was something rigged and insincere about the enterprise; but if we look at what Frost wrote, rather than jumping to what his "real" motive may have been in writing it, we find his attempt at self-definition of great interest. He reiterates to Braithwaite the by then well-rehearsed talk about the speaking voice's importance, but goes on to say that all this attention to voice leaves out something crucial, and that in writing "The Death of the Hired Man" he realized he was "interested in neighbors for more than merely their tones of speech—and always had been. I remember about when I began to suspect myself of liking their gossip for its own sake."

Here the curious reader may wonder whether this something "more" is really very different fom the "tones of speech" he had previously been interested in, and this uncertainty is not resolved by the next paragraph, particularly valuable as it refers to *North of Boston:*

> I like the actuality of gossip, the intimacy of it. Say what you will effects of actuality and intimacy are the greatest aim an artist can have. The sense of intimacy gives the thrill of sincerity. A story must always release a meaning more readily to those who read than life itself as it goes ever releases meaning. Meaning is a great consideration. But a story must never seem to be told primarily for meaning. Anything, an inspired irrelevance even to make it sound as if told the way it is chiefly because it happened that way.

More than likely, Frost did not know quite what he had created with this second book of poems, and was working hard to find a plausible way of explaining himself as a story-teller poet. Many of his predecessors would have been in favor of "actuality," certainly, and intimacy, perhaps, as desirable aims for the artist in making his poems. But no poet I can think of, with the possible exception of Oscar Wilde, put forth "gossip" as an ideal vehicle to express those qualities—though Chaucer would have understood. In raising a warning finger at the notion of an intrusive "meaning," in stressing the virtue of "an inspired irrelevance" as good for the poem's health, Frost pointed to what his friend Thomas called being "free": writing as if one had no purpose but to express *something;* an "it"; gossip in all its intimacy and actuality.

A number of poems would do to illustrate what in actual practice this inclination amounted to. "The Black Cottage" will serve my purposes since, while not one of Frost's better known pieces, it is a good example of his procedures at their most pure. And it has special interest in that years before, while living at Derry, he had worked the materials of the poem into a totally different form. "The Black Cottage" is about an old lady whose husband served and died in the Union Army and whose sons then moved away, leaving her alone. In the Derry version, the woman was presented, in rhymed stanzas, as a figure of pathos:

> And if by guide-post sent astray,
> At eventide one passed that way
> And paused for sadness, would he guess,
> I wonder, by one outward token
> The solitary inmate there
> Who bows her head with snowy hair
> The bread of loneliness to bless
> With lips that shape the words unspoken.

Somewhat reminiscent of a sketch by Edwin Arlington Robinson, its overall tone is sadly respectful and "poetical," ending in a portentous evocation of the place itself—"The cottage that without a lamp / Sinks darkly upon darker hours." Its elaborate rhyme pattern, again reminiscent of certain stanzas of Robinson's, reveals it to be an object made with care; but the form is not enough to redeem the overbroad pathos with which its subject is handled, and Frost had no luck when he sent it out to editors.

In rewriting the poem, he thoroughly reimagined it, dispensing with the all-seeing, all-wise poet-narrator equipped with a stock of beautiful phrases (like "the bread of loneliness") to grace the saddest situation. He also dispensed with the rhymed stanza and he no longer set the old woman inside the house, bowing her head "with snowy hair," an object of irresistible pathos. In the reimagined poem she is a presence rather, a memory in the mind of the character who tells her story—a minister in whose congregation she once sat. Such an approach by itself could, of course, be as productive of Norman Rockwellism as the earlier poem in stanzas: the minister could speak throughout in a folksy, sincere, winning manner, designed to make us love the old lady all the more. Instead, Frost hit upon the good idea of putting another character into the poem and making him a narrator who, knowing nothing of the lady and her story, is content to listen to the minister as he rambles on. This quiet narrator, the audience for the minister's story, speaks to us only at the beginning and end of the poem, framing the story in a detached, coolly observant manner:

> We chanced in passing by that afternoon
> To catch it in a sort of special picture
> Among tar-banded ancient cherry trees,
> Set well back from the road in rank lodged grass,

The little cottage we were speaking of,
A front with just a door between two windows,
Fresh painted by the shower a velvet black.
We paused, the minister and I, to look.
He made as if to hold it at arm's length
Or put the leaves aside that framed it in.
"Pretty," he said. "Come in. No one will care."

In Edward Thomas's phrase, the medium is the good old English one of blank verse, but there is nothing homemade or indulgent about that first sentence, extending over seven lines, postponing the "it" (which is caught as in a picture) as in apposition ("The little cottage we were speaking of"), suggesting a conversation previous to the poem into which we are being brought, and eventually coming to a vivid close with the nice doubleness of "fresh painted"—an epithet appropriate both to the nature of showers and to the human nature of artists as they render something "a velvet black."

Although these opening seven lines have almost no tone, the sentence sound is there, especially when contrasted with the eighth line ("We paused, the minister and I, to look") and its single, flat declaration; or with the sentence in lines nine and ten which mimes the connoisseur's satisfaction in what he has to show. Then follows line eleven, made up of three tiny sentences, as the minister begins to speak by inviting narrator and readers into the "special picture": "'Pretty,' he said. 'Come in. No one will care.'" It is all a matter of pace; Frost's accomplishment is to make that pace expressive of the activity supposedly going on, so if "We paused, the minister and I, to look," "we" do so in a line that is a complete sentence and whose commas create the pause. If garrulousness is in order to simulate the activity and intimacy of gossip, Frost lets the minister ramble on, double back on himself, drop all sorts of little confidences and parenthetical asides, clear his throat at some length, and generally hem and haw.

In fact, speaking of pace and length, the poems in *North of Boston,* including "The Black Cottage," demand and try the patience of a reader, by the very principles on which they are written. Consider as an example a passage where the minister muses in front of a crayon portrait on the wall—"done sadly from an old daguerreotype"—of the woman's husband who went off to war:

"He fell at Gettysburg or Fredericksburg,
I ought to know—it makes a difference which:

> Fredericksburg wasn't Gettysburg, of course.
> But what I'm getting to is how forsaken
> A little cottage this has always seemed;
> Since she went, more than ever, but before—
> I don't mean altogether by the lives
> That had gone out of it, the father first,
> Then the two sons, till she was left alone.
> (Nothing could draw her after those two sons.
> She valued the considerate neglect
> She had at some cost taught them after years.)
> I mean by the world's having passed it by—
> As we almost got by this afternoon."

By some standards of judging poetry, a passage such as this is simply not very interesting. Pound's remark quoted earlier about how nobody expects Jane Austen to be as "interesting" as Stendhal (nobody expects books about dull or provincial people to be as interesting as ones about cosmopolitans) is irrelevant in a way, since Jane Austen presents her limited and often garrulous characters through narrative comment of the highest intelligence and wit. But this is exactly what Frost does *not* do in "The Black Cottage" and in the other dialogues or monologues from *North of Boston* which lack perceptive or ingenious speakers. How much can the poet assume about our willingness to put up with garrulity when it seems to have (and *must* seem to have, in Frost's insistence) no burning desire to convey a "meaning," but exists rather just for itself, is "free" in the nature of its expressiveness? In the long and important review Edward Garnett wrote of *North of Boston* after it had been published in this country in 1915, he came finally to noting a few defects in Frost's method, one of which was its tendency sometimes to be "both a little casual and longwinded," another of which was that his interest in rendering "fineness of psychological truth" was in excess of his interest in creating "poetic beauty." But Garnett added that these were inevitable defects in the realistic method. With reference to the above passage, we note the three lines in which the minister muses about how he cannot remember which town it was where the husband was killed, and how it does make a difference ("Fredericksburg wasn't Gettysburg, of course") but that what he is getting to is how forsaken the wife was after the husband's death. One's irritation at this extended playing with somewhat less than compelling content can only be tempered by the reminder that, unlike the minister, Frost isn't "getting to" anything;

that his purpose is importantly served by such "digressive" moments which, when broken out of—as the minister eventually does here—enhance the actuality and intimacy of the art, though they may try our patience in the process.

What the minister "gets to" eventually, as he delineates for us the old woman's stubborn innocence, is her adherence to certain truths, whatever contemporary experience said against them. So he decided to leave the phrase "descended into Hades" in the Creed (over the objections of other parishioners) because its deletion might have upset "her old tremulous bonnet in the pew." He warms to an eloquent homeliness in imagining her sense of loss:

> "But suppose she had missed it from the Creed,
> As a child misses the unsaid Good-night
> And falls asleep from heartache—how should *I* feel?
> I'm just as glad she made me keep hands off,
> For, dear me, why abandon a belief
> Merely because it ceases to be true.
> Cling to it long enough, and not a doubt
> It will turn true again, for so it goes."

This is the essential homely speech Frost created in *North of Boston,* heard most strongly in "The Death of the Hired Man," in "A Servant to Servants," or in the humorous exchanges of "The Mountain." With the appearance of this second book, readers began to hear that speech less as an artistic creation than as an expression of the real man himself, who was able on more than one occasion to provide uplifting wisdom—as here in the minister's portrait, or in Mary's description of "home" in the hired man poem, or in the woman's confession of her exhaustion in "A Servant to Servants."

There is no doubt that some of Frost's success in "reaching out," in being a poet to all sorts and kinds rather than caviare to the crowd, had to do with the easy way members of that crowd could identify the homely voice of a character with an inspiriting "country" man who disdained fancy or obscure poeticisms in the name of something more basic and wholesome. Yet the voices of those characters were created by artfully varied sentence sounds. What makes Frost's presence so much larger than the folksy model some would have had him fill, is the designed inclusiveness of his poetry. In "The Black Cottage," as the minister becomes fascinated with his notion of the timelessness of certain truths, of how most "change" we see is but a matter of one or another truth being "in or out of favor," he warms to an eloquence far above the homely sort previously heard. Now he imagines or wishes himself to be "monarch of a desert land" dedicated to timeless truths, and he develops at length and with intensity a figure of how the land would protect them:

> "So desert it would have to be, so walled
> By mountain ranges half in summer snow,
> No one would covet it or think it worth
> The pains of conquering to force change on.
> Scattered oases where men dwelt, but mostly
> Sand dunes held loosely in tamarisk
> Blown over and over themselves in idleness.
> Sand grains should sugar in the natal dew
> The babe born to the desert, the sand storm
> Retard mid-waste my cowering caravans—"

In this peak moment from the poem, the minister is vouchsafed a glimpse of that "freedom" which Frost experienced when writing at his best; another word for it could be "idleness," as in the lines above—the diligent idleness (or "indolence" in Keats's word) that is essential to the writing of poems.

But part of the reason this passage assumes importance is that the style in which it is composed is altogether different from the "absolutely unliterary" one Frost claimed he was employing in *North of Boston*. Rather than dropping "to a level of diction even Wordsworth kept above," he permits the minister to speak in a sweeping éxtended blank verse which gathers propulsive force as it moves along ("So desert it would have to be, so walled/ By mountain ranges"), catching up reader as well as character in its visionary splendor. It is a style filled with elaborate ornamental and assonantal effects ("Sand grains should sugar in the natal dew") and its diction is high enough to accomodate words like "natal" or "retard" or "cowering" or "covet." It feels stately and elevated because it contrasts sharply with the earlier, folksier ramblings of the minister ("I ought to know, it makes a difference which"). The presence here and in other poems from *North of Boston* (like "Home Burial" and "The Death of the Hired Man") of a relatively dignified and formal verse, should indicate that Frost's designing was too elaborate to be understood as "realism," as an attempt to imitate the way people actually talk. And the presence of these "higher" moments is his way of giving modulation and lifelike variety to what might otherwise have been monotonous, overlong sequences of the colloquial.

As suggested earlier, it is as an artful exploiter of rhythmic pace that Frost succeeds in these poems, one of the most dramatic instances of which occurs at the very end of "The Black Cottage," just as the minister seems to be winding up for a lengthy piece of rhetorical spinning-out of his desert fantasy. For suddenly he breaks off with a dash ("Retard mid-waste my cowering caravans—") and changes the subject:

> "There are bees in this wall." He struck the clapboards,
> Fierce heads looked out; small bodies pivoted.
> We rose to go. Sunset blazed on the windows.

Just that and no more; no final summary to let us know what it all meant, what was signified, finally, by the "special picture" we have chanced to catch. Only the bees remain, looking out and pivoting with no special motive except their bee-ness to keep them going. "We rose to go," and "Sunset blazed on the windows," are two further facts which along with the bees' agitation don't add up to any explanation or "symbolic" statement of innocence, permanence, or any such ultimate concern. We may be reminded once more of the lines from "Mowing"—"The fact is the sweetest dream that labor knows." Our departure from the house is effected in an atmosphere of fact, tersely expressed as noun and verb, subject and activity. When Pound said in the final sentence of his *North of Boston* review that "'The Black Cottage' is very clearly stated," he was probably admiring such statement in the final lines. But merely to speak of clear statement is an inadequate measure of the poem's whole method of expression. Frost is larger than Pound's vocabulary could encompass.

In fact Wordsworth, more than Pound, is relevant here, since one of his interests in writing the *Lyrical Ballads* was to demonstrate "the manner in which we associate ideas in a state of excitement." Like Wordsworth's, Frost's interest was psychological; in "The Black Cottage" the focus of interest is not the old woman who is talked about, but the association of ideas revealed in the shifting, intricate pattern of speech given to the minister. This speech—or "gossip"—in its actuality and intimacy is the substance of *North of Boston*. But Frost's interest in many of these poems was psychological in the more extended sense that he was concerned with the motives and hidden natures of men and women, particularly of women. When Randall Jarrell interviewed him at the Library of Congress in 1959, he questioned Frost closely about *North of Boston* and the fact that many of its poems featured women, often speaking out of conditions of deprivation, with secrets long held back but now—given the occasion of the poem—finally able to be uttered. Frost told Jarrell that "the woman always loses" but added that "she loses in an interesting way. She pulls the whole thing down with her." This remark attributes power to "the woman" even as it designates her the loser in whatever she suffers at the hands of her husband or her family or of "life" generally.

Such an engagement with the idea of loss meets its counterpart in Frost's insistence in the same interview that he had tried to write poems for *North of Boston* without villains. "In tragic life no villain need be," he said, quoting George Meredith, and he recalled telling Amy Lowell that she was like Shakespeare because she couldn't get along without villains in her poems. (Lowell riposted that he was really saying she should be more like Frost in constructing villain-less poems; Frost replied that no he hadn't said that, just that she was more like Shakespeare.) To write a poem in which something terrible happens and no one is to blame—as in "Home Burial" with the different responses of husband and wife to the death of their young child—Frost felt as a challenge, as it was a challenge to write a poem about a worn-out old hired man who has come home to die, and to bring out an interplay of sympathy and judgment by setting in motion the contrasting voices of man and woman. His effort was to attempt, through language, moral feeling, and a truly represented "life," not to load the dice in favor of one idea, but to strive rather for inclusiveness.

The "personal" narratives from the book—"Mending Wall," "After Apple-Picking," and "The Wood-Pile"—also strive for inclusiveness although they are spoken throughout by a voice we are tempted to call "Frost." This voice has no particular back-country identity, nor is it obsessed or limited in its point of view; it seems rather to be exploring nature, other people, ideas, ways of saying things, for the sheer entertainment they can provide. Unlike poems such as "Home Burial" and "A Servant to Servants," which are inclined toward the tragic or the pathetic, nothing "terrible" happens in the personal narratives, nor does some ominous secret lie behind them. In "The Wood-Pile," for example, almost nothing happens at all; its story, its achieved idea or wisdom, the whole air with which it carries itself, is quite unmemorable. A man out walking in a frozen swamp decides to turn back, then decides instead to go farther and see what will happen. He notes a bird in front of him and spends some time musing on what the bird must be thinking, then sees it settle behind a pile of wood. The pile is described so as to bring out the fact that it has been around for some time. With a reflection about whoever it was who left it there, "far from a useful fireplace," the poem concludes. And the reader looks up from the text, wonders if he has missed something, perhaps goes back and reads it again to see if he can catch some meaning which has eluded him. But "The Wood-Pile" remains stubbornly unyielding to any attempt at ransacking it for a meaning not evidently on the surface.

This surface is a busy one, as when the speaker meets the bird:

> A small bird flew before me. He was careful
> To put a tree between us when he lighted,
> And say no word to tell me who he was
> Who was so foolish as to think what *he* thought.
> He thought that I was after him for a feather—
> The white one in his tail; like one who takes
> Everything said as personal to himself.
> One flight out sideways would have undeceived him.

The bird is teased for its egoism in thinking that the world revolves around his subjective hopes and fears, and his nervousness is amusing because never was there a less predatory or even purposeful figure than the walker in this poem, who early along—in deciding to continue rather than turn back—put it this way: "No, I will go on farther—and we shall see." See what? See things like a bird lighting in a tree, and be free to make up a story about why it doesn't speak, or how jealously protective it is of the white feather in its tail? Being free to "see" means indulging in such harmless playful fantasies the freedom of whose play is a measure of its solitary creation, far from any human or social situation. Perhaps the point of maximum play occurs in the lines about the bird's caution as he lights in the tree and determines to look only: "And say no word to tell me who he was / Who was so foolish as to think what *he* thought." The monosyllabic tongue-twisting aspect of these lines is effective in mixing up the reader: *who* is more "foolish," man or bird, and how on earth can one tell?

Then there is the wood-pile itself, a cord of maple, split, piled and measured

>                  . . . four by four by eight.
> And not another like it could I see.
> No runner tracks in this year's snow looped near it.
> And it was older sure than this year's cutting,
> Or even last year's or the year's before.

> The wood was grey and the bark warping off it
> And the pile somewhat sunken. Clematis
> Had wound strings round and round it like a bundle.
> What held it, though, on one side was a tree
> Still growing, and on one a stake and prop,
> These latter about to fall . . .

This is a thoroughly unexciting presentation of what might lay claim to be the world's most unexceptional phenomenon, yet it engages the man enough to occupy him for the remainder of the poem. More interesting than anything it "says" is the way the presentation resists, as solidly as does the sunken woodpile, our readerly efforts to find a message in it, to take it as a symbol for something or other important. In so resisting us, the woodpile confirms the teasing character of the whole poem, always leading us on, promising that around the next corner, past the next tree, we shall see something, if we but have faith to follow the walker: and then, sure enough, there it is—an old woodpile with clematis wound round it, its very situation (its "stake and prop" about to collapse) precarious.

This is all we see, except that Frost moves to reflection, concluding the poem with these lines in which the pile of wood is extended into something more:

> . . . I thought that only
> Someone who lives in turning to fresh tasks
> Could so forget his handiwork on which
> He spent himself, the labor of his ax,
> And leave it there far from a useful fireplace
> To warm the frozen swamp as best it could
> With the slow smokeless burning of decay.

The final line has been rightly admired, but its brilliance almost blinds us to the fact that the reflection which it concludes is in no sense a stunning or profound one. The thought that "someone" who abandoned this pile of wood must be one who "lived in turning to fresh tasks," is certainly uncontroversial and hardly provocative of further speculation. Again the interest lies not in "content" but in the way a sentence develops over seven lines, winding from the "I" to the "someone" and finally to the "handiwork" whose thermal activity is celebrated in the ingenuity of the final three lines. As with other moments in the poem, no great claims are made, no meanings are held out for everyone to use, no praise or blame is assigned to motive or action.

Early in "The Wood-Pile" the walker is surrounded by "tall slim trees / Too much alike to mark or name a place by / So as to say for certain I was here / Or somewhere else . . ." By the poem's end a marking has been taken, a place named, though in a way so fanciful as to establish that it is poetry we are responding to when we try to think of that decaying pile, warming the frozen swamp as best it can.

To alter the walker's final thought: only someone, like a poet, who lives in turning to fresh tropes could write a poem like the one Frost has written here, and it is an appropriate conclusion to what remains the most original, even revolutionary, book he would ever write. We need to recall once more the language Edward Thomas used in defining and in praising it, about how Frost trusted his convictions about the validity of speech in poetry, of sentence sounds employed with "no purpose to serve beyond expressing it, when he has no audience to be bullied or flattered, when he is free, and speech takes one form and no other." Despite the presence of back-country characters and scenes in this "book of people," it is as a book of sentence sounds that it most truly exists, as a triumphant vindication of the poetic theory Frost had designed, and as a monument to how much could be accomplished by trusting to the rendering of speech. At the end of "Home Burial," the wife lashes out at her husband in exasperation: "*You*—oh, you think the talk is all . . ." But for the composer of these poems, the talk *is* all, whether that of his imagined characters or of himself speaking aloud.

In a recent, critically intelligent book, *Robert Frost and New England,* John Kemp notes that when Frost wrote to Bartlett in August of 1913 about a book to be called, tentatively, *New England Eclogues,* made up of "stories" from between one to two hundred lines, he sent along a list of eleven poems, one of which bore the title "Swinging Birches." The other poems from the list duly appeared in *North of Boston* (one of them, titled "The Wrong" appearing as either "Home Burial" or "The Self-Seeker") but "Swinging Birches" did not: it was later to be published as "Birches" in Frost's next volume, *Mountain Interval.* Mr. Kemp thinks it appropriate for Frost to have excluded it since, and unlike the other "meditative lyrics" (Kemp's phrase) which he added to the list of eleven—"Mending Wall," "After Apple-Picking," and "The Wood-Pile"—"Birches" is more overtly philosophical, offering sage observations about life and love which the *North of Boston* poems, rooted in the realism of experience, do not offer. Kemp argues, plausibly, that "Birches" is an important poem because it is predictive of so much in Frost's later work, but that it is also ominously predictive. For the poet will soon begin to believe his own myth, believe in himself as a wise New England farmer-moralist, and will turn into the cracker-barrel sage who became the favorite poet of thousands. At least one other critic, Louise Bogan, agreed, and in her brief survey of American poetry she took a similar line by saying that Frost in *North of Boston* "briefly possessed himself of a humane realism and insight which he was never quite able to repeat."

Such judgments are the product of hindsight, of inestimable use to critics but unavailable to the poet engaged in his work of composition. Their implication is that Frost would have been a better poet if he had kept on writing in the mode of *North of Boston;* that he should have suppressed his inclinations to play—however much in earnest—the New Hampshire or Vermont sage. But aside from the appropriateness of taking a slightly reproving tone toward a poet's career (which unlike the critic he never got the chance to look at dispassionately, from the outside), there is the specialness of Frost's situation to which the critics have not fully responded. This situation might be viewed in the following manner: an aspiring poet at age forty puts together a collection of "farm" narratives using incidents and stories heard about or remembered. He is at all times careful to keep his hands off the characters, as if their speech were issuing forth of its own accord, untouched by the creator's thumb of moral judgment and assessment. On the whole the technique works brilliantly, even though the reader—in 1914 or seventy years later—must struggle with questions about the sort of poetry it is, or whether it has to go on for quite so long, or if the rendering of sentence sounds and speech rhythms is enough in itself to justify the enterprise. These questions do not arise in connection with poems written contemporaneously with *North of Boston* by Thomas Hardy ("The Convergence of the Twain"), or W. B. Yeats ("The Fisherman"), or Wallace Stevens ("Sunday Morning"). By contrast, Frost's poems are as experimental as Eliot's "Prufrock" or "Portrait of a Lady," and to wish that he had gone on writing more of them, rather than returning to the mode only on occasion— as with "The Witch of Coös," say—is to run him, retrospectively, another kind of risk. Imagine the reader of 1916 waiting for a new volume which he hopes will contain "more *North of Boston.*" Like Eliot, one might guess that Frost was unwilling to repeat himself, to work a familiar vein even if it had proved a good one. The question that we should ask ourselves, as perhaps he did, is whether one *North of Boston* isn't enough.

England went to war in August of 1914. Frost had hoped to stay there long enough to see one more book through the press, feeling somehow that three was the number that would "clinch" things. But as he wrote home to Cox on August 20, the war ended all such thoughts of publishing further books. "Our game is up," as he put it— with some disregard for world politics—more than once. He claimed to approve of the war, of the idea of "abolishing Prussia," but also said he had no business approving of something he was not himself ready to die for. In September he and the family left their cottage at Little Iddens and moved in to share Abercrombie's house in nearby Ryton, Dymock. The plan was originally to stay on through the coming winter; but as the Germans increasingly made their presence felt at sea, Frost began to ask how long he dared stay, reasoning that it might become more dangerous to leave later rather than sooner, and that having money sent across the Atlantic might become ever more difficult. By Christmas he was feeling the uselessness of pursuing a poetic career in England at this unpropitious time, and feeling also that his children should be removed from any possible danger. Holt had agreed to bring out both *A Boy's Will* and *North of Boston* in America, and was interested in publishing further books assuming sales were successful. One way to help those sales would be for the poet to mastermind things by being on the scene rather than an ocean's distance away. That fall, for the first time, Frost expressed in a letter to Cox the desire for "a quiet job in a small college where I should be allowed to teach something a little new on the technique of writing and where I should have some honor for what I suppose myself to have done in poetry." He warned himself not to dream; at the same time, with the example to hand of his success in England, he knew that his dreams had a way of coming true.

Concurrently, he managed to convince himself that American education was in a bad way, especially as it concerned the teaching of literature. Reading the American critic G. E. Woodbury's article on American literature in the eleventh edition of the *Britannica,* an article which concluded with some pessimistic thoughts about how the university went about teaching "English," Frost decided that the emphasis was wrongly on knowledge rather than on aesthetic response: "No one is taught to value himself for nice perception and cultivated taste'" he wrote to Cox. But he believed that literature—

like love and friendship and religion—must not be regarded as something to be studied professionally. What it needed rather—and what was thoroughly lacking in the "German thoroughness" of the professional "knowledge" approach—was "the light touch." By January as he made plans for a February departure, he had decided on looking around for "a small college with the chance of teaching a few ideas." If that didn't work out, why then "I shall get me a farm where between milking one cow and another I shall write Books III IV & V and perhaps draw a few people about me in time in a sort of summer literary camp." The astonishing thing about these sentences of course is the way they stake out Frost's major activities over the next decade or so: teaching at Amherst College; milking one cow or another at his farms first in Franconia, New Hampshire, then at South Shaftsbury, Vermont; summer associations with the Bread Loaf School of English beginning in 1926; and last but not least—indeed the purpose animating all the others—the composition and publication of those next three books of poetry: *Mountain Interval* (1916), *New Hampshire* (1923), and *West-Running Brook* (1928). He was still "not undesigning."

The Frosts sailed from Liverpool on February 13, navigating with success and with the aid of British destroyers the hazards of possible mines and submarines. Before sailing he wrote a short note to F. S. Flint, with whom he had been out of touch since his break with Pound. But at this final moment of his English adventure, and surely with the sense that his success thus far as a poet was at least as much as he could have anticipated, he looked back to the person who more than anyone else he felt was responsible for it:

Dear Flint

I ought to know by the length of your silence that you don't want to write to me any more—cor silicis. And if you don't I ought to have pride enough not to ask you to. But no matter: I must at least say goodbye to the man who opened England to me. You are good. Sincerely yours Frost.

It is one last and typical performance just before the boat sailed. There is the slightly aggrieved opening about being neglected, leavened by the Latin pun *cor silicis*—heart of stone, or flint, then the expressed compunction ("if you don't I ought to have pride enough not to ask you to") magnanimously waved aside with "But no matter," after which he moves out into a romantic tribute to Flint as the opener of all England to him. Finally a three word tribute: "You are good." That done and with those words written, it was certainly time to go home.

# IV

## Forms of Guardedness

Frost's return to the United States in 1915 was accompanied by one piece of good fortune after another and marked the bursting forth of a career which would come to its first peak nine years later, when he won the Pulitzer Prize for *New Hampshire,* his fourth book of poems. From the moment when, on Washington's birthday, the SS *St. Paul* docked in New York City with the Frost family aboard, his return— as with the departure two and a half years earlier to "the land of *The Golden Treasury*"—was infused with the impulsive and the poetic. The man who had stolen away to England had now returned with two published books of poetry and the beginnings of a literary reputation. So it had transpired, as naturally as breathing. Of course this sense of a new life as just somehow transpiring ("That will transpire presently") rather than being planned out in advance, was partly a product of Frost's way of looking at his own past, and was indicative of the wish to have things occur as if without grim forethought or too obvious manipulation. Yet we have observed how assiduous he was, during his stay in England, at keeping track of reviews and reviewers, and of trying—through letters home to Bartlett and Cox—to mitigate any possible offense that Pound's championing him as a poet unappreciated by American editors might cause. If anything, he was in the years ahead to intensify and orchestrate ever more complexly such public relations work. Still, through it all shines the kind of happening in which fact and sweetest dream are, for a moment, indistinguishable—the true reward for the labor of years. Here then was the just-returned poet, strolling out in the neighborhood of Grand Central Station to view the great city once more, when, passing a newsstand, his eyes alighted on a new magazine called the *New Republic.* This, when examined, revealed Amy Lowell's admiring review of a book called *North of Boston* by a newcomer to the poetry scene, Mr. Robert Frost. He had come home in a large way, on the birthday of his country's founder, to find himself saluted—in a new magazine with a boldly promising title—as a distinctively American poet, by one of the apostles of what was termed the The New Poetry. To be "American" in Amy Lowell's sense of the word was to work, as Frost did in *North of Boston,* in "local color," and with a realism that she called "photographic." She insisted on distinguishing this kind of American writing from something she called rather awkwardly "the subtler sense in which Poe ranks as the greatest American poet." Frost could not have been overjoyed either by this qualification or by the insight provided by her criticism of his poetry. As others had already done, she saluted him for his simplicity and directness, while claiming that various things he lacked, like "exotic music" and "subtleties of expression," would be out of place in so elementary a talent. But, after these reservations, she came down very much on the side of the book, and, as with the earlier headline about England being "in the grip of Frost," he accepted the omen.

Choosing to remain in New York after he put his family on the train for their destination at the home of a family in Bethlehem, New Hampshire, he put his time to beneficial use. The ostensible occasion for delaying in New York was a problem about the status of Edward Thomas's son, who had accompanied the Frosts to America and was going to live with friends in New Hampshire. Immigration difficulties made it necessary for Frost to return to Ellis Island to show evidence that the boy, an alien under sixteen years, would be properly looked after financially. Yet one feels that something more was at work in Frost's lingering, especially since one thing led to another so perfectly: the discovery of Amy Lowell's review; a visit to the offices of his American publisher, Henry Holt; his meeting at the Holt offices with Alfred Harcourt, the trade books editor, who gave Frost a check for "The Death of the Hired Man" which had appeared in the *New Republic* a couple of weeks previously. From Harcourt came the urging that he attend a meeting of the Poetry Society, also a small luncheon with members of the *New Republic* staff, including Herbert Croly and Walter Lippmann. And Frost went on to look up Mrs. Holt, whose original interest in *North of Boston* had been responsible for bringing it to the attention of the publishing house.

These professional and literary operations were conducted with Elinor and the children safely off in New Hampshire, and it would be silly to seize upon this fact as in itself particularly telling, since Frost had done a fair amount of such activity during the last two years in his trips to London. But the small round of visits marking his New York reception is important as the beginning of what was to be an altogether larger, public literary life than Elinor or even her husband dreamed might be the case. One is reminded of this fact by a vivid outburst Frost made in a letter to his new friend Louis Untermeyer two years later, in response to Amy Lowell's chapter about him in her *Tendencies in Modern Poetry*. Frost pointed out various ways she had gotten him wrong, such as overstating the influence on him of Gibson and Abercrombie, or insisting upon his "morbid" side while overlooking the sense of humor she mistakenly thought he didn't possess. But he was annoyed mainly by a remark of hers about how he owed "an immeasurable debt to the steadfast purpose of his wife," whom Amy Lowell spoke of in another place as a "spur" to his creative success. Frost responded with the following disclaimer to Untermeyer:

> That's an unpardonable attempt to do her as the conventional helpmeet of genius. Elinor has never been of any earthly use to me. She hasn't cared whether I went to school or worked or earned anything. She has resisted every inch of the way my efforts to get money. She is not too sure that she cares about my reputation. She wouldn't lift a hand or have me lift a hand to increase my reputation or even save it. And this isn't all from devotion to my art at its highest. She seems to have the same weakness I have for a life that goes rather poetically; only I should say she is worse than I . . . And it isn't that she doesn't think I am a good poet either. She always knew I was a good poet, but that was between her and me, and there I think she would have liked it if it had remained at least until we were dead.

He went on to mock the idea that his wife received satisfaction from her "housekeeping" since it was in the service of feeding a poet ("Rats! She hates housekeeping"), and also noted that "She's especially wary of honors that derogate from the poetic life she fancies us living."

This typically complicated response faces more than one way. It can be read as rescuing Elinor from the unthinking clichés through which Amy Lowell portrayed her, all "steadfast purpose" and "spur" to her husband's ambition. She is above such clichés, as she is above caring about such worldly things as her husband's reputation. But if she is above such things, she is also apart from them, in a way Frost has mixed feelings about. "Elinor has never been of any earthly use to me": is it going too far to hear just the hint of a complaint in that declaration? Or a puzzled wonderment that she hasn't "cared" enough about any of the enterprises in which he has been actively engaged, to take a hand in encouraging them? And does Frost need to exaggerate her unconcern so that he and nobody else will be responsible for his success as a poet? Elinor, like him, has a weakness for "a life that goes rather poetically"; yet, unlike her, Frost is taking most aggressive steps to insure that he will receive just that public acclaim which may put such a life in danger. No deference toward their privately shared secret—the "secret" of his poems—will deter him from taking steps to widen his reputation beyond the private sphere. So there is something of a thin line being walked here in this vigorous correction of Amy Lowell's portrait.

The letter to Untermeyer about Elinor was written in 1917. In 1915, newly arrived back and on his own in New York, Frost had a sense that the time to embark fully upon his American literary career was now. Not content with a more than satisfactory reception in New York, he continued his operations in Boston, remaining there for a time after visiting Wilbur Rowell (executor of his grandfather's estate) and other Lawrence acquaintances. Here, even more than in New York, one thing led quickly to another, and by the time he headed home to New Hampshire—as he put it later to Sidney Cox— he had become further involved in publicizing his career. One of the publicizers was Ellery Sedgwick, editor of the *Atlantic Monthly,* to whom Frost had previously sent some poems from *North of Boston* which Sedgwick turned down. This time the editor was charmed, genuinely so it appears, since he later wrote to Edward Garnett—whose lengthy appreciation of Frost's second book would be published in the *Atlantic* (it stands as permanently useful criticism)—that he found Frost "quite delightful—as unspoiled as when he left his Vermont plough for his quite extraordinary adventures in poetical England." Never mind the Vermont plough, which hadn't yet been wielded by this unspoiled person, and whom Sedgwick had of course never met in his earlier, presumably unspoiled state. The point was that Frost managed to weave, through his appearance, tone of voice, the things he said and the way he said them, a benign spell over one of Boston's culture guardians. Sedgwick invited him home to supper, and suggested he get in touch with two Boston literary men, Nathan Dole and Sylvester Baxter, who were reading aloud poems from *North of Bos-*

*ton* at the Boston Authors' Club. Dole not only put up Frost for the night, but introduced him to the *Transcript's* W. S. Braithwaite who had begun to edit a yearly *Anthology of Magazine Verse* and whom Frost used both as conduit and stimulus for the letter referred to earlier, with its interesting formulations about gossip, the vernacular, and the speaking voice. Last but not least there was Amy Lowell, who had already alerted Sedgwick to Frost's virtues and who upon receiving a phone call from Frost invited him to dinner at her Brookline mansion, at which occasion John Gould Fletcher, enjoying some reputation at the time, was also present.

The heady freshness of all these meetings, which are of less interest in their individual occurrences than when taken together as indication of how the wind was blowing, was surely enhanced by Frost's having so recently returned to his home country. As anyone knows who comes back from a long stay abroad, there is a sense of possibility and newness available in one's first days back that releases new kinds of adventuresome energy: in the words of "The Trial by Existence," "To find that the utmost reward / Of daring should be still to dare." Of the people he met in New York and Boston, with the exception of Alfred Harcourt (with whom he remained on warm terms for many years), none became Frost's friends for long; in the case of Braithwaite and Lowell there was a large disparity between the way he dealt with them publicly and what he said about them in the privacy of letters to people he trusted. A remark from one of his notebooks puts with candor his sense of himself in relation to other people who might be of use to him in his attempt, in poetry, to reach out, not ever to become "caviare to the crowd": "You have to be attractive enough to get people within striking distance." This formulation need not be reduced to the literal-minded supposition that Frost was looking to do them violence; but he did want to "strike" them, and that depended on being "attractive." At a certain point in his relations with them, neither Sedgwick nor Braithwaite nor Lowell needed to be kept within such distance.

The most important of his new acquaintances, who would develop into a lifetime friend, was Louis Untermeyer, who had first read Frost in the December 1913 issue of Monro's *Poetry and Drama* where "The Fear" and "A Hundred Collars" appeared. Untermeyer assumed Frost was English until disabused by Abercrombie, and they met for the first time in 1915 soon after Untermeyer published a laudatory review of *North of Boston,* hailing it as the beginning of a great career. In his memoir, *Bygones,* Untermeyer nicely describes the first time he ever heard Frost read his poetry aloud. It was in Malden, Massachusetts, at a small gathering where Frost read badly, too conscious of being on exhibition and unsure of the sort of role he should play. Untermeyer remembers with clarity

the proper Bostonians, fashionably dressed, listening with a mixture of curiosity, skepticism, and tolerance to a "rustic" from the Northeast Corner who had teased the imagination of the metropolis; Frost, declining to comment on his work, reciting or, as he called it, "saying" a couple of lyrics and a few of the monologues from *North of Boston,* refusing to be quaint (he was deeply offended when someone introduced him as "our farmer-poet"), and underplaying, actually throwing away, line after line. His readings, like his poems, were the essence of understatement.

This shrewd observation is typical of Untermeyer's perspicacity and suggests something of why Frost was drawn to him. Although from the very beginning he was the strongest of admirers, giving Frost pride of place in his survey of American poetry since 1900, it would be mistaken to see Untermeyer as merely an adoring sycophant. For one thing, the appreciation in his chapter on Frost in the survey is just and intelligent; for another, Untermeyer was a humorous man who loved to pun and generally carry on with language in a manner congenial to Frost. So for all the use he was to Frost as a publicist, a New York-based poetry enterpreneur who edited many anthologies, the affinity ran deeper.

More than any of Frost's other early critics, Untermeyer recognized what he later termed his "irrepressible sense of play," a "delight in fooling for its own sake," and he was willing to play along with it, indeed play back to it. By November of 1915 Frost was writing him in this manner: "You and I are not clever, Louis: we are cunning, one with the cunning of race [Untermeyer was a Jew] the other with the cunning of insanity. (All women are cunning with the cunning of sex.)" A few years later he would fill Untermeyer in on plans for an "epic of dentistry" he claimed to be about to write concerning "the life of a dentist I used to know who had gone out from a New England hill farm to learn dentistry and became dentist to the crowned head of South America, the emperor Dom Pedro of Brazil." This is pure fooling, an example of the sort of thing Frost had asked for at the outset of their correspondence. In the first letter he wrote which addressed Untermeyer by his first name, he wished that they could be on "emotional" terms, without "controversy" or the need to credit "one or the other with more or less than we mean. Then we shall know when we are fooling because we shall be always fooling like a pair gay with love." This "security," Frost went on to say, was what he meant by the beauty of friendship, and (he said) it was the opposite of enmity, the beauty of which lay in its insecurity.

To claim that there is a beauty in "enmity," or that "all women are cunning with the cunning of sex," is to make formulations designed to startle and shock, also to entertain, whether the audience is Untermeyer or a reader of the correspondence today. Some critics of Frost's life feel that only a man suffering from deep personal insecurities would say such things, would actively warm to the disparaging of another's accomplishments or personality, would be seriously pained to see the work of a contemporary meet with applause comparable to what his own was receiving. But the impulse toward satire, the "curse of humor"—as a character in a Wyndham Lewis novel referred to it—will not be easily dislodged by such psychological "understanding." The satiric impulse is deliberately *unfair* in that it refuses to treat other people as human beings with real feelings, with inner lives—refuses to try to understand all and thus forgive all. Rather, it seizes on a single aspect of a person, or a person's work, a partial truth, and exaggerates it by developing it into a simplification, a caricature which it is comically satisfying to contemplate.

Except for moments in the humorous poems from *North of Boston,* Frost's published poetry up to 1915 had showed very little of the satiric impulse and nothing of the "enmity" he talked about to Untermeyer. But the letters home from England were full of sharp and sometimes bitterly turned comments, less than flattering character portrayals of Pound and W. H. Davies, critical ridicule directed at the theories or poems of Robert Bridges, Rupert Brooke, Alfred Noyes and others. In 1915, back in America and very much concerned with protecting his growing reputation, he used Untermeyer's willing ear as a recipient of increasingly satiric thrusts at some of the other figures in the "poetic renaissance" which Harriet Monroe and Amy Lowell were touting. Untermeyer himself had enthusiastically described the New Poetry as having swung back, in Whitmanesque manner, "to actuality, to heartiness and lustihood." Besides *North of Boston,* two major contributions to actuality and heartiness, perhaps to lustihood also, were Edgar Lee Masters's *Spoon River Anthology* (1915) and Carl Sandburg's *Chicago Poems,* published the following year. Masters's sequence of vignettes of small-town life was especially popular: Untermeyer had praised it, and Braithwaite in his *Anthology of Magazine Verse* for 1915 referred to Masters, along with Frost, as "the two great successes of the year."

Edgar Lee Masters had published a number of volumes before *Spoon River,* all of them conventional in sentiment and form; now he had hit upon the sort of "unconventional" procedure seen in "Ollie McGee," one of the earliest portraits in the new book:

> Have you seen walking through the village
> A man with downcast eyes and haggard face?
> That is my husband who, by secret cruelty
> Never to be told, robbed me of my youth and my  beauty;
> Till at last, wrinkled and with yellow teeth,
> And with broken pride and shameful humility,
> I sank into the grave.
> But what think you gnaws at my husband's heart?
> The face of what I was, the face of what he made me?
> These are driving him to the place where I lie.
> In death, therefore, I am avenged.

Such strokes of heavy-handed melodramatic gesture, though bereft of rhythmic distinction or unity, found an audience eager to hear small-town life debunked in what was soon to be a popular sport. But Frost was not at all interested in seeing small-town life debunked, especially by a competitor; furthermore he was predisposed to like neither the tone of Masters's sentiments nor the irregular verse in which they were couched. Although he claimed to Untermeyer that he had a "real liking" for the book, he also called it "too romantic for my taste, and by romantic I'm afraid I mean among other things false-realistic." Three years later he returned to the subject in a complicated manner ("I can't say for certain that I don't like Spoon River. I believe I do like it in a way") by wishing the book "weren't so nearly the ordinary thing in its attitude toward respectability":

> How shall we treat respectability? That is not for me to say: I am not treating it. All I know with any conviction is that an idea has to be a little new to be at all true and if you say a thing three times it ceases to be so. Mind you I am not finding fault—I never am—only—to be frank, the book chews tobacco I'm afraid. Perhaps that's *why* I like it.

Emerging from this elaborately drawn apology for why he doesn't (or does) like Masters, is an absolutely telling and final criticism of the whole Spoon River enterprise. Masters's book is "against" respectability; it delights in bringing bankers and other successful citizens to grief and to the grave where they lie side by side with the town drunk, the abandoned woman, the prostitute, and other types. But since the poem goes on for a long time, drumming in its idea, that idea ceases to be true—too "romantic" because of its crude notion of what constitutes realism. In other words, it "chews tobacco," which is fine for a baseball player but not so fine for a poet whose hardboiled Illinois realism was merely the reverse of his earlier, poetical efforts.

Masters's reputation was soon to fade, as too many books too quickly succeeded *Spoon River,* and Frost began to refer to him condescendingly as "poor old Masters," or mock-heroically as "my hated rival." Sandburg, whose *Chicago Poems* were also published by Holt, and in the same year as Frost's *Mountain Interval* (1916), was not similarly destined to fade, and came eventually to be thought of by many as—along with Frost—the archetypical American poet, fine white hair and all. For Sandburg's free verse Frost felt contempt, and it later provided the stimulus for his famous remark that he would as soon write free verse as play tennis with the net down. But Sandburg's manner—that of the popular bard full of (in Untermeyer's words about the New American poetry) heartiness and lustihood—bothered him even more, finally provoking him to write the following to his daughter Lesley in 1922, after Sandburg had visited the University of Michigan where Frost was teaching at the time:

> We've been having a dose of Carl Sandburg. He's another person I find it hard to do justice to. He was possibly [three] hours in town and he spent one of those washing his white hair and toughening his expression for his public performance. His mandolin pleased some people, his poetry a very few and his infantile talk none. His affectations have almost buried him out of sight. He is probably the most artificial and studied ruffian the world has had . . . I heard somebody say he was the kind of writer who had everything to gain and nothing to lose by being translated into another language.

Thompson calls this a "bitter" reaction, neglecting to point out what a forceful study in satiric reduction it presents. Frost's picture of the poet preparing for his performance by washing his hair and "toughening" his features, is a truly creative one; in bringing together carefully chosen adjectives ("artificial," "studied") with the manly noun ("ruffian"), it casts a fresh perspective on Sandburg's midwest heartiness, while the sentence beginning "His mandolin pleased some people" is a little masterpiece of rhythmic dispatch. (On a later occasion he remarked that while Sandburg said "The People, Yes!" he, Frost, said "The People, Yes and No!")

These formulations about Masters and Sandburg are something more than malicious or envious—even though envy and malice went into their composition—since not only are they expressed with satiric originality but they penetrate to the heart of another poet's performance. On a different level they can be understood as ways of staving off troubling thoughts about what it meant to be an acclaimed "best-selling" poet, as he had become when *North of Boston* went into a number of printings. Frost had determined, he wrote from England, to "reach out to all sorts and kinds"; now he looked round him and noted the character of two other poets who were having similar success at reaching out. In the Masters of *Spoon River* he saw a "realism" which wasn't really realism, but sentimental, tough-guy romance; in Sandburg he saw affectation and guitar-playing and free verse. Yet they were linked with him, as apostles of the New American Poetry. It become important then for Frost to be able to say why—to friendly ears like Untermeyer's or, later, Lincoln MacVeagh's, his new editor at Holt—that linkage was a mistake; why his brand of realism, his brand of romance, the form of his verse, possessed kinds of oppositions and balances, possessed a delicacy of utterance and of spirit, which theirs did not.

The point of stressing the positive element in Frost's friendship with Untermeyer, and his expressive distaste for the poetry of Masters and Sandburg, is to suggest that these instances of friendship and enmity had their base in intelligent feeling and cannot be reduced to cynically self-furthering or desperately self-protective acts. This does not mean he was above manipulating others out of the desire to advertise himself, and when this manipulation went on with a person for whom he had little intellectual or personal respect, the spectacle is unpleasant. Perhaps the most embarrassing instance of Frost's opportunistic behavior occurred with the journalist-anthologist Braithwaite, who wrote a couple of newspaper articles on the basis of information Frost provided him in 1915. Soon afterwards he invited Braithwaite up to his Franconia farm, and gave a sympathetic ear when Braithwaite mentioned an annoyed letter Pound had published in the *Transcript,* claiming credit for helping to discover Frost and also referring, slurringly, to Braithwaite as "your (?negro) reviewer." The fact that

Braithwaite was black was guaranteed not to raise him in Frost's eyes, whose prejudices in racial matters were automatic and unquestioned. But that he commanded readers in his newspaper, and would publish "The Road Not Taken" and "The Death of the Hired Man" in his *Anthology,* made him worth cultivating.

The level of taste and discrimination at which Braithwaite operated may be gathered from the opening of his Introduction to his 1915 anthology, titled "The Eternal Reality of Poetry—An Analogue":

> The very name of April has a quiet mystery when spoken: as if at the sound of those soft and liquid letters some haunting memory begins to glow wth indefinable ecstasies. The name leads one to sense a curious kind of secrecy, wherein some stirring and changing miracles are happening. It lures one into harmony with something intangibly but delightfully and poignantly strange.

He goes on to speak, rapturously, about poetry as "A Breath, a Vision, a Realization of Immortality" whose "one message is Life!" Here we have the last dregs of popular romanticism, and the writer of such indefinable ecstasies was the man Frost was warmly inviting to visit him in New Hampshire, which visit would presumably include much talk about poetry. (The event is hard to imagine, and, in fact, never took place.) Summing up the best poems of 1915 in the *Transcript,* Braithwaite made a list of five, including ones by Amy Lowell and Wallace Stevens ("Peter Quince at the Clavier," which Frost didn't like, he said, because although it used the word "bawdy" it also purported to make us think), and one by a less familiar name, Marjorie French Patten, whose "Needle Work" has the following lines evoking a woman's imagined journey as she sews:

> Friends to greet on the jolly road,
> Lopeing rabbit, and squatting toad,
> Beetle, trundling along with your load;
> Hey, little friends,
> Good-day, good-morrow,
> You see me to-day,
> You forget me to-morrow.

If this poem, rather than "Birches" or "The Road Not Taken" or "The Death of the Hired Man"—its companions in the 1915 anthology—was an especially notable achievement, then what kind of conversation about poetry could Frost have had with Braithwaite? The annoyance, but more likely the embarrassment or self-con-

tempt Frost probably felt in "reaching out" to a reader with such pro-
miscuous literary tastes as Braithwaite's, expressed itself in an outburst to Untermeyer, shocking in its vengeful crudity, as in a pre-
Christmas note Frost wrote "Sometime at a worse season I will tell
you what I think of niggers and having said so much to pollute this
letter I will break off here and begin over on a fresh sheet which I will
mail under a separate cover." When he published Frost's letters in
1963 after his death, Untermeyer couldn't quite bear to pollute them
with that word, so he substituted "Braithwaite" for "niggers," and he
also omitted the opening paragraph of a follow-up letter in which
Frost made heavy and unpleasant play with the words "niggardly"
and "niggerly." Yet a couple of months later Frost wrote an amiable
letter to Braithwaite, saying that he could "have the poem on Shakespeare" if he, Frost, could write it (he never did, unless it was " 'Out,
Out—' " which appeared later that year) and saluted him in sugary
language such as Braithwaite himself used about poetry: "These are
piping times and surely you are one of the pipers." It is difficult to
ascertain the exact degree of cynicism which lay behind such unmemorable words. But the relationship with Braithwaite was a cautionary instance of the perils of "reaching out," of seeking to widen that
reputation which Frost said his wife would not "lift a hand" to widen.
There would be more of such instances to come.

---

He had purchased, in the spring of 1915, a farm in Franconia, New
Hampshire, within striking distance of Lafayette Mountain, the highest of the Franconia range of White Mountain peaks, and while making preparations to occupy it the Frosts continued to board with the
Lynch family in nearby Bethlehem. The children, who had been pretty
much out of school during their English sojourn, would begin in the
fall to attend the local grammar and high schools, and a tone of nervous apprehension, so characteristic of Elinor Frost's letters, can be
heard as she wrote in June of that year to Margaret Bartlett about
the prospect of settling in Franconia:

> I think we shall enjoy our new home very much. I wish the house was
> just a little larger, but its such a cheerful, cosy place that I am willing
> to endure some inconveniences. The view is very fine, and the village of
> Franconia is exceptionally attractive. All I ask is that the children will
> like the school there and will find a few nice children for companions.

They have been out of school for so long that it will be a bit difficult for them to fit in, I fear, and I tremble at the possibility of their disliking the whole place, and if they *should*—well, it would be still harder to sell the farm than it has been to buy it, I am afraid.

From her tone, one could predict that going to school for the Frost children would not possibly be anything less than "a bit difficult." Meanwhile Elinor, now forty-two and having borne six children, feared she was pregnant once more. Writing to Abercrombie in September 1915, Frost described her as "altogether out of health"; he worried about the condition of her heart and looked forward with foreboding to the prospect of another child. Two and a half months later he wrote again, telling Abercrombie they were "out of those woods," "still six in the family, no more, and, thank God, no less." To Bartlett he confided that Elinor had been "unspeakably sick" for the past three months.

Her illness would be a recurring theme in letters over the next ten years. In August 1917 he wrote Bartlett from Franconia saying he couldn't get down to see him, since "Elinor has been sick for a long time. We don't know what is the matter with her unless it is something that may come to an end abruptly at any moment," suggesting that she may have been pregnant again. Two years later in a letter to Lesley, Elinor spoke of being "in such a nervous condition with these electric treatments that I don't like to think of the responsibility of entertaining." Years later, in June 1925, Frost wrote his Amherst colleague, George Roy Elliott, that "Elinor had a serious nervous collapse early last week" and blamed it at least in part on his "way of life"—his "campaigning" (as he called it) was putting too much strain on her. Three years after that, during a trip to Paris and England for the improvement of his daughter Marjorie's health, he wrote from Paris to his English friend John Haines, telling him how bad things were and not just with his daughter: "Elinor has had too much on her. I am afraid it will take her a long time to recover. Something radical will have to be done, & I will have to be the one to do it. She is in a state past doing anything for herself." Again he blamed himself, in part, for filling up their calendar with too many visits to old friends, and for his overengagement with the literary world generally. But there is no indication that he did "something radical" to effect Elinor's recovery.

In 1915, of course, Frost's "way of life" was still very much in the making, his "campaigning" still in its early stages. Yet he was taking a most active part in turning that way of life into the stuff of myth, a myth of the farmer-poet. He had said to Cox just after returning from England that he couldn't afford to live in the city, thus chose the country at present out of necessity, though it might also be out of real preference (Cox was directed to recall Browning's "Up in a Villa; Down in the City," for appropriate commentary). In retrospect it looks as if Frost determined he must get right down to business and establish himself on his Franconia farm, far from the madding crowd, so as to be "discovered" by the metropolis and its media. Holt brought out *A Boy's Will* in its first American edition in April of 1915, one month after *North of Boston* had appeared. By summer, a fourth printing of the latter book had been ordered. So it was only to be expected that by February of the following year, a Boston newspaper reporter would show up one morning and knock at Frost's door, eventually interview him, then go back and publish a piece titled "Finds Famous American Poet in White Mountain Village." What could be more fitting! The famous poet was extremely willing to talk about himself, deprecating the amount of farming he did, claiming he liked it but wasn't successful at it, and that "I always make a failure of it, and then I have to go to teaching. I'm a good teacher, but it doesn't allow me time to write. I must either teach or write, can't do both together." What he did in this interview was to take a slice from his past—the years on the Derry farm, followed by teaching at Pinkerton and Plymouth Academies—and translate it into a timeless repetitive pattern—the stuff of myth. Evidently, we gather from his remarks, teaching and writing don't go together; but farming and writing do, which leaves us wondering how much the farming amounted to (the Franconia farm seems to have consisted mainly of some cows and a vegetable garden). Frost told the reporter that someday he'd have a "big farm where I can do what I please"—which, by the logic established, would have to be just about no farming at all. But the reporter wrote it all down and went back to Boston fulfilled, and prepared— we may imagine—to pass it along to his readers.

In the latter part of 1915 and the early months of the following year, Frost's schedule of poetry readings at various colleges became increasingly busy. It may thus seem inevitable that one of them would suggest a more permanent association by inviting him to become a member of its faculty and give students the benefit of what was seen as his sagacity, a wonderful ability to put into words new thoughts about poetry. But really such an invitation was not inevitable; Frost had no college degree, and the notion of a writer-in-residence had not come into being. So it is of some interest that Amherst College, the institution at which he began teaching in January 1917, was itself a place out of the ordinary, or at least was attempting to become so. This Congregationally-founded school for "young men of piety and indigence" was now, almost a century after its founding, presided over by a newly appointed president with a very large idea about the aims of education and its relation to the undergraduate. Alexander Meiklejohn, who became president of Amherst in 1912, was passionately committed to the idea of a college as an "experimental" place where students would not just "learn" the facts but would actively engage with "ideas," with economic and political issues of world concern, and even more centrally with the philosophical questions which have occupied mankind. Years later, looking back on his experience at Amherst and Meiklejohn with an irony that could scarcely be called gentle, Frost wrote Untermeyer that

> The boys had been made uncommonly interesting to themselves by Meiklejohn. They fancied themselves as thinkers. At Amherst you *thought,* while at other colleges you merely *learned.* (Wherefore if you love him, send your only son and child to Amherst.) I found that by thinking they meant stocking up with radical ideas, by learning they meant stocking up with conservative ideas—a harmless distinction, bless their simple hearts.

But these remarks were made well after the fact, and the circumstances leading up to Frost's coming to Amherst College were marked by cordiality and high hopes on both sides. The precipitating agent in the whole matter was Stark Young, whom Meiklejohn—at the suggestion of John Erskine—had brought to Amherst from the University of Texas. Young (now remembered mainly for his drama criticism) was a Southerner, an aspiring poet and novelist whose relation to the teaching of English bore little resemblance to that of scholars trained in the field. Perhaps for that reason his courses were extremely popular at Amherst, his cultivated Southern manner something out of the ordinary for a small college in western Massachusetts. Young made it his business to get to know as many important artists as possible, and it was at his suggestion that the college literary society invited Frost to read from his work in April of 1916. At that time, George Whicher was a young English instructor at the college, and thirty years later, in one of his morning chapel talks, he described his first meeting with Frost, as the curious gathered in the Christian Association Room to greet the sage:

> We found a sturdily built man in his early forties, wearing rumpled clothes and a celluloid collar, with unruly brown hair, blunt features, and eyes of seafarer's blue that had a way of magically lighting up. As he talked, he seemed to be constantly inviting his audience to help him find just the right form of words. He spoke slowly, often rolling up a phrase with many heaves as though it were a stone to be placed in a wall that needed mending. We felt that we were watching an arduous creative triumph, the shaping into form of ideas drawn from the dark abyss of the unconscious mind. It was a dramatic, a memorable hour that we spent with him.

Confined to the brief compass of a nine minute talk, Whicher had recourse to metaphor to express the magic of this moment: Frost's blue eyes are "seafarer's blue"; putting phrases into sentences is mending a stone wall. Whereas Untermeyer's account of first hearing Frost read and talk stressed the way he understated things, Whicher speaks of him as drawing ideas up "from the dark abyss" of his unconscious. Indeed the process becomes Miltonic in character, as at the opening of *Paradise Lost* we hear of the Spirit who "with mighty wings outspread / Dove-like sat'st brooding on the vast abyss / And mad'st it pregnant." One could carry Whicher's metaphor further and say that the students and faculty at Amherst were somehow to be made pregnant, productive of ideas, under the creative ministerings of this remarkable spirit. Frost himself grew fond of the birth metaphor, informing Untermeyer in the letter about Meiklejohn and Amherst quoted above, that "I put them [the students] on the operating table and proceeded to take ideas they didn't know they had out of them as a prestidigitator takes rabbits and pigeons you have declared yourself innocent of out of your pocket trousers legs and even mouth." He was not merely an impregnator, but an obstetrician as well.

One doubts that Stark Young was similarly awed. Although he took pleasure in acting as host at the Amherst reading, he had in mind the specific goal of obtaining Frost's assistance toward the end of publishing a volume of his own poetry. This poetry he read to Frost, took as truly meant the older man's dutiful response, and proceeded to send the poems to Alfred Harcourt at Holt, with what he thought was Frost's approval. In fact, when Harcourt received the book and wrote

Frost to ask him about it, Frost replied with a telegram the essence of which was "Thumbs Down." But by then President Meiklejohn, and surely with Young's encouragement, had offered Frost a job as a replacement for George Bosworth Churchill of the English department who was about to serve a term in the Massachusetts Senate. Young showed up in Franconia with the offer, which Frost finally accepted in December—his teaching to begin in the following month. On December 16, 1916, he received a warm letter from Meiklejohn, looking forward to his presence at Amherst and saying that that morning in chapel he had read aloud "The Road Not Taken," "and then told the boys about your coming. They applauded vigorously and were evidently much delighted by the prospect."

Alexander Meiklejohn was an exceptionally high-minded educator whose principles and whose moral tone toward things may be illustrated most briefly and clearly by some statements from his essay "What the College Is." This, his inaugural address as president of Amherst, was printed for a time as an introduction to the college catalogue. What the college was, or should be—what Meiklejohn hoped to make Amherst into—was a place to be thought of as "liberal," that is, "essentially intellectual": "The college is primarily not a place of the body, nor of the feelings, nor even of the will; it is, first of all, a place of the mind." Introducing "the boys" to the intellectual life led for its own sake, would save them from pettiness and dullness, would save them from being one of what Meiklejohn referred to as "the others":

> There are those among us who will find so much satisfaction in the countless trivial and vulgar amusements of a crude people that they have no time for the joys of the mind. There are those who are so closely shut up within a little round of petty pleasures they they have never dreamed of the fun of reading and conversing and investigating and reflecting.

A liberal education would rescue boys from stupidity, its purpose being to draw from that "reality-loving American boy" something like "an intellectual enthusiasm." But this result could not be achieved, Meiklejohn added, without a thorough reversal of the curriculum: "I should like to see every freshman at once plunged into the problems of philosophy," he said with enthusiasm.

Now, five years after his address, he was bringing to Amherst someone outside the usual academic orbit, a poet who lacked even a college degree. But despite—or perhaps because of—this lack, the poet had escaped triviality, was an original mind who knew about living by ideas. For he had written among other poems "The Road Not Taken," given pride of place in the just-published *Mountain Interval* as not only its first poem but also printed in italics, as though to make it also a preface to and motto for the poems which followed. It was perfect for Meiklejohn's purposes because it was no idle reverie, no escape through lovely language into a soothing dream world, but a poem rather which announced itself to be "about" important issues in life: about the nature of choice, of decision, of how to go in one direction rather than another and how to feel about the direction you took and didn't take. For President Meiklejohn and for the assembled students at compulsory chapel, it might have been heard as a stirring instance of what the "liberal college" was all about, since it showed how, instead of acceding to the petty pleasures, the "countless trivial and vulgar amusements" offered by the world or the money-god or the values of the marketplace, an individual could go his own way, live his own life, read his own books, take the less traveled road:

> I shall be telling this with a sigh
> Somewhere ages and ages hence;
> Two roads diverged in a wood, and I—
> I took the one less traveled by,
> And that has made all the difference.

The poem ended, the boys "applauded vigorously," and surely Meiklejohn congratulated himself just a bit on making the right choice, taking the less traveled road and inviting a poet to join the Amherst College faculty.

What the president could hardly have imagined, committed as he was in high seriousness to making the life of the college truly an intellectual one, was the unruliness of Frost's spirit and its unwillingness to be confined within the formulas—for Meiklejohn, they were the truths—of the "liberal college." On the first day of the new year, 1917, just preparatory to moving his family down from the Franconia farm into a house in Amherst, Frost wrote Untermeyer about where the fun lay in what he, Frost, thought of as "intellectual activity":

> You get more credit for thinking if you restate formulae or cite cases that fall in easily under formulae, but all the fun is outside saying things that suggest formulae that won't formulate—that almost but don't quite formulate. I should like to be so subtle at this game as to

seem to the casual person altogether obvious. The casual person would assume I meant nothing or else I came near enough meaning something he was familiar with to mean it for all practical purposes. Well, well, well.

The "fun" is "outside," and lies in doing something like teasing, suggesting formulae that don't formulate, or not quite. The fun is not in being "essentially intellectual" or in manifesting "intellectual enthusiasm" in Meiklejohn's sense of the phrase, but in being "subtle," and not just subtle but so much so as to fool "the casual person" into thinking that what you said was obvious. If we juxtapose these remarks with his earlier determination to reach out as a poet to all sorts and kinds of people, and if we think of "The Road Not Taken" as a prime example of a poem which succeeded in reaching out and taking hold, then something interesting emerges about the kind of relation to other people, to readers—or to students and college presidents—Frost was willing to live with, indeed to cultivate.

For the large moral meaning which "The Road Not Taken" seems to endorse—go, as I did, your own way, take the road less traveled by, and it will make "all the difference"—does not maintain itself when the poem is looked at more carefully. Then one notices how insistent is the speaker on admitting, at the time of his choice, that the two roads were in appearance "really about the same," that they "equally lay / In leaves no step had trodden black," and that choosing one rather than the other was a matter of impulse, impossible to speak about any more clearly than to say that the road taken had "perhaps the better claim." But in the final stanza, as the tense changes to future, we hear a different story, one that will be told "with a sigh" and "ages and ages hence." At that imagined time and unspecified place, the voice will have nobly simplified and exalted the whole impulsive matter into a deliberate one of taking the "less traveled" road:

> Two roads diverged in a wood, and I—
> I took the one less traveled by,
> And that has made all the difference.

Is it not the high tone of poignant annunciation that really makes all the difference? An earlier version of the poem had no dash after "I"; presumably Frost added it to make the whole thing more expressive and heartfelt. And it was this heartfelt quality which touched Meiklejohn and the students.

Yet Frost had written Untermeyer two years previously that "I'll bet not half a dozen people can tell you who was hit and where he was hit in my Road Not Taken," and he characterized himself in that poem particularly as "fooling my way along." He also said that it was really about his friend Edward Thomas, who when they walked together always castigated himself for not having taken another path than the one they took. When Frost sent "The Road Not Taken" to Thomas he was disappointed that Thomas failed to understand it as a poem about himself; but Thomas in return insisted to Frost that "I doubt if you can get anybody to see the fun of the thing without showing them and advising them which kind of laugh they are to turn on." And though this sort of advice went exactly contrary to Frost's notion of how poetry should work, he did on occasion warn his audiences and other readers that it was a tricky poem. Yet it became a popular poem for very different reasons than what Thomas referred to as "the fun of the thing." It was taken to be an inspiring poem rather, a courageous credo stated by the farmer-poet of New Hampshire. In fact, it is an especially notable instance in Frost's work of a poem which sounds noble and is really mischievous. One of his notebooks contains the following four-line thought:

> Nothing ever so sincere
> That unless it's out of sheer
> Mischief and a little queer
> It wont prove a bore to hear.

The mischievous aspect of "The Road Not Taken" is what makes it something un-boring, for there is little in its language or form which signals an interesting poem. But that mischief also makes it something other than a "sincere" poem, in the way so many readers have taken Frost to be sincere. Its fun is outside the formulae it seems almost but not quite to formulate.

Frost's teaching at Amherst should likewise be seen as a move to the outside, to some road not taken by the academics around him. To do that he needed a firm structure of regular course and classroom procedures, against which he could define himself as an extraordinary phenomenon. But President Meiklejohn also saw himself as outside the usual academic routines, as committed to subverting traditional procedures and instigating radical methods for promoting learning rather than mere teaching. In bringing Stark Young into the English department, he had chosen someone who was a poet rather than a scholar, whose inclinations were homosexual, and whose manner was Southern courtly-aesthete. That manner and those inclinations struck Frost as repellent. By April 1917 he was writing Untermeyer about Young in this manner:

> He has spoiled everything here that the coming of the war hasn't spoiled. And he's so foxy about it. He walks up close to me on the street and passes candy from his pockets to mine like a collier passing coal to a warship at sea. It makes everybody think that he must say with sorrow everything he says against me when he loves me so much in spite of all.

There is another reference at the same time to Young's "stark disingenuousness" which Frost says makes the Franconia farm beckon all the more attractively. A student of Frost's that spring, Gardner Jackson, told him that he, Jackson, and another student, had been unsuccessfully wooed by Young in an attempt to initiate them in the joys of single-sex love, and Jackson says that Frost pressed them for details which he would later bring to the attention of Meiklejohn, in an unsuccessful attempt to get Young fired. So the "Stark Young imbroglio" Frost told Untermeyer he was sick to death of by April in his first term of teaching, was fed and fueled by Frost's creative imagination, enlarging the jealousy and repulsion he felt toward Young. Surely it was a way, in part, of dealing with the fact that Young was a very popular teacher and, like Frost, unconventional—though in a way Frost found disgusting. "I only go / When I'm the show," ran a seemingly light-hearted but firmly meant ditty he liked to use when invited to read with other poets. Early along in his Amherst teaching he found, annoyingly enough, that he wasn't the only show.

By April he had also to compete with the war into which America had entered. At that time he was teaching three courses—more than he would ever teach again—formerly taught by his predecessor Churchill: pre-Shakespearean drama, poetry, and Freshman composition. The following academic year, his first full one, he is listed as teaching only one course, Advanced Composition ("Hours arranged at the convenience of the instructor and students"). During the academic year, 1917–18, many students withdrew from Amherst to work on farms or to enlist, and by September of 1918 the war department had taken over the college, created a Students Army Training Corps and geared any classroom work to its demands. At one point during this period just before the armistice, Frost wrote to Untermeyer that Amherst was now "a war college" and that he was teaching something called "war issues." Whether he was able to make his concerns about the sound of sense relevant to such matters is uncertain. But earlier in his Amherst teaching, he did what looks like a continuation of what he had done in the New Hampshire academies a decade before: he would assign the students a specimen from early English drama, from Marlowe or Shakespeare, then have them abridge the play and eliminate less than essential material, then have them read it aloud taking different parts, and, finally, put on a public performance of it.

At the same time he had no interest in enforcing classroom discipline, thinking of himself rather as "there" for those students who were imaginative enough to make use of him. One of those was Henry A. Ladd, who contributed a retrospective portrait twenty years later to an Amherst undergraduate magazine which put out a "Frost issue." Ladd, who graduated in 1918, and thus knew Frost near the beginning of his term, recalls that the writing course he took with him met in a fraternity house in the evening, usually lasting until midnight. There was much reading of and talk about poetry, with Frost sprawled in a chair asking them questions to which, Ladd says, there was almost always no possible answer:

> It would be something like "Why do they have classes anyway?" And then the talk would begin: he would broaden it, turn it this way and that; occasionally ask questions in the middle and sometimes throw the answers out the window with contemptuous phraseology which was also picturesque so that we all laughed—on and on it would go. Then there would be long silences where some of us who were appalled at the informality and wanted things "to go well" would try asking questions . . .

Some evenings, Ladd recalled, not much happened; some evenings it all seemed to come together. But for a member of the faculty to ask, at an institution like Amherst College, why "they" had classes anyway, was to practice the "sheer mischief" Frost recommended as essential for avoiding boredom, in education as in poetry as in life.

Ladd also etches in unsparing terms the moral personality of his teacher, as one evening Frost began to denounce the life of "Bohemian" intellectuals in New York:

> I can recall being shocked at the moral intolerance, the scorching anger behind his words . . . I was under the assumption that he was liberal in thought, broad-minded, humanistic. I found none of this kind of thing. He had violent prejudices and hatreds; he descended to gossip with a

genuine relish and abused even teachers close to him on the campus; but always with a fine turn of phrase or the selection of instances of behavior which were significant as the lines of a brilliant entertainer.

This penetrating description suggests how ill-suited such behavior was to the atmosphere of the liberal college Meiklejohn was trying to nurture, with its commitment to ideas and intellectual debate and social relevance, to the disinterested search for truth and the extirpation of prejudice. Frost was such a creature of prejudice that he once insisted, "I'd no more set out in pursuit of the truth than I would in pursuit of a living unless mounted on my prejudices." Henry Ladd felt the incongruity of Frost and the liberal college, yet was also much taken with his compelling, if sometimes disturbing, performance. Here was a way of teaching "English," of teaching writing, which knew that it was necessary to talk about something besides good grammar, sentence structure, or arresting imagery. In very much his own way, Frost was as moral an educator as was President Meiklejohn. He wrote to Lesley in 1919, when she was studying at Barnard, that he was increasingly unhappy about his situation at Amherst, and complained about the pettiness of what he termed "intramural college standards," by which he meant discouragements to originality. A student of his, in response to one of Frost's remarks, had asked him, "Do they say that?"

> I told him, "No, *I* say it but *they* would say it too if I pointed it out to them." They know of nothing not gotten from somebody else. Quotation is the height of scholarship and scores ten. It is best if you have an idea to attribute it to someone else so that they will feel that it has the weight of authority. They are always asking Who is your authority? I suppose their attitude of mind can hardly be helped in college where acquirement is the main object. But it is deadly and deathly. How to escape it!

By the following fall he had decided to escape it by escaping from Amherst College. Certainly it cannot be said that Meiklejohn and the English department had made heavy demands on his time by assigning him too many teaching hours. Beginning in the fall of 1917 the arrangement was that he would teach no more than two courses and could be absent as much as needed for the poetry readings he gave in the greater world. In the spring of 1918 he was awarded an honorary degree, was appointed professor at full salary in the department, was to teach only in the first semester of the following year. But that same spring he wrote to the widow of the poet William Vaughn Moody (who was interested in bringing Frost into association with a summer school she had plans for) to say that he hoped her scheme could be put off a bit so he could have it as "some thing ahead to prolong life a moment if I should burst my bonds as a teacher and run wild again. I strain at those bonds all the time and of course they only cut deeper the more I strain." By the fall of 1919, Elinor Frost was writing Lesley that the atmosphere at Amherst was unpleasant, that Frost was having nothing to do with Meiklejohn, and that the president "will make things so disagreeable in return that papa will want to leave." She added that this might not be a great misfortune, since he was wasting his life there—"The boys are after him nearly every evening, and he is tired all the time" (a not unheard of wifely complaint).

In fact Meiklejohn did nothing to make things disagreeable for Frost, and Stark Young—about whose presence Frost had made so much fuss two years previously—was spending the 1919–1920 academic year abroad. Nor was it the case that being the only fish in a small pond, he was constantly bedeviled by hordes of students. Meiklejohn had brought a number of distinguished professors to the faculty, and the immediate postwar mood of social concern carried many students in directions away from Frost's poetic interests. Although his presence would be missed by some, it was not an indispensable one. Or so he must have convinced himself when in the fall of 1919 he tried to persuade Meiklejohn that, because of his sexual orientation, Stark Young had to be fired. Meiklejohn—as Frost was to tell the story—replied reasonably enough that since the "boys" would encounter such things in later life, why protect them in college? Indeed, he went on, Amherst was a place where a man like Frost could "counteract" the influence of a Stark Young. "I did not come here to counteract," Frost supposedly responded, with dramatic flair and finality. And that was that: he moved his family back to Franconia at the beginning of February and resigned officially in the following May of 1920. On the eve of his departure from Amherst he wrote to an alumnus explaining why he would not be speaking at a dinner he had been invited to, saying that he was too much out of sympathy with what Meiklejohn was doing "with this old New England college"—even though he, Frost, had had plenty of "academic freedom" there: "While he detests my dangerous rationalistic and anti-intellectualistic philosophy, he thinks he is willing to have it represented here. But probably it will be better represented by someone else who can take it less seriously than I."

"Detestation" is the wrong word for what the high-minded Meiklejohn thought of Frost's "philosophy," but the really curious thing in the sentence is Frost's use of the word "rationalistic" to describe that philosophy. For what Frost brought to Amherst, in a very powerful form, was not rationalism, but the imagination. That imagination operated on the students who were themselves imaginative enough to respond to it, to produce an educational exprience they never forgot, as can be seen from the testimonies of a number of them in the college magazine mentioned above. It also ran wild on the subject of Stark Young to produce a fantasy that the man was really an evil spirit, endangering the purity of fine young Amherst boys. This imagination—in its splendid manifestations and in its inglorious ones—was too much, finally, for the liberal college as defined by Meiklejohn to hold in bounds. Or that is one way of putting it. Another would be to say that in insisting to the president that he fire Young, Frost lost his sense of humor, and thus opened himself up to the censure of not being imaginative enough. A few years later, in an especially rich letter to Untermeyer about style, he wrote that

I own any form of humor shows fear and inferiority. Irony is simply a form of guardedness. So is a twinkle. It keeps the reader from criticism ... Humor is the most engaging cowardice. With it myself I have been able to hold some of my enemy in play far out of gunshot.

At Amherst Frost eventually exhausted his resources for play and lost his irony, his "form of guardedness," in the effort to impose his will on an equally unironic Meiklejohn. Yet the benefits which accrued to both the college and Frost far outweighed the troubled embarrassments of his leavetaking. He would return, once the president had lost his own battle.

The steady outpouring of verse over the next three years triumphantly culminated in the Pulitzer Prize for *New Hampshire,* and in the publication, also in 1923, of Frost's first *Selected Poems,* the privilege of a veteran who had been publishing his books for a decade and could now choose favorites from them. Not long after his relationship with Untermeyer began, he wrote a playful letter claiming that the poet in him "had died nearly ten years ago," and that he was revealing this secret for the first time. What he had done to offset the coming of evil days after age thirty ("I tell you, Louis, it's all over at thirty") was to hoard up a number of poems ("Did you ever hear of quite such a case of Scotch-Yankee calculation?") into which he could dip at the appropriate time and come up with enough for a "new" volume. As Frost's fantasy went, he had taken measures accordingly:

> And now my time is my own. I have myself all in a strong box where I can unfold as a personality at discretion. Someone asks with a teasing eye, "Have you done your Phi Beta Kappa poem yet?" "No, I don't know that I have, as you may say." "You seem not to be particularly uneasy about it." "Oh, that's because I know where it's coming from, don't you know." Great effect of strength and mastery!

Now although it was true that in 1916, when he published *Mountain Interval*, Frost dipped into his hoard for poems like "Range-Finding," or "An Old Man's Winter Night," or "Meeting and Passing" (poems which had been written wholly or in part during the years at Derry) the fantasy as he unfolded it here deliberately exaggerates the facts. If, as he called it, "irony" was "simply a form of guardedness," then the elaborate form of guardedness embodied in the strongbox might be a way of assuring oneself that one would not run out of poems. For the "great effect of strength and mastery" is not merely an effect on the person inquiring whether Frost has written his Phi Beta Kappa poem; it works as well on Frost himself by convincing him that he really *does* know where his poems are coming from. In this case then, the strong box is never empty even when it appears to be, and Frost could leave Amherst at the beginning of 1920 after a period in which he had published scarcely anything, and proceed to write the poems which would make up *New Hampshire*.

In those immediate post-Amherst years, other forms of guardedness, ways in which he was determined to maintain himself as a metaphorical strongbox may be observed. There was, for example, the vexing question of his sister Jeanie, with whom for years he had had a troubled relationship. There had been a stormy visit from her back at the Derry farm, culminating in Frost's chasing her out of the house with a revolver, then handing it over to her when she promised to go away. Upon returning from England he visited her in western Pennsylvania, where she was teaching school, and with his encouragement she had gamely entered the University of Michigan at age thirty-nine, taking a degree there. In 1919, when he was at Amherst, Jeanie showed up suddenly in hysterics, claiming to have been run out of a nearby mill town (in which she was teaching school) for professing pro-Kaiser sentiments. The following year word came from Wilbur Rowell that she had been taken into custody by the authorities in Portland, Maine, still obsessed with the war and (Frost wrote Untermeyer) presuming the police to be German officers intent on carrying her off for immoral purposes. She had been living with a female companion who was unsympathetic to Frost and whom he suspected of having designs on his sister's annuity. With Frost's consent, Jeanie was committed to the State Hospital in Augusta where she spent the remainder of her life until her death in 1929.

A few years before she died she wrote a long letter to her brother (who visited her from time to time) trying to explain what had gone wrong. She told him that her blood "doesn't flow in such a way as to cause me pleasure," that people had always slighted her and that her heart was steel, that she was "very peculiar and didn't start right," and that "I've hardly ever been pleased at anything else in my life except when I drank coffee or when people praised me." It is the touching detail about the coffee which gives this letter its grotesque, sad air, found even more painfully in the following sentence: "I read The Cloister and the Hearth but everything almost I read or look at seems to me like eating blueberries slightly sprinkled with salt." This is poetry, the poetry of what Frost referred to as "dementia praecox," and he held it and Jeanie away from him and his family, writing to Lesley in 1920 that she should not trouble herself too much about her aunt's condition, assuring her that they would "keep track of her." To Untermeyer he sent a most powerful and candid statement of the limits of his own sympathy for Jeanie's condition, which he saw as an expression of her "antiphysical" and "sensibilitist" nature:

> She had had very little use for me. I am coarse for having children and coarse for having wanted to succeed a little. She made a birth in the family the occasion for writing us once of the indelicacy of having children. Indelicacy was the word. Long ago I disqualified myself for helping her through a rough world by my obvious liking for the world's roughness.

His sister's dislike for roughness, for the coarseness or indelicacy of sexual matters, finally expressed itself madly in her hysterics over the war. In her view, Frost said, "One half the world seemed unendurably bad and the other half unendurably indifferent. She included me in the unendurably indifferent. A mistake. I belong to the unendurably bad." He was "bad" insofar as he had committed himself to the coarseness of sex and of ambition, to the world's roughness. He had married, fathered children, and reached out in his poetry and his public relations to all sorts and kinds of people, with not always a due regard for their sensitivities. But there was a limit to the extent to which he would reach out toward his sister, and the letter ends with a paragraph making a virtue of this refusal:

> And I suppose I am a brute in that my nature refuses to carry sympathy to the point of going crazy just because someone else goes crazy, or of dying just because someone else dies. As I get older I find it easier to lie awake nights over other people's troubles. But that's as far as I go to date. In good time I will join them in death to show our common humanity.

Even after repeated readings, these sentences are still shocking in their assertive, sardonic finality—in the roughness of play with which his "crazy" sister is handled. One of his notebooks contains an entry titled "Pushing Things Around—things & people," and says "It may be affectionately or hatefully; It may be affectionately & still roughly and the more roughly the better. But whether affectionately or hatefully it is always playfully." But he also wrote that "any form of humor shows fear and inferiority," and the dark humor of this letter about his sister shows how much Frost feared diminishment of himself by a flow of pity into the life of another which would leave him unguarded. In the face of a demand for selflessness, he insisted upon the self's right to persist, and without the qualifications of cultivated ambivalence.

His feeling indicated in this letter, that Jeanie Frost's madness sprang from her recoil from the world's roughness, particularly from the roughness of sexuality, did not make him willing in the least that his own daughters should encounter such roughness. When in 1918, Lesley, having left Wellesley and doing war work in an airplane factory, wrote to him describing a boat ride she had taken with an older man, one "Mr. Wheeler," Frost responded by telling her please to restrict her "adventures" to her work at the factory. He doubted that Wheeler should have taken her into his boat, though he didn't want to think too much about such things "lest we grow too suspicious and even evil-minded." But clearly he had grown suspicious enough to set down this advice "for keeping out of danger where men and women meet": "Be conventional *pretty* nearly always with men and always with those fellows 'old enough to be your father.'" He tells her that she wouldn't want to "have scared as reckless a father as I am into chronic sleeplessness," which suggests that he found it easier to lie awake over other people's "troubles" than he suggested was the case in connection with his sister. Two years later, when Lesley was in New York and working for a publisher, he wrote her that Raymond Holden, a young poet who admired Frost and had come to Franconia to live near him, was about to go to New York on "business" but really planned to see Lesley. Frost suggested that she might "get rid of him as I got rid of Walter Hendricks, so that not a word was said out about what was the matter." (The "matter" with Hendricks, a student and disciple of Frost's from Amherst College days, was that Frost decided he was paying improper attention to Lesley, and Hendricks—who was visiting them in Franconia—was forthwith dismissed from the farm with no explanations given.) As for Holden, Frost suggested that Lesley

> Be away, be otherwise engaged, be anything you please to show your self-possession. He is no sort of person for youthful folly to trifle with. He's been talking all the bold bad stuff of the books he derives his poetry from—talking it right and left. I simply tell you and leave the rest to your common sense.

But of course this was no simple telling, rather a powerful parental thumb pressed down in the attempt to protect Lesley from another example of "Bohemianism" and to protect for her the "self" he feared she might lose possession of. Never trust a poet, especially if he's an older one, seems to be the burden of this sermon in defense of guardedness.

After discounting what could be called ordinary fatherly concern for the innocence of his daughter and the possible wiles of men, we must recognize that Frost's imagination on the subject of sex was at least as lively as it was with respect to other human occupations. Gardner Jackson's memory of him as someone of Puritan background with perhaps an excessive interest in "the stuff that was anti-Puritan," makes sense when we note that his contempt and disgust at Bohemian extravagances of behavior, in Greenwich Village and other places of "free love," combined with a strong tendency to detect such excesses under every bush. There is his oft-repeated story—until Joseph Warren Beach asked him to stop repeating it—of how he "made" Beach marry his research assistant, drove them across the state line (in 1918, when Frost gave a reading at the University of Minnesota) to get a marriage license, and generally made things proper which had previously not been so. He wrote at that time to Lesley, boasting of having "personally conducted the elopment of Joseph Warren Beach that awful sinner with an assistant of his in the graduate school . . . It was cruel of me to marry him off, but I had to do it. I was cutting up." He "had to do it," presumably, because his nature demanded it, just as it demanded that Stark Young not inhabit the same college in which he taught. The double attitude of disgust at sexual "irregularities" and a creative fascination with them (to the extent of "cutting up") is memorably caught in Robert Lowell's sonnet about Frost in which the older poet is understood to speak about one of his daughters—presumably Irma, who eventually entered a mental institution:

> "One of my daughters thought things,
> thought every male she met was out to make her;
> the way she dressed, she couldn't make a whorehouse."

Though Lowell put the words together, it is not inconceivable that Frost once said something like them. As with the response to his sister's madness, it is both callous and enlivening, guarding the individual self by creating a harsh poetry about others.

Showing self-possession, as he advised Lesley to do with respect to the attentions of Raymond Holden, was not a piece of advice which had to do with relations between the sexes only. As can be seen from the letter to Untermeyer about all the unpublished books of verse he had stored up in his "strong box," Frost's poetry-writing self had to be guarded and possessed at all costs. When Lesley began to attend Wellesley in 1917, he wrote her about the importance of indulging in "outbursts of writing without self-criticism." This letting-go would only later be succeeded by a critical watchfulness, and only then would a teacher's comment be of any use. As he strikingly put it, "A teacher's talk is an outrage on fresh work that your mind still glows with. Always be far ahead with your writing. Bring only to class old and cold things that you begin to know what you think of yourself." To be "far ahead" in one's writing was necessary so as to preserve the self, providing it with material always in advance of fully articulate criticism. We are to hear and see and possess more than we can as yet understand—this way, he insists, lies sanity and productivity.

It was also advisable to be as far ahead in one's financial situation as possible, or so he seems to have believed judging from the circumstances of his sale of the Franconia farm. Raymond Holden was well-to-do, and admired Frost enough to buy the upper half of the Franconia property for $2500 (Frost had purchased the entire property for $1000), further agreeing that, if at some point Frost should wish to sell the remainder of the farm, Holden would buy it for another $2500. Holden purchased the upper half in the summer of 1919, and by the following spring Frost was looking hard—in Connecticut, Massachusetts, and Vermont—for a new farm, which he soon found near South Shaftsbury in Vermont. Holden later confessed that at the time he thought Frost was taking advantage of him; at any rate it was economic dealing not of the gentlest sort, but of the sort required to put Frost as far ahead for the moment as he needed to be. It provides another, less admirable, instance of how in the poet's terminology one had to "score": "They say not, but you've got to score—in all the realms—theology, politics, astronomy, history, and the country life around you."

In dealing with Raymond Holden, Frost scored in real estate at the expense of morality; in daring President Meiklejohn to fire Stark Young, he may have scored what he thought was a principled victory, but at the expense of his sense of humor. "Scoring" does not necessarily consort well with the detached, playful Frost encountered in so many poems and letters. Further, the insistence that one has to score, even though "they"—who are presumably gentler souls of a liberal persuasion—don't say so, came increasingly to be connected in his mind with the necessity that his country perform with similar success. Given the fact of world war, especially after America's entry into it and the attempt by Meiklejohn and others to maintain a critical attitude toward their country even in the face of commitment, Frost began to insist more loudly on the continuity of interest between person and nation. To the Englishman John Haines he wrote after his return to the United States that "My politics are wholly American. I follow my country in regions where the best of us walk blind. I suppose I care for my country in all the elemental ways in which I care for myself. My love of country is my self-love." At this point in 1916 he was convinced that only immediate danger to America would cause her to enter the war. A few years later he teased Harriet Moody, whom he suspected of being too partial to British poets, by saying that "I do love a country that loves itself . . . that insists on its own nationality which is the same thing as a person's insisting on his own personality." And he was to speak more than once of his love for "definiteness of position," no matter how intellectually admirable or not that position might be seen to be. Keeping watch over the ramparts of one's native land was of a piece with guarding one's self, with staking out a definite territory and defending it. Thus firmly planted, on one's prejudices or politics or self-love, one was in a position not to drift, but to *express* drift by giving shape and form to it in art.

———————

That his departure from Amherst represented no long-term commitment to farming rather than teaching, is shown by the immediacy with which he returned to the academy, accepting in 1921 what was to be a two-year term as Fellow in the Creative Arts (Writer in Residence we would call it now) at the University of Michigan. The salary offered—$5000—was attractive, the official duties presumably minimal, and the idea of a large university quite unlike the small college he had left, had its attractions. His sister had been a special student there and he knew well at least one professor who had been a summer neighbor in Franconia. But more significant than his return to the academy was his return to publishing poems, and with a vengeance. Between his departure from Amherst and his move to Michigan in the fall of 1921, twenty-three poems appeared under his name in various magazines; these poems would make up the bulk of his almost completed next book, *New Hampshire,* and so he was "far ahead" enough in his writing to feel comfortable about risking the Michigan venture.

The three years of his term there (he was to return for one final year in 1925–26, after he had again resumed teaching at Amherst) were in no way a disaster, could surely be called a successful enterprise, yet somehow do not engage the imagination as—for all their difficulties, and partly because of them—the earlier term at Amherst does. The most notable, certainly the most publicly significant thing Frost did at Michigan was to bring in a number of his contemporaries to give readings of their poems at the university: Padraic Colum, Sandburg, Amy Lowell, Vachel Lindsay and others came, performed, and doubtless helped create a more receptive atmosphere for the writing of verse. Sometimes these performances were broad ones indeed, to which Frost made his own contribution. After Amy Lowell's visit, he wrote Untermeyer that she "upset a lamp and a water pitcher" (Thompson claims rather that Frost was responsible) and was herself upset when Frost told her that Untermeyer had once remarked that she not only carried a chip on her shoulder, but an entire lumber yard: "She called the janitor fool and damn fool to his face—that was out back before she went on—and she called Conrad [a student of whom Frost was fond] 'boy' in the sense of slave." Such behavior gave Frost a chance to "cut up" moderately, at least to write about it afterward, yet look like a sober fellow compared to his extravagant guest. But it appears that one of the differences between his presence at Michigan and at Amherst, was that at Michigan he seized the opportunity to become a popularizer for poetry, a cultural propagandist who brought in good acts to delight the students and stimulate their curiosity. It was, in other words, still *his* show.

When he agreed to return to Michigan for the second year, it was with the understanding that he might be away from the campus as much as he wanted; for example, it was accepted that he be absent for the first few weeks of the fall term because of prior reading engagements. As at Amherst, the movement was toward more freedom, less required time spent in the classroom. Increasingly he became the eminence who talked, whose "teaching methods were 'nonexistent'," as one of his students recalled about a seminar he offered in 1926, when he was there for the last time as a faculty member. Another student remembers Frost sitting at the end of a long table in a library seminar room: "The time is early evening, but his seated figure, with the undeniable poet's head, is always radiant with light, though the many student figures around the table . . . become shadowy, except that they always listen to what the poet has to say." Here then was the figure who *inspired,* not perhaps so much because of anything in particular he said, but because of the situation he created, thick with implication and the promise of wisdom.

He had by then developed his lecture-reading appearances into an extremely winning operation, and his person bore little resemblance to the ill-at-ease figure Untermeyer remembered from that early reading at Tufts in 1915. In April of his second year at Michigan, he wrote Cox that he had had "fluenza" no less than five times during the winter, also that he had been "fairly absent from Ann Arbor this year." Some of those occasions for absence were heavily and successfully advertised, such as the one at Baylor University where the chairman of the English department wrote a special message to all students instructing them to buy their tickets in advance for the reading by one of America's greatest poets—much like the great English poet, Browning; the chairman also urged them to buy copies of Frost's books and have him autograph them. From Thompson's description of the evening, and as must have been the case more often than not, Frost employed his great charm and wit to demonstrate that, for example,

Amy Lowell was far off the mark in finding the writer of *North of Boston* devoid of humor. In fact—and partly in response to the poems he had been writing over the past two years, including the long title poem for *New Hampshire*—Frost began to conceive of himself as a writer whose satiric abilities were considerable. When given a large and agreeable captive audience in some college auditorium or other, he was not about to deny himself the pleasure of entertaining them and himself at Amy Lowell's or whomever's expense.

Although he had not planned to return to Michigan after serving the second of his one-year appointments, it was even less likely he should have expected to find himself recalled to Amherst. But that is what happened in 1923, President Meiklejohn having been dismissed by the trustees and a good number of the professors he had appointed having handed in their resignations. Clearly a powerful move toward stabilizing things and healing wounds would be to bring back the poet who had gotten out early, before the battle became most fierce between a divided faculty, a recalcitrant president, and a worried board of trustees, which was stirred finally to take the action of removing Meiklejohn. When the newly appointed president, Professor George Olds, made a special trip to Frost's South Shaftsbury farm urging him to return, the temptation was too much to resist. To return, indeed to be called back to the institution from which he had parted—at least to some extent out of principle—only three years back, was satisfaction in itself. To be offered an attractive teaching schedule of any two courses, with no other duties but to be the residing poet, and with a good three-year stretch of poems almost ready to go to the press—the omens looked to be worth accepting, especially if that acceptance on his part were a little less than simply wholehearted. When Wilbur Cross, who was publishing a good many of Frost's poems in the *Yale Review,* which he edited, congratulated him on returning to Amherst, Frost responded by insisting that he "ought to have been poet enough to stay away" but that as a philosopher he had to go back and see that a liberal college went about its business in a proper, un-Meiklejohnian way. And he added the qualification: "I never could keep out of things. But I can get out of them. That's my saving virtue. I *will* bite the hook if it is baited with an idea, but I never bit one yet that I couldn't wriggle off before it was too too late." This proud boast was consistent with the kinds of "saving virtue" Frost's various forms of guardedness had been displaying.

The following spring, a couple of weeks before he was to turn fifty and win the Pulitzer for *New Hampshire,* he wrote a long, marvelous letter to Untermeyer, filled with the confidence and daring of a man who had finally arrived, who knew what he believed and knew how interesting he was. In this letter Frost formulated most memorably his sense of what "style" was, throwing off in the process literary judgments of other writers that went to the heart of each one's respective genius. Style in prose or verse, he said,

> is that which indicates how the writer takes himself and what he is saying. Let the sound of Stevenson go through your mind empty and you will realize that he never took himself other than as an amusement. Do the same with Swinburne and you will see that he took himself as a wonder. Many sensitive natures have plainly shown by their style that they took themselves lightly in self-defense. They are the ironists.

Some writers never manage to make a style, Frost goes on to say, and then there are the novelists who can make a name without a style. Ideas and "deeds" are important, but a man's style is the way "he carries himself toward his ideas and deeds":

> The style is out of his superfluity. It is the mind skating circles round itself as it moves forward. Emerson had one of the noblest least egotistical of styles. By comparison with it Thoreau's was conceited, Whitman's bumptious. Carlyle's way of taking himself simply infuriates me. Longfellow took himself with the gentlest twinkle.

One of the things to be observed about Frost's own style, the manner in which he "took" or "carried" himself in relation to his ideas and deeds, is that it was one not eager to be too quickly found out and named—in the way he himself so effortlessly named the style of Swinburne or Whitman. Whether in his poems or his life, he needed to make it difficult for those who thought they had the right names for him or for his work. The little poem "Revelation" from *A Boy's Will* warns at its end that all of us need to be "found out"; that those "who hide too well away / Must speak and tell us where they are." But it also laments the occasion of such revelation, opining earlier that

> 'Tis pity if the case require
> (Or so we say) that in the end
> We speak the literal to inspire
> The understanding of a friend.

Speaking "the literal" ran counter to everything that made up a style—the superfluity with which the mind skated circles round itself while moving forward. While he never said anything quite so radical or "conceited" as did Thoreau, who called it "a ridiculous demand which England and America make, that you shall speak so they can understand you," Frost did say that he hoped to be so subtle at his game of making sentence sounds as to appear "altogether obvious to the casual ear." And when he remarked in one of his notebooks that "Dry humor is the kind that doesn't seem to appreciate itself. I wish all literature were as dry in the same sense of the word," he was yearning for a kind of unemphatic subtlety, beyond the appreciation of people who used phrases like "dry humor" to name what they couldn't quite understand. At any rate, the style of life observed in Frost's post-England years combined elaborate forms of guardedness, of withholding, of being and staying "ahead" in his writing—with the promise of revelation, the willingness to speak largely, nobly, and to an enlarging general public about central matters of experience, of life. Like "The Road Not Taken," Frost's style kept back as much as it gave away.

# V

## Mountain Interval *and* New Hampshire

This chapter departs from my usual procedure in that it pays no attention to Frost's life, but concentrates exclusively on his third and fourth books of poetry, with an eye to naming recurrent attitudes and concerns. *Mountain Interval* (1916) and *New Hampshire* (1923) both solidify and enlarge his achievement, and they contain many of his finest poems. In fact, the two books were farther apart in time than their dates suggest, since twelve of the thirty poems from *Mountain Interval* were written, or at least written in part, before *A Boy's Will* was published—some of them dating from the years at Derry—while the poems in *New Hampshire* were almost all written after he left Amherst, during the years 1920–23. He had expressed some disgruntlement or uncertainty about getting his third volume ready in time to appear in the fall of 1916, so soon after *A Boy's Will* and *North of Boston* had been published in America, and wrote in August of that year to Harriet Monroe that it looked as if he "were not going to get out of giving Harcourt another book this fall." *New Hampshire* on the contrary came fresh from a burst of creativity in the early 1920s and was a book most carefully arranged, as if he had a notion it might in fact win him the Pulitzer. This burst of creativity can be thought of as a consequence both of his release from the vexing Amherst situation, and of his knowledge that the strongbox of poems he boasted about keeping filled was a good deal depleted from what ideally he would have liked it to contain.

Compared with the success *New Hampshire* was later to have, *Mountain Interval* had a relatively lukewarm reception, eliciting no particularly interesting or fresh reviews, and was certainly responded to less imaginatively than *North of Boston* had been. Indeed Thompson claims that after this third volume Frost's reputation declined sharply, with few editors bothering to ask him for poems for their magazines. If there was any such "decline," it probably had more to do with the fact that America's entry into the war in 1917 drew public attention away from poetry; Frost, meanwhile, busy with academic and other matters at Amherst College, did much less publicity work on his own behalf.

But any decline or increase in reputation these two volumes may illustrate is of much less note than how strong and impressive they remain as individual collections. Although neither etches itself on the mind as indelibly as does *North of Boston,* that may be in part because they are more various books and show less of the consistent unity of purpose he maintained in the earlier collection—his "book of people." Instead, both *Mountain Interval* and *New Hampshire* show the poet putting together different kinds of performance within the covers of a single book, as if to insist that—if there were any readers so deceived—he could not be understood as, or reduced to, a merely lyric or merely narrative writer. In fact, mixtures of song-like and speech-like sounds were already evident in the poems from both *A Boy's Will* and *North of Boston:* a "talking" poem such as "Home Burial" or "The Death of the Hired Man" contained, at crucial dramatic moments, elevated diction and elaborated sound effects, as in the climactic moment of "Home Burial" when the grieving wife recalls, to her husband, how he had dug the grave of their dead child:

> I saw you from that very window there,
> Making the gravel leap and leap in air,
> Leap up, like that, like that, and land so lightly
> And roll back down the mound beside the hole.
> I thought, Who is that man? I didn't know you.

In contrast to the last line, with its inclination toward the plain style expressive of what someone might say, the previous four lines sound like a poem composed by the suffering woman into a portrait in sound, repetitive and alliterative in its formality, as the remembered moment is obsessively dwelt upon. By a similar, reverse token, one of the most obviously composed and musical pieces in *A Boy's Will*—"The Tuft of Flowers"—can accommodate a marked flexibility of speech within its rather unpromising form, the two-line couplet stanza. The presence of syntactical energies and of larger rhythmic units makes the poem feel less purely song-like, and gives it solid affinities with the spoken word:

> The mower in the dew had loved them thus,
> By leaving them to flourish, not for us,
>
> Nor yet to draw one thought of ours to him,
> But from sheer morning gladness at the brim.
>
> The butterfly and I had lit upon,
> Nevertheless, a message from the dawn,
>
> That made me hear the wakening birds around
> And hear his long scythe whispering to the ground,
>
> And feel a spirit kindred to my own . . .

These are only two instances of Frost's early exploitations of the sound of sense, each one breaking down the barrier between "lyric" and "narrative" verse.

There were, however, a number of ears in need of further training, such readers and reviewers who not only, like Amy Lowell, didn't hear any "exotic music" in *North of Boston,* but heard no music at all, so presumed the poems were really short stories, character sketches broken up into lines without "poetic" quality. Or like the anthologist Braithwaite, who wrote as if he admired what Frost was doing, but also admired contemporaries whose practices contradicted everything Frost was committed to. At any rate, there is little indication from the response, or lack of it, to *Mountain Interval* that it was generally recognized how many poems of extremely high quality there were among the thirty ones constituting the original volume. Consider the following list as permanently valuable work on Frost's part: first, five sonnets, most or all of them written before he returned to America— "The Oven Bird," "Hyla Brook," "Putting in the Seed," the strange, toneless "Range-Finding" (included in his Christmas packet to Susan Ward in 1911), and the graceful "Meeting and Passing." Next, two long narratives, each of which could have belonged to *North of Boston*—"In the Home Stretch," an exceptionally warm treatment of marriage, and "Snow," an overlong but dramatically intense vehicle, as close to a play as anything Frost had written. Then there were "realistic" vignettes such as "An Old Man's Winter Night," or "'Out, Out—,'" or "The Exposed Nest," a poem now all but forgotten. And there were the introductory and concluding poems from the book, printed in italics to make them not quite of a piece with the other ones in *Mountain Interval:* "The Road Not Taken" and "The Sound of Trees" (originally "The Sound of the Trees"), artful musical evocations of what might have been. Finally, there was "Birches," the soon to be popular favorite in which he attempted an inclusive posture toward experience and gave the illusion of revealing more of "Robert Frost" than anything he had yet written. This is to say nothing of interesting and entertaining moments from the remainder of the poems.

However hastily put together *Mountain Interval* may have been, it showed the power that came from having a strongbox to raid, in which poems like "Range-Finding" had been held back against the day they would be needed. And although there was nothing in the volume discontinuous with work he had done earlier, it exhibited a new thematic insistence which could hardly be missed. Sidney Cox was certain he had put his finger on it, when after an excited perusal of *Mountain Interval* he wrote Frost a fan letter and instead of addressing him with the careful "Mr. Frost," hitherto used as appropriate to their relationship, threw caution to the winds with the salutation "Dear Oven Bird." Cox said that "The Oven Bird" was the poem from the book which had most stirred him, perhaps because of a "discovery" it had enabled him to make. In a postscript to the letter he explained himself: "I doubt if you intended any reference to your poetic aims when you described the oven bird. Perhaps no such significance suggested itself to you even after it was written. Your voice as a poet is not loud, certainly." (The poem begins, "There is a singer everyone has heard, / Loud, a mid-summer and a mid-wood bird".) He hoped Frost would not be offended at the connection he had made between the voice of the bird who "knows in singing not to sing" and the voice of his favorite bard. Frost may not have been offended, but was surely ungracious in a reply designed to take the wind out of Cox's sails. After saying Cox had done "awfully well" with the book (the pupil gets a pat on the back), he warned him against "exaggerating the importance of a little sententious tag to a not over important poem," adding that surely Cox knew better than to think it was one of the book's "larger things" like "An Old Man's Winter Night," which had been deemed such by "the consensus of opinion among professors." He ended by assuring Cox that he wouldn't have minded his overpraising "The Oven Bird" had his reasons for doing so been better.

Frost was doubtless annoyed at being addressed as "Dear Oven Bird," but surely Cox had a point and not just with reference to that one particular poem. We may recall the burden of the oven bird's song, or not-song:

> He says that leaves are old and that for flowers
> Mid-summer is to spring as one to ten.
> He says the early petal-fall is past,
> When pear and cherry bloom went down in showers
> On sunny days a moment overcast;
> And comes that other fall we name the fall.
> He says the highway dust is over all.

In the deliberately monotonous repetition of "He says," beginning three lines out of seven, or in the use of noncommittal verbs like "says" or "is," Cox may have heard an artful fitting on Frost's part of manner to subject. In fact, as the poem develops, we see that its subject is "manner." In what manner does a bird, a singer, a poet, behave when he comes late in the game, after "the early petal-fall is past" and with another "fall" on the way? The poem's final quatrain suggests how to understand such persistence:

> The bird would cease and be as other birds
> But that he knows in singing not to sing.
> The question that he frames in all but words
> Is what to make of a diminished thing.

In a sense the poet's lines provide an answer to the bird's question by framing it in words; but a very minimal answer it is. What annoyed Frost about Cox's "discovery" was really a manner on the part of his disciple which the master found inappropriate. Flushed and excited, Cox presumed to have found Frost out, to have discovered the "key" to his art; so Frost responded by brushing it off, saying that altogether too much was being made out of a minor poem.

Yet when "An Old Man's Winter Night" is put next to it—the poem Frost claimed was judged best in the volume—it is the continuity of concern, indeed of manner, which strikes one. Here, more so than in "The Oven Bird," the comfort of a warmly human subject is held out; no one who ever responded to a Norman Rockwell magazine cover could but be taken by the old man, alone in his house ("All out-of-doors looked darkly in at him"), unable to summon up the resources to hold the winter night at bay:

> What kept his eyes from giving back the gaze
> Was the lamp tilted near them in his hand.
> What kept him from remembering what it was
> That brought him to that creaking room was age.

But if lovers of Rockwell had paused over these lines and tried to read and listen to them, they might well have noted how odd is their disposition. The "sense" of them is that the old man can't see out because the lamp won't permit him to see out—all he gets back is an image of himself. And if he cannot see out, neither can he see in; he is so old that he can't remember how or why he is where he is. But what, in the prose paraphrase are concerned and sympathetic insights into the plight of old age, sound rather different when experienced through the sing-song, rather telegraphic formulations of the lines. As with "The Oven Bird" there is a heavy use of the verb "to be": "was" occurs three times in four lines, something a novice writer of poetry would try to avoid. And there are also three "whats," two of which occur in a single line ("What kept him from remembering what it was"), designed to make it hard to indulge in sad feelings about old age— one notices the way that "age" is quietly buried at the very end of the next line.

Apropos of his sister Jeanie, Frost claimed that as he grew older he found it easier to lie awake and worry about other people's troubles. But he is at least as much a critic of such sympathetic identification with others—lonely old men or oven birds—as a practitioner of it. Or rather, some of the best poems in *Mountain Interval* derive their energy from the play of movement toward and withdrawal from the subject contemplated, play such as can be seen in two lines further on which summarize the old man in his setting;

> A light he was to no one but himself
> Where now he sat, concerned with he knew what.

By itself, the first of these lines could figure as a compelling and moving statement of the human condition, eyesight and insight failing as death comes on. And, typically, Frost won't let us read it just that way, although having said it the poem lodges it in our minds. But the inspiring saying does not stand by itself, isolated in a memorable line; instead, it continues over into the next one, flattening out the ringing declaration by moving it to the homely, revealing, "Where now he sat," then continuing by acting as if the old man's concerns *can't* be our concern—we can't know the "what" that only he is concerned with. An even more forceful, because final, example of this movement toward and away from the subject of contemplation occurs in the poem's final three lines which look at the man, now fallen asleep after "he consigned to the moon" not his soul to keep, but "his snow upon the roof, / His icicles along the wall to keep":

> One aged man—one man—can't keep a house,
> A farm, a countryside, or if he can,
> It's thus he does it of a winter night.

The voice becomes broadly expansive as it moves from "aged man" to the generic "man," separated by expressive dashes; then from house to farm to the larger countryside, as if it is about to break under the weight of all this intimidating, alien nature. And having arrived at just the point where such a break might be imagined, the sentence turns itself around in the middle of a line, with the important "or"—"or if he can, / It's thus he does it of a winter night." That is where we are to end, with the "what" encountered earlier now transformed into an equally blunt "thus." We know how "thus he does it," but all we know is what we have been shown about it by the poem. Frost's procedure, again typically so, is not to send us out into a "real" world of lonely, aged men on New England farms (they could as well be Minnesotan or Nebraskan ones) but back into the poetic life given sound and shape in a particular, even a noticeably peculiar, order of words and sentence sounds. It is there that any house-keeping, or life-keeping, will have to be accomplished.

As is evident from these rather detailed observations about verse, I see a continuity between the forms of guardedness observed in Frost's life, and the temperamental inclinations of many poems in *Mountain Interval* and in the books to come. But it is here, in this his third book, where for the first time we are made fully conscious of the value he places on guardedness—on knowing in singing not to sing; or on the value of somehow "keeping" a farm or a life—even as that farm or life has become a diminished thing, and more precious for its being so, perhaps. "Hyla Brook" precedes "The Oven Bird" and is written in celebration of a brook that is scarcely a brook at all, whose bed is only "a faded paper sheet / Of dead leaves stuck together by the heat." All the more sharply, then, is the poet challenged to speak adequately and truly about it. Although the extra line added to this sonnet carries a sententious ring, announcing that "We love the things we love for what they are," the line cannot be used as a provocative incitement to further thought or enhanced understanding of "life." For what does it mean, when we stop and ponder, to love the things we love for what they *are?* It is exactly as true as to say "We love the things we love for what they might have been, or for what they may yet become." Yet it sounds more flat and "ultimate" than those revised formulations; its wisdom rather is as ultimate-sounding, yet as elusive, as "The fact is the sweetest dream that labor knows."

Frost's guardedness can be beautifully protective and unexploitative of his New England material (that material which allowed his publisher recently to produce something called a "Robert Frost Engagement Calendar," with a gorgeous piece of nature and an appropriate poem for each month). In "The Exposed Nest," for example, a poem which he did not even see fit to include in his 1923 *Selected Poems,* two people discover

> ... a nest full of young birds on the ground
> The cutter-bar had just gone champing over
> (Miraculously without tasting flesh)
> And left defenseless to the heat or light.

This diminished nest becomes an object of concern to the people, who want to protect the young birds from "too much world at once," yet wonder whether their "meddling" with this natural disaster may not serve to make the mother bird, when she returns, more fearful of assisting her babies. But they decide to take "the risk ... in doing good," even if harm should come of it:

> ... so built the screen
> You had begun, and gave them back their shade.
> All this to prove we cared. Why is there then
> No more to tell? We turned to other things.
> I haven't any memory—have you?—
> Of ever coming to the place again
> To see if the birds lived the first night through,
> And so at least to learn to use their wings.

One needs to imagine the possible kinds of archness and coy self-congratulation a less subtle writer than Frost might have lavished on such materials. We might observe love strengthened between the two people because of their act of caring; or we might have baby birds and mother reunited in a benign stroke of fortune. Instead, Frost's question bursts out in the middle of a line—"Why is there then no more to tell?"—as if the questioner is suddenly pricked with disappointment at the incompleteness or unfulfilledness of the tale told. Turning to other things, the pair can't even remember returning to the spot. Yet of course there could have been as much to "tell" as Frost the poet had cared to invent. Not to invent it, but to leave us and the speaker grasping for something more, is another instance of attractive realism, of unwillingness to exploit nature in "moving" ways.

The act of turning to other things is a significant part of Frost's world, a recurring metaphor in the poems. In "Home Burial" it was exactly the husband's ability so to turn which maddened his wife, when only a few moments after having dug the grave of their dead child, he sat in the kitchen and remarked on the inability of birch fences to stand up against the rigors of New England weather. This moving on to something else, rather than staying fixed in grief, prompts her to deplore all human grief as sporadic rather than lasting:

> Friends make pretense of following to the grave,
> But before one is in it, their minds are turned
> And making the best of their way back to life
> And living people, and things they understand.

Such a turning to "things" is similar to—though more radical in its consequences than—the one made jointly by the couple in "The Exposed Nest." One of Frost's notebooks contains the following thought: "Like a person hard pressed in an argument we shift the ground to our children & begin the defense of life all over." But if, as in "Home Burial," the child is dead, then that ground shifts away into some other aspect of "life," perhaps even one as mundane as a birch fence. The woman's impulse not to "have grief so, if I can change it" is an impossible, poignant protest against the world's evil way in such matters. Yet her way madness lies, as with the lonely Hill Wife (in the five-part poem of that title, also from *Mountain Interval*) who, without child, occupation, or other human company except her husband, has nothing whatsoever to turn to, so turns inward and obliterates herself:

> Sudden and swift and light as that
>> The ties gave,
> And he learned of finalities
>> Besides the grave.

By contrast, to turn to something, somehow, is to put off finalities and begin the defense of life all over. Frost's moral passion informs and dignifies that impulse: if, as "Birches" has it, "Earth's the right place for love," it is also the only place ("I don't know where it's likely to go better").

The human impulse to turn to other things is most shocking when there is neither a dramatic clash of one position with another (as there is in "Home Burial") nor (as in "The Exposed Nest") a thoughtful, concerned narrator to report on what "we" saw and did. "'Out, Out—' " is by any standards one of Frost's grimmer poems (a boy's hand is cut off by a saw and the boy dies forthwith) but all the more so because of the way its narrator provides no guiding tone of response— tragic or otherwise—to the event. The moment of disaster is rendered by someone about whom we know nothing and who possesses no identifying characteristics except that he sees everything happen, and reports it in a manner which sounds dangerously close to callous. The boy's sister has announced "supper":

> At the word, the saw,
> As if to prove saws knew what supper meant,
> Leaped out at the boy's hand, or seemed to leap—
> He must have given the hand. However it was,
> Neither refused the meeting. But the hand!

This strained fancy about saws and supper, and the pretense that one can talk about the destructive "meeting" of animate and inanimate as if it were a social matter, a politeness not to be refused, keeps the reader on edge, not knowing what sort of event he is observing. It would not do to imagine some mythical New England farmer speaking about the event with that famous laconic understatement said to be characteristic of the territory—not when ingenuities of expression are so perversely applied. Yet there is no more likely presence to be imagined speaking these words.

"'Out, Out—'" proceeds at a rapid pace, as the doctor is summoned, the boy sinks fast "in the dark of ether" and the whole scene takes on a bare abstractness as of figures moving or unmoving in a shadowy dance:

> He lay and puffed his lips out with his breath.
> And then—the watcher at his pulse took fright.
> No one believed. They listened at his heart.
> Little—less—nothing!—and that ended it.

> No more to build on there. And they, since they
> Were not the one dead, turned to their affairs.

If this were a moral or satiric attack on the people who turned away to their "affairs" it would be intolerably crude—a smug, put-up job on the part of an unfeeling writer. But the event is so compressed, the refusal to indulge in any sort of narrative posture—of regret, horror, or even acceptance—so absolute, that the effect is of a weird unforgettable bluntness: "No more to build on there," as if that were the right thing to say to a child's death. The crazy nursery lilt of "And they, since they / Were not the one dead" makes it seem as if the survivors skipped away because in fact they were still alive. And that, the poem says, is what happened. What is there to say—by anyone, including the poet—in the face of such a finality? The answer is that we are powerless, except to change the subject.

John Kemp's *Robert Frost and New England* admires many of the poems in *Mountain Interval* but identifies it as the book where Frost began to turn away from the impersonal genius of his realistic poetry (as practiced in *North of Boston* or in sonnets like "The Oven Bird" or "Putting in the Seed" or "Range-Finding") and to indulge himself, instead, in a more personal brand of entertainment. Putting himself on stage as the New England farmer-poet-sage, purveyor or sceptical inspector of wisdom, Frost airs his prejudices and inclinations in ways which invite (but for Mr. Kemp don't usually command) appreciative assent. The poem which signals the beginning of Frost's use of the Yankee as wise spokesman about all matters, is "Birches," and Kemp finds that other, lesser poems in *Mountain Interval* exploit the myth to the point where they seem mannered, coy, and self-satisfied. Because of these failings, they matter less than do the best poems Frost had published previous to 1916. And after *Mountain Interval,* Kemp proceeds to argue, Frost's most compelling poems usually turn out to be the non-regional, non-New England pieces in which he drops the "Yankee" pose and writes about "something he *cared* about instead of something he thought *others* might find impressive."

Kemp reserves special scorn for "New Hampshire," the long title poem of Frost's volume of 1923. "New Hampshire" serves as an introduction to that volume, alluding to various materials which will figure in its individual poems, as well as to (for the first time in his poetry) names of real people and places in New Hampshire. It also exhibits (and for the first time) in Randall Jarrell's phrase "the public figure's relishing consciousness of himself." This self-advertising poet confesses, though always humorously, that he has written "several books against the world in general"; or he confides that lately, visiting New York City, he became engaged "in converse with a New York alec / About the new school of the pseudo-phallic"; or allows as how he is pleased to be "a plain New Hampshire farmer / With an income in cash of, say, a thousand / (From, say, a publisher in New York City)." If then, one reads through this long poem and thinks back, by contrast, to the style of address and treatment of material in "Death of the Hired Man" or "Home Burial," one may lament the decision Frost took to relax his energies and perform before an audience in a manner partly derived from his heavy service on the circuit, his "barding around" to all those colleges. The trouble with this way of understanding and adversely judging the shape of Frost's career, is that it achieves a neatly drawn outline of his rise and fall as a poet at the expense of the truth. For rather than being a falling-off from earlier work, *New Hampshire* (the volume, not the poem) is an extremely varied and powerful collection, with enough fine poems to convince us that it is not just a prize-winner, nor a "falling-off" from something, but a book whose quality is comparable to any Frost had published before.

Like the remaining books he would write, *New Hampshire* contains a considerable number of poems which are by no stretch of the imagination major, nor do they command a place in any essential anthology of his work. But there is in Frost much un-major poetry that is nonetheless extremely appealing and engaging, and some of this poetry is found in the title poem "New Hampshire." One instance may suffice: having asserted that the two best states in the union are (of course) New Hampshire and Vermont, and having neatly described the physical way in which they lie together on the map ("like wedges, / Thick end to thin end and thin end to thick end,") the unbuttoned narrator tells us another reason for admiring them:

> Both are delightful states for their absurdly
> Small towns—Lost Nation, Bungey, Muddy Boo,
> Poplin, Still Corners (so called not because
> The place is silent all day long, nor yet

Because it boasts a whisky still—because
It set out once to be a city and still
Is only corners, crossroads in a wood.)

With the sense of how, in "Mending Wall" or "An Old Man's Winter Night," Frost writes the most flexible and dramatically artful blank verse, there is pleasure in the way these lines from "New Hampshire" sprawl about and dawdle over from one to the next, intent only (so is the pretence) on giving us the facts. Or on instructing us in the psychology of relativity by considering the instance of a New Hampshire town named Easton which (so it was flashed on a movie screen one presidential election night) had gone Democratic, giving Wilson four votes and Hughes two:

> . . . And everybody to the saddest
> Laughed the loud laugh, the big laugh at the little.
> New York (five million) laughs at Manchester,
> Manchester (sixty or seventy thousand) laughs at
> Littleton (four thousand), Littleton
> Laughs at Franconia (seven hundred), and
> Franconia laughs, I fear,—did laugh that night—
> At Easton. What has Easton left to laugh at,
> And like the actress exclaim, "Oh, my God" at?
> There's Bungey; and for Bungey there are towns,
> Whole townships named but without population.

The best moment here occurs at the seeming end of the population rope, when Frost comes up with (or rather comes back to) the "Bungey" he mentioned previously, and provides one last out for its six inhabitants: "Whole townships named but without population." Vistas of emptiness suddenly open out of this embryonic tall tale.

Without claiming too much for good moments like this one, of which there are a number in "New Hampshire," they should not be undervalued. In 1923, American poetry had begun to descend somewhat from its heights of idealistic poeticality, but often the grittier versions of experience—as in Masters or Sandburg or Amy Lowell— were just as humorless, because just as idealized, as the poetical ones. (Remember how Frost complained that Masters's poetry "chewed tobacco.") The lines from "New Hampshire" quoted above are amusing partly for the way in which their rough and ready pentameter serves to pass along all those vital population statistics. This humor is part of the verse, depending for its life on the way that verse moves—

or rather lurches—along. In other poems from *New Hampshire* Frost puts himself forward at stage center, more theatrically than in his previous work, indulging in large gestures and assertions of what he might do or say if things were not as they are, and titling the poem in which such gestures occur, "An Empty Threat." The threat, as it was in the earlier "The Sound of Trees" is to "make the reckless choice" and really, one day, set out for somewhere. In the later poem this "somewhere" figures as the wilderness: "I stay; / But it isn't as if / There wasn't always Hudson's Bay / And the fur trade, / A small skiff / And a paddle blade," it begins, continuing through irregular lines and stanzas to place the threat-maker somewhere up North in his tent, dealing with an "Exquimaux" fur trader named Joe, and trying to figure out what is fascinating about "so much bay / Thrown away / In snow and mist." He is not sure,

> Unless it be
> It's the old captain's dark fate
> Who failed to find or force a strait
> In its two-thousand-mile coast;
> And his crew left him where he failed
> And nothing came of all he sailed.

But Frost never really leaves home, since the whole fancy of lighting out for the territory is but "An Empty Threat" (the poem begins with the words "I stay").

An objection to this procedure is that it too cleverly covers all bets, so as to take the risk out of them, and that Frost's poetry contains more of that sort of hedging as he grows older. One answer to the objection is historical. In the oddity of its playfulness, "An Empty Threat" is a daring peom to have appeared in 1923, and it can be seen now that *New Hampshire*, along with Stevens's *Harmonium* and W. C. Williams's *Spring and All* (each also appearing in 1923), as well as work that had been published recently by e. e. cummings and Marianne Moore, was an important part of the renaissance of humor in American verse. But, as usual, Frost is serious when he is humorous; the end of "An Empty Threat" makes, with appealing poignancy, an identification of spirit and of imagination with the dead captain, Henry Hudson:

> It's to say, "You and I—"
> To such a ghost—
> "You and I

> Off here
> With the dead race of the Great Auk!"
> And, "Better defeat almost,
> If seen clear,
> Than life's victories of doubt
> That need endless talk talk
> To make them out."

Better defeat almost, though he has stayed home to write a poem, a small victory of doubt about the expense of spirit in a waste of exploration. "An Empty Threat" succeeds in making us care, just for a moment, about what has become an inert schoolroom legend only.

The poem originally appeared in *New Hampshire* under the rubric "Notes"—relatively long poems which were followed by a section of shorter lyrics titled "Grace Notes." The "Notes" section contains more fanciful, indeed fantastic, poems than Frost had hitherto written, and they sometimes reach a higher level of intensity than humorously entertaining ones such as "New Hampshire" or "An Empty Threat." One thinks, for example, of "The Witch of Coös," a poem strange enough so that it cannot be understood merely as a post-*North of Boston* exercise in portraying the real lives of rural people through faithfully recorded speech. In this poem we hear of how the bones of a murdered lover of the "Witch" who tells the story, ascended from the cellar one night and were artfully encouraged to proceed all the way up to the attic ("up attic"), whereupon the woman and her husband bolted the door, locking them up there forever. Sensing that the skeleton was looking for a way out, the woman suggests to her husband that

> It's looking for another door to try.
> That uncommonly deep snow has made him think
> Of his old song, 'The Wild Colonial Boy,'
> He always used to sing along the tote road.
> He's after an open door to get outdoors.

Surely it is impossible to infer from this utterance a "real" person behind it; yet the conceit is wonderful, as is the notion that now, sometimes the bones

> Come down the stairs at night and stand perplexed
> Behind the door and headboard of the bed,
> Brushing their chalky skull with chalky fingers,
> With sounds like the dry rattling of a shutter . . .

Noteworthy for its weirdly inventive originality of storytelling, "The Witch of Coös" shows to what a pitch of improvising brilliance Frost had by now brought his art.

If *New Hampshire* has more fantasy than earlier volumes, more poems where Frost risks the charge of being too ready to buttonhole us with the latest clever thing that has come into his mind, too mainly or merely frivolous in spirit, it has concurrently more self-explication. Richard Poirier has remarked on this fact, as well as on Frost's tendency to dogmatize himself, to show "a satisfaction so smug, an irony so steeped in the vanity of popular acclaim, as to invite repudiation." I don't think this dogmatizing happens enough in *New Hampshire* to make repudiation inviting, and it cannot happen as long as Frost is able to resist temptations to be solemn about his own imagination and other profound matters. The remarkable "A Star in a Stone-Boat," which Poirier has been the first to notice for the quite original way it is "about" the poetic imagination, behaves so as to display, in its individual lines and stanzas, the truths of freedom and waywardness it celebrates.

> Never tell me that not one star of all
> That slip from heaven at night and softly fall
> Has been picked up with stones to build a wall

it begins, proceeding over the course of its three-line stanzas to tell a story of how once a laborer picked up a falling star and lugged it away in a stone-boat, rather than in a "flying car" with Pegasus leading— which would have been more appropriate to its stellar qualities. At the poem's end, the "I" speaks about his own labor, how as if "commanded in a dream," he spends his time attempting "To right the wrong that this [the laborer's mistake] should have been so." He pursues the task of "following walls" endlessly, never lifting up his eyes except at night, and then "to places in the sky / Where showers of charted meteors let fly." Others, he tells us, find what they are seeking in "school and church," but the poet's vocation is "measuring" stone walls, in the conviction that "though not a star of death and birth"

> Though not, I say, a star of death and sin,
> It yet has poles, and only needs a spin
> To show its worldly nature and begin
>
> To chafe and shuffle in my calloused palm
> And run off in strange tangents with my arm,
> As fish do with the line in first alarm.

And having viewed one of these strange tangents in the poem which has just been written, its speaker concludes his affirmation:

> Such as it is, it promises the prize
> Of the one world complete in any size
> That I am like to compass, fool or wise.

Like the speaker of "An Empty Threat," the "I" in "A Star in a Stone-boat" need not be identified with the wise rural philosopher or farmer-poet who, it is fair to say, does speak in "Birches." There when we hear that "Earth's the right place for love" or "It's when I'm weary of considerations / And life seems too much like a pathless wood," we may think our experience has been gathered up and made momentarily comprehensible in such truths. "A Star in a Stone-boat" (not to speak of "An Empty Threat") has less appeal, in such terms, for an audience that hopes to have Frost speak for them; but it is every bit as authentic and distinct an expression of another kind of poetic caring, and is really bolder than "Birches" since it dares to risk the creation of a speaker who is oddly and unsettlingly at variance with things as they are.

One can pause for some time over poems from *New Hampshire* which have never been anthology favorites but which after many readings still are strong and satisfying. There is "I Will Sing You One-O" where a man lying in bed hears the clock strike one and is moved to a series of cosmic thoughts—expressed in short, unpretentious lines which tumble from one to the next—about the "utmost star." It is a witty yet grave meditation on singleness. For doubleness, on the other hand, there is "Two Look At Two," a poem with as much tenderness as is ever found in Frost, where two people, in love, climb a mountain and (before turning back as night comes on) halt before a "tumbled wall / With barbed-wire binding." There they encounter a doe who looks at them "Across the wall as near the wall as they." Unafraid, the doe passes along, and as the lovers again prepare to turn home there appears, with a snort, a buck who views them quizzically, then eventually passes, also unscared, along the wall. The "spell-breaking" as the poet names it, has occurred:

> Two had seen two, whichever side you spoke from.
> "This *must* be all." It was all. Still they stood,
> A great wave from it going over them,
> As if the earth in one unlooked-for favor
> Had made them certain earth returned their love.

Of the many "as if" moments in Frost's poetry, none is more touching than this one, and on "whichever side you spoke from." The line from "Mowing" about the fact being the sweetest dream is borne out in a fresh way here, where "two had seen two" and where the lovers have few words beyond saying "This *must* be all" (earlier in the poem they have said "This is all," then again "This, then, is all"). Now they stand wordless, feeling the great wave, and it is the poet who dreams for them the "as if" of a grace note—"As if the earth in one unlooked-for favor / Had made them certain earth returned their love." The figure a poem makes, as Frost was to say later in the essay of that title, is the same as for love.

In praising the variousness of the poetry in *New Hampshire,* I am countering the argument that Frost's work suffered a decline from the impersonal realism of *North of Boston* into something much less substantial. But even if the longer poems in the "Notes" section don't convince the sceptic, and if my claims for their value as entertainment are excessive, the "Grace Notes" section contains some of the best poems Frost ever wrote. Most of these are short lyrics, and a list in order of appearance shows "Fire and Ice," "Nothing Gold Can Stay," "Stopping By Woods on a Snowy Evening," "For Once, Then, Something," "The Onset," "To Earthward," and "The Need of Being Versed in Country Things." It is a pity that in collected editions of his poems, Frost did not preserve the original subheadings of individual volumes, since "Grace Notes" is such a perfect one for these lyrics. The word "Grace" opens up a range of possibilities, from the "One unlooked-for favor" granted to the lovers in "Two Look at Two," to the whiteness discerned in the well of "For Once, Then, Something," to the "dust of snow" in the poem of that title which saved part of a hitherto regretted day. Or there is the grace, in its various senses, with which the idea of a returning spring is invested in "The Onset," when a man, almost overwhelmed by a snowstorm and deciding that his life is ineffectual ("nothing done to evil, no important triumph won") is granted the promise—because there is a precedent for it—of spring:

> Yet all the precedent is on my side:
> I know that winter death has never tried
> The earth but it has failed: the snow may heap
> In long storms an undrifted four feet deep
> As measured against maple, birch, and oak,
> It cannot check the peeper's silver croak . . .

Grace notes are also short, ornamental and elegant enhancements the musician must take care to measure correctly in performing, since they are easy to mar if touch and attack are unsure. In this section so titled from *New Hampshire*, Frost included the shortest poems he had ever written: eight lines in "Nothing Gold Can Stay," "Dust of Snow," and "Fragmentary Blue"; nine in "Fire and Ice"; sixteen in "Stopping By Woods . . ." It may have been that after writing many long poems in the years of *North of Boston* and after, then placing the longest one he had ever written (413 lines) as the introductory poem to *New Hampshire*, Frost was eager to show that his excellence extended also to the shortest of figures, as in the perfectly limpid, toneless assertion of "Nothing Gold Can Stay":

> Nature's first green is gold,
> Her hardest hue to hold.
> Her early leaf's a flower;
> But only so an hour.
> Then leaf subsides to leaf.
> So Eden sank to grief,
> So dawn goes down to day.
> Nothing gold can stay.

The elegant "subsides" gently names the process of natural changing and metaphorical couplings within the poem; as "green is gold," as "Her early leaf's a flower" (where the contraction makes even more imperceptible the seeing of one thing in terms of another), as "dawn" changes both in fact and in words (from "dawn" to "day"). The poem is striking for the way it combines the easy delicacy of "Her early leaf's a flower" with monumentalities about Eden and the transient fading of all such golden things, all stated in a manner that feels inevitable. It is as if in writing "Nothing Gold Can Stay," Frost had in mind his later definition of poetry as a momentary stay against confusion. The poem's last word proclaims the momentariness of the "gold" that things like flowers and Eden, dawn and poems share. So the shortness of the poem is also expressive of its sense.

Randall Jarrell once commented on how little Frost's poems look like "performances," by which one supposes he meant that they possessed enviable ease and the appearance of casualness; they felt no need to raise their voices or gesture histrionically to capture a reader's attention. But the shorter a poem is, the more strongly its performance aspects stand out, as when we praise the poet for operating so deftly within such a small compass. Frost himself claimed that he wanted his readers to notice and talk about such things; "what a feat it was to turn that that way, and what a feat it was to remember that, to be reminded of that by this"—as he put it in the *Paris Review* interview. With respect to his most anthologized poem, "Stopping By Woods . . ." which he called "my best bid for remembrance," such "feats" are seen in its rhyme scheme, with the third unrhyming line in each of the first three stanzas becoming the rhyme word of each succeeding stanza until the last one, all of whose end words rhyme and whose final couplet consists of a repeated "And miles to go before I sleep." Or they can be heard in the movement of the last two lines of stanza three:

> He gives his harness bells a shake
> To ask if there is some mistake.
> The only other sound's the sweep
> Of easy wind and downy flake.

As with "Her early leaf's a flower," the contraction effortlessly carries us along into "the sweep / Of easy wind" so that we arrive at the end almost without knowing it.

Discussion of this poem has usually concerned itself with matters of "content" or meaning (What do the woods represent? Is this a poem in which suicide is contemplated?). Frost, accordingly, as he continued to read it in public made fun of efforts to draw out or fix its meaning as something large and impressive, something to do with man's existential loneliness or other ultimate matters. Perhaps because of these efforts, and on at least one occasion—his last appearance in 1962 at the Ford Forum in Boston—he told his audience that the thing which had given him most pleasure in composing the poem was the effortless sound of that couplet about the horse and what it does when stopped by the woods: "He gives his harness bells a shake / To ask if there is some mistake." We might guess that he held these lines up for admiration because they are probably the hardest ones in the poem out of which to make anything significant: regular in their iambic rhythm and suggesting nothing more than they assert, they establish a sound against which the "other sound" of the following lines can, by contrast, make itself heard. Frost's fondness for this couplet suggests that however much he cared about the "larger" issues or

questions which "Stopping By Woods ..." raises and provokes, he
wanted to direct his readers away from solemnly debating them;
instead he invited them simply to be pleased with how he had put it.
He was to say later on about Edwin Arlington Robinson something
which could more naturally have been said about himself—that his
life as a poet was "a revel in the felicities of language." "Stopping By
Woods ..." can be appreciated only by removing it from its pedestal
and noting how it is a miniature revel in such felicities.

Frost's poetic forms of guardedness both invite and withhold. They
are self-sufficient, sharing with us only a part of themselves; like an
old man on a winter night or a persistent oven bird, they keep on doing
what they are doing without our help. When Frost is most personal,
as he is in "To Earthward," the finest poem in *New Hampshire* and
one of the best he ever wrote, the same pattern of inviting and withholding can be seen. In a letter to Bernard DeVoto written years later,
a few months after the death of Elinor Frost in 1938, he admitted that
even though he once concluded an early poem by announcing that
"They would not find me changed from him they knew— / Only more
sure of all I thought was true," he had in fact endured a few changes
and that "One of the greatest changes my nature has undergone is of
record in To Earthward and indeed elsewhere for the discerning." The
relative obscurity of the poem suggests that few have paid attention to
the great change he said it recorded. "To Earthward" has eight stanzas rhymed ABAB with a high percentage of monosyllabic words—
as in its first few lines:

> Love at the lips was touch
> As sweet as I could bear;
> And once that seemed too much;
> I lived on air
>
> That crossed me from sweet things,
> The flow of—was it musk
> From hidden grapevine springs
> Down hill at dusk?

The remembered sensuous pleasure of love's smells and taste is both
delicately and compactly evoked, while the short two- and three-beat
lines make for the opposite of garrulity, make for sentence sounds
unlike those produced by longer blank verse and couplet groups. This

poetry seems to exist more on the page than it does in the speaking voice, if the distinction can be made:

> I had the swirl and ache
> From sprays of honeysuckle
> That when they're gathered shake
> Dew on the knuckle.

Nothing about such lines tags them as distinctively Frost, which is another way of suggesting why "To Earthward" is special. The sweets of youthful love have, in the poem's first half, been celebrated—"I craved strong sweets, but those / Seemed strong when I was young"; but then in one of the more curious pieces of expression to be found anywhere in the poems, we are directed to the present condition of things:

> Now no joy but lacks salt,
> That is not dashed with pain
> And weariness and fault:
> I crave the stain
>
> Of tears, the aftermark
> Of almost too much love,
> The sweet of bitter bark
> And burning clove.

His fondness for negatives has never been more strikingly demonstrated than in this presentation of "Now," and the lines are initially difficult to smooth out into a coherent sense. Is he lamenting the change which has occurred in his nature between back then and "Now"? This is the first assumption we make, noticing, instead of dew and honeysuckle, "pain / And weariness and fault." It may have been such an assumption which caused the editor of his collected poems to "improve" the punctuation of "To Earthward" by inserting a comma after "salt"—

> Now no joy but lacks salt,
> That is not dashed with pain . . .

But in the original edition of *New Hampshire* and in all subsequent printings of the poem while he was alive, Frost made no separation of the lines with a comma. The rightness of his choice is evident when we see that the stanza is saying something more like "Now" any "joy" I may experience is going to lack salt, lack savor, if it is not "dashed," not seasoned liberally with "pain / And weariness and fault," with tears, with a different kind of "sweet" from the ones which seemed strong in my youth. "Now" the sweet must be "of bitter bark and burning clove." Alluding to its title, the poem concludes in a similar key:

> When stiff and sore and scarred
> I take away my hand
> From leaning on it hard
> In grass and sand,
>
> The hurt is not enough:
> I long for weight and strength
> To feel the earth as rough
> To all my length.

What is so revealing—yet not entirely—about "To Earthward" is the way it expresses one of the "greatest changes" in Frost's nature, the change into an insistence upon the mixed nature of experience, into a hunger for an "aftermark," for the "sweet of bitter bark and burning clove" rather than for a pure sweet. The poem's images translate only with much awkwardness into the language of paraphrase, an indication perhaps of how seriously Frost took the change he was writing about. It is the poem of a man about to turn fifty years of age, but rather than creating an "I" who speaks to us eloquently and persuasively and at length about what he once had or now demands, the speaker of "To Earthward" adopts a sort of laconic telegraphese one has to listen carefully to in order to follow at all. "Now no joy but lacks salt, / That is not dashed with pain / And weariness and fault": the effect is that of scarcely addressing the reader at all even while a matter of intimate concern is being spoken about. Another way of putting it is that in this poem Frost is wholly at the service of the language, letting it take him (so is the illusion) where it will, where it must in order to say what has to be said.

Frost followed the procedure of his previous two volumes by putting the final poem in *New Hampshire*—"The Need of Being Versed in Country Things"—in italics. Since *New Hampshire,* illustrated with woodcuts by J. J. Lankes, is an especially handsome book, probably the finest looking one Frost ever published, concluding on the italic note made for a gesture of typographical eloquence. But it is also satisfying the way the poem, particularly its final stanza, frames the whole volume in a richly compressed and memorable way. "The Need

. . ." tells of desolation, of a farmhouse which burned leaving only its barn, into and out of which the birds now fly through broken windows, "Their murmur more like the sigh we sigh / From too much dwelling on what has been." Yet, the poet corrects himself, the murmur is only *like* it, not the same as it. Birds do not grieve over what the human imagination finds desolate and sad; instead, nature seems to renew itself for them, lilacs, dry pump and fence post are still there, still carrying on in the way things do. In the final stanza Frost insists that

> For them there was really nothing sad.
> But though they rejoiced in the nest they kept,
> One had to be versed in country things
> Not to believe the phoebes wept.

The diminished thing, so often celebrated in *Mountain Interval,* can be viewed here in the way the phoebes persist in their housekeeping, and to recognize this persistence for what it is one needs to be versed in country things. It is a nice stroke that Frost does not end the poem with the positive security, potentially complacent, of being so versed, as if the speaker were a wise know-it-all. Rather, the last line reaches out to what one would believe if one were deluded. That possibility is strongly there in the stanza's first line—"For them there was really nothing sad"—where the "really" acts as a check on the equally strong impulse (and a traditional poetic one all the way back through pastoral poetry) to believe that the birds are responsively grieving at the spectacle of human loss. Thus, in the last line, "Not to believe" doesn't cancel out the impulse to believe. After all, the poem's last word is "wept."

One could say something similar about *New Hampshire* as a whole, a book distinguished by its ability to include rather than leave out, and by its variety—of styles, verse forms, poetic speech. As in the poem of that title, the impulse is to earthward, to the substantiation of country things; yet really to be "versed" in such matters is to insist on imagining "pain / And weariness and fault," the tears of things which birds don't weep but poets must. Such variousness, such unwill- ingness to be located or fixed in one position—however solid it may seem—also has its comic aspect. To title one's book after a state is, after all, a rather dangerous thing to do, inviting patronization as a self-proclaimed "regional" writer who promises to offer us glimpses of charming New England things. Frost therefore dedicated the book to a couple of other states ("To Vermont and Michigan") and concluded

his long poem in celebration of New Hampshire with a carefully
worked-out declaration of what he had chosen and where he stood:

> I choose to be a plain New Hampshire farmer
> With an income in cash of, say a thousand
> (From, say, a publisher in New York City).
> It's restful to arrive at a decision,
> And restful just to think about New Hampshire.
> At present I am living in Vermont.

# VI

## *Further Rangings*

After Frost resigned from Amherst College in 1920, he divulged to Wilbur Cross his plan to "return to print hurling fistfulls [of poems] right and left." He had "kicked himself free from care and intellectuality," leaving the academy because he had seen through the Amherst idea as expounded by President Meiklejohn. That idea was "Freedom for taste and intellect," but a freedom which turned out to be only a freedom from prejudice, especially (Frost added ironically) when the prejudice was in favor of "home church morality, etc." Too much himself a creature of prejudice to listen to "such stuff," he insisted to Cross (in a phrase quoted earlier) that "I'd no more set out in pursuit of the truth than I would in pursuit of a living unless mounted on my prejudices." Two years later he wrote his Amherst colleague George Whicher, apropos of the Bread Loaf School of English (for the staff of which he had recommended Whicher) that "The strength of the teacher's position lies in his waiting till he is come after. His society and audience are a privilege—and that is no pose." Increasingly in the years after 1923, the Pulitzer Prize winner could wait until he was come after; and he made sure that before he engaged in anything, teaching a class, making a living, or setting out in pursuit of the truth, he was securely mounted on his prejudices. If his use of the word "prejudice" sounds provocatively reactionary, we may suppose Frost wanted it to sound that way. But he was serious about what it signified, and in response to a letter from the young B. F. Skinner in 1926, fresh from college and wondering whether he had any future as a writer of fiction, Frost told him that "All that makes a writer is the ability to write strongly and directly from some unaccountable and almost invincible personal prejudice." R. L. Stevenson, Thomas

Hardy, Sinclair Lewis had it, he went on to say; indeed everybody has it but usually ends up by acting out the prejudices of someone else. By contrast, the true writer finds out his own prejudice and writes from it.

One can imagine the mixture of triumph and trepidation with which he prepared to return to the college he had so recently left. Writing to Cross in the August preparatory to his return, he praised him for striking "just the right dubious note in congratulating me about going back to Amherst. I ought to have been poet enough to stay away. But I was too much of a philosopher to resist the temptation to go back and help show the world the difference between the right kind of liberal college and the wrong kind." There is a dramatic and adversary flare to this admission—or boast—which suggests how unpeacefully Frost returned. That is, he was not only firmly mounted on his prejudices, but was on the lookout for any signs of what he referred to as "Meiklejaundice," or the wrong kind of liberal education. In the satirical terms he put it to Untermeyer after his first year back, this disease meant fancying that in Amherst College you were doing something called "thinking" rather than mere "learning" (which was what they did at colleges other than Amherst). A related fancy, in Frost's opinion, was the idea that the pupil "taught himself," rather than was taught by the teacher. What he "taught" himself, in Frost's scornful view, was really only a replacing of conservative ideas with "radical" ones. So he and his students in the philosophy course Frost offered that first year back in "Verdicts" or "Judgments," inquired into what thinking really was: "We reached an agreement that most of what they had regarded as thinking, their own and other peoples, was nothing but voting—taking sides on an issue they had nothing to do with laying down."

"Thinking," for Frost, was deeply involved with the associative act of metaphor, of saying one thing in terms of another, of saying one thing while meaning another. When he complained that the Amherst students had been affected by Meiklejaundice, he meant that they were unable to recognize a metaphor when they saw or made one. But discounting his eagerness to lay blame on the departed president's shoulders (surely he could have made a similar complaint about his students at Michigan), the complaint was inevitable from one who had committed himself to education by poetry. What Frost meant by such education—for him, the only true liberal education—was, in the language of the essay he would write in 1930 ("Education by Poetry"), "enthusiasm tamed by metaphor." But another word for enthusiasm was prejudice. If one were ready to speak and write strongly and directly out of that prejudice, it was also imperative to recognize that speaking and writing involved the making of metaphors, and that to know what you were doing when you used a metaphor—indeed *that* you were using one—you needed to know when and where the metaphor broke down. As an example, he mentions someone once telling him that the universe was a machine, whereupon Frost suggested to the metaphor-maker that what he meant was that the universe was *like* a machine, but was unlike a machine (it didn't have pedals or levers or button, etc.). "All metaphor breaks down somewhere. That is the beauty of it," he wrote, adding that it was "touch and go with the metaphor, and until you have lived with it long enough you don't know when it is going." The endeavor in the Amherst classroom, in any classroom where "thinking," according to his standards, was going on, would necessarily involve practice in this "touch and go" activity; would be concerned with tracing when various metaphors were "going," what they touched, when they broke down.

The more firmly planted Frost imagined himself to be, the more he could entertain possibilities for drift. At least he could introduce his students in the literature course at Amherst to books written by some exceptional drifters, men and women very unlike college professors. The list of titles in English 9 featured Melville's *Typee,* George Borrow's *Lavengro,* and Thoreau's *Walden,* books which were made out of the writer's adventures somewhere else, and whose styles ("style is the way the man takes himself") were indicative of the forcefulness of an individual choice. The list went on to include Plutarch's life of Coriolanus and Shakespeare's play about the hero who insisted, to his death, that there was a world elsewhere. Other titles (the idea was to read about a book a week) were Hazlitt's *Table Talk,* autobiographies by Cellini and Gibbon, Emerson's *Representative Men,* and Christina Rossetti's *Poems.* Frost later insisted that the function of a college was to show there was a "book side" to everything, and his course list of books is notable for its lack of concession to anyone's possible desires for "light" reading. It hung together as a list not in the usual dutiful "course" sense of having a theme which unites them (Frost's did so up to a point), but rather as having been chosen for their individual distinctivenesses, their varied styles of composition. The notion was that the particular creation should have priority; that it was enough to trust one book to suggest another one; that there was no place to stop, no culminating truth to be learned; and that becoming aware of the "book side" to everything was a heady and a lifetime experience.

But it was evidently not so heady for Frost to be back at the Amherst stand, at least as indicated by a brief line to Untermeyer in March of the first year: "Amherst goes sadly, I'm afraid I have to admit. I'd like to look at it receding from the deck of an outward bound ship" (he was contemplating a visit to England in the summer). It may very likely have been that the complaints about leftover "Meiklejaundice" were not so much explanations of his discontent as rationalizations of it, of the fact that he was once again a member of an academic faculty he did not think any poet should be part of, for all that the money was an attractive lure. Already that first year back at Amherst, he had been tempted again by Michigan, by an offer of a larger salary and no official duties connected with his appointment. As always, the acceptance of an academic routine brought with it the wish for more freedom than was available under the existing arrangement, probably under any conceivable arrangement. And of course his insistence, in the letter to Untermeyer quoted above, that "the strength of a teacher's position lies in the waiting till he is come after," could also be construed on occasion as the hope that the students would not come after him too frequently. (If you don't bother them too much, perhaps they won't bother you, and you may be permitted to get on with writing poems—surely Frost cannot always have been above such less than high-minded impulses.)

There is then an ironic relation between public protestations—students should be responsible for their own education; a teacher should wait until he is "come after"—and private feelings (the teacher is disinclined to spend time marking student papers; the teacher desires to be let alone rather than be pestered by the eager young). But to judge this divergence of motive as hypocritical on Frost's part, or to regard it solely with cynicism, one must be very clear and fairly inflexible about what constitutes *real* as opposed to "symbolic" teaching—the kind Frost said he did. A number of his colleagues on the Amherst faculty were perfectly clear about the matter and wondered just what the duties were for which he drew a salary. That feeling grew stronger after he returned in 1926 from his one year, last-shot flirtation with Michigan, and took up once more the position he would fill for the next twelve years. A full professor, he was expected to be in residence only during the ten weeks of the winter term (later, when Frost began to go to Florida in December the time was changed) and to have no official duties beyond giving an occasional lecture or reading. One can imagine the sort of grumbling this arrangement produced among those not so favored, and how any discrepancy between what was professed and what was practiced might be eagerly seized upon as evidence of bad faith. Yet, in a sense, there was no discrepancy at all between belief and practice; Frost professed a sort of academic laissez-faire and also carried it out.

There was a more evident lack of fit between his public statements and his private feelings when the subject was a literary compatriot or rival such as Amy Lowell. While her review of *North of Boston* had been a pleasant surprise to be greeted with upon returning to America in 1915, Frost was annoyed with the charge that he lacked humor, and with her later remarks about Elinor Frost as loyal helpmate. Nor could he have admired the mixture of dogmatic assertion and thrown-off hunches of which her criticism was made. By 1920 he wrote Untermeyer that he didn't believe her anything but a "fake"—that her prose statements were nothing but "Nonsense and charlatanry." In 1925 a fiftieth birthday celebratory dinner was held for him at the Hotel Brevoort in New York (he wrongly supposed he had been born in 1875). Amy Lowell was invited but did not attend, and in retaliation Frost stayed away from her Boston dinner party on the occasion of her fiftieth birthday and her just-published biography of Keats (Frost called this occasion the "Keats eats"). She died suddenly soon afterward, and Frost responded first by writing what he characterized to Untermeyer as "a little compunctious prose to her ashes." This tribute appeared in the *Christian Science Monitor* and was incisive, even eloquent, about what he called the "breathless swing between subject matter and form" which could be seen in successive poetic movements. Amy Lowell had "helped make it stirring times for a decade to those immediately concerned with art and to many not so immediately." In other words, she had made a good deal of publicity. The only words dealing directly with her poetry were in Frost's closing paragraph:

> The water in our eyes from her poetry is not warm with any suspicion of tears; it is water flung cold, bright and many-colored from flowers gathered in the formal garden in the morning. Her Imagism lay chiefly in images to the eye. She flung flowers and everything there. Her poetry was forever a clear resonant calling off of things seen.

The writing here is itself so resonant that we almost neglect to notice how it fixes Lowell's poetry as appealing merely to the eye, flinging "flowers and everything there." But Frost believed in "ear-reading" rather than "eye-reading." In "The Figure a Poem Makes" he was to speak of poetry as a "happy-sad blend of the drinking song" and warn that "No tears in the writer, no tears in the reader." There were no tears in Amy Lowell's poetry, thus no tears in our eyes but cold water instead.

In addition to this *Monitor* tribute, Frost spoke about her to the students at Amherst, saying in effect (he told Untermeyer in the same letter) that no one minded her outrageousness because it never thrust home: "In life she didn't know where the feelings were to hurt them, any more than in poetry she knew where they were to touch them." Whether said "in effect" or straight out, it was a devastating thing to say. But as Frost's dislike of spending too many hours in classrooms or grading student papers was a practical carrying out of his theoretical principle that a student is responsible for his own education, so his remark that Amy Lowell didn't know where "the feelings" were, either in life or poetry, is an extension of his Imagist portrait of her in the *Monitor* article. In his response to Lowell, Frost was well-mounted on his prejudices: against the rich; against poets (especially female ones) who spoke, too loudly, various dubious pronouncements; against Imagism; against any contemporary who might be construed as a rival. Yet what issued from this mixture of antipathies were extraordinarily rich pieces of expression—both in the newspaper tribute and the letter to Untermeyer—which have in them the essential surprise of poetry. Whatever one may think about his judgments of her, they are in no sense an obvious way to talk, but original, rather, and in their freshness repay a second look.

In the fall of 1925 Frost returned to the University of Michigan for what was to be his last year of teaching there, although he had accepted a permanent post at Michigan as Fellow of Letters. Various family illnesses seem to have given him the sudden sense that he had made a mistake in returning to Michigan, at such a geographical and spiritual distance from what he now imagined to be the security and solidity of farming in New England. The most immediate cause for his guilty concern was the illness—which in various forms was to last for years—of his youngest child Marjorie, whose difficulties at that moment included appendicitis, pericarditis, and a general nervous listlessness. Frost wrote Untermeyer in February of 1926, from Ann Arbor, that Elinor had stayed in the East to care for Marjorie, while he had

come to Ann Arbor to make some show of teaching a little for my year's pay. I'm sad enough about Marj, but I am more busted up than sad.

All of this sickness and scatteration of the family is our fault and not
our misfortune or I wouldn't admit it. It's a result and a judgement on
us. We ought to have gone back farming years ago or we ought to have
stayed farming when we knew we were well off.

The letters to Untermeyer are almost always playful, but this one is
perhaps rather less controlled in its distraction. For "our fault" we
may choose to read "my fault" and entertain the notion that the "scatteration" was indeed Frost's fault, insofar as his returning to Michigan
was not a popular decision among members of his family. But to
talk—however seriously or playfully—about a "judgement on us"
transforms the situation from a moral one to a religio-poetical one: if
"sickness and scatteration" are really a "result and judgement" on
"us" for "our" not having stayed on the farm, it all seems larger than
anything the individual Robert Frost could have done to stave it off.
Elinor and Marjorie and the rest of the family become accomplices,
rather than individuals who may be suffering as a result of it.

Marjorie's ill-health was complemented by Elinor's. In a letter the
previous June to George Roy Elliott, Frost had spoken of a "serious
nervous collapse," a phrase which covered the fact of another pregnancy and the miscarriage which ended it. Frost—who must have
blamed his own sexual drive also—blamed explicitly the "way of life"
he had been leading which put too much strain on Elinor. "All this
campaigning goes against her better nature," he told Elliott, announcing that it was time to get "back into the quiet from which we came."
But this of course was extremely unlikely given the continuing
demands of maintaining his literary career and reputation. In addition
to Marjorie's illness and Elinor's "nervous collapse," there was the
possibility that his son Carol's "incipient tuberculosis" (in Elinor's
phrase) of a decade before had returned. Carol had married in 1923
and his wife Lillian had presented Frost with his first grandchild the
next year. Frost wrote Untermeyer that summer about his pride in
Carol's work as a farmer on the South Shaftsbury farm, which by now
he had given outright to his son and daughter-in-law. But Carol's wife
underwent major surgery the year after their child, Prescott, was born;
then she developed tuberculosis (it was diagnosed in Marjorie in 1930)
and eventually (in 1931) moved with her husband to California. In
response to the "sickness and scatteration" of his family, Frost held
out the farm and "the quiet" as wistful pretenses that there was a
place or a condition to which, somehow, they could return if only he
took the "judgement" on him seriously enough. In fact there was no
going back.

Lesley Frost, 1921.

Carol Frost, 1921.

Marjorie Frost, 1921.

He took different tones toward his children, tried to speak to and about them as if they were distinct people with different capacities and needs. When Lesley was at Wellesley he vigorously enlisted himself on her side in her difficulties with a Latin teacher, or her failure to make the tennis team. He was more than ready, also, to warn her about the dangers of the male sex and the importance of not giving them any "wrong ideas" about her behavior. But he could also indulge himself, especially with Lesley, in the kind of destructive comic fantasy he enjoyed constructing for Untermeyer. When Lesley was living in New York in an apartment of an acquaintance, Frost revealed a plan for getting rid of some "cooccupants" whose presence she must have complained about:

> You can get in a kerosene can a gallon of gasolene (price 36 cents) and pour, literally pour, it into every crack and corner of the wood work of the beds or cots and soak the canvass of them all along where it is nailed to the wood . . . You must do the deed very early in the day . . . You may have to buy a cheap kerosene can. It is the best thing to buy the gasolene in and to put the stuff on with. Don't spare it. Make the wood bubble. Go over the beds twice perhaps. Then open the windows and get out.

(He confesses he should hate to mail this from the local Franconia post office for fear it would be opened and his evil discovered.) There is no indication that Lesley followed his directions, even if she enjoyed the fantasy.

In his reminiscence of Frost, Raymond Holden says that he did his best to "crush the poetic instinct" in Carol and Lesley. Nothing which his oldest daughter ever wrote suggests that such was the case. In contrast with Lesley, Carol was a shy, inarticulate person whose ambitions to succeed first at farming, then at poetry, were to be unrealized and would end in suicide. Elinor was especially protective of him, fearing that her husband's impatience and high standards might cripple the struggling son. Yet in the letters he wrote to Carol after Carol and Lillian had moved to California, Frost shows a touching attempt to be encouraging about his son's efforts to write poetry, yet not lay it on too thick and run the risk of patronizing or misleading him. Carol's questions to his father about how to proceed in the matter of poetic composition are embarrassing in their naivete: "I don't under[stand?] the system of blank verse. Is there some way of grouping the words? I'm sending along thoughts I had and would like to know what type of verse they would best be adapted to." Of course the notion of gathering a bunch of "thoughts" and then trying to figure out the sort of verse they should be expressed in, was contrary to everything Frost believed about how poetry got written. But though he blamed himself at times for not encouraging the children enough in their efforts, he responded to the poems Carol sent him with sympathetic and encouraging criticism.

Irma Frost's presence is a shadowy one, as she figures very little in the fascinating volume of the Frost family letters, and her main role, sadly, never makes itself felt until late in Frost's life. At that time, divorced by her husband and having lost custody of her children, she was finally committed by her father to the state hospital in Concord, New Hampshire. In her delusions of persecution and (on the strength of her husband's testimony in his letter to Frost after he had determined to divorce her) in her sexual fears and prudery, she brings to mind his sister Jeanie. For a time Irma studied art in New York City, but it led to nothing lasting. Her marriage to John Cone was a troubled one from the beginning and relations with her father were similarly uneasy.

It was the fourth child, Marjorie, whose spirit was most truly a poetic one, and not just because she wrote poems (privately printed after her death in a volume titled *Franconia*). This spirit can be felt unmistakeably in a letter she wrote home to her parents in 1932 when she was undergoing rehabilitation in Boulder, Colorado, after tuberculosis had been diagnosed. In it she thinks back to times spent boarding with the Lynch family in Bethlehem, New Hampshire:

> Dear Mama and Papa. A wonderful rainy night. With the windows wide open & the old, fragrant air coming in, all the places I have ever been come back to me just as they were then, not as I found them to be since. The years between are as if they had never been, & for a moment I am sitting on the steps of the old stoop back of Lynches, inhaling horse-radish tips, listening to the pump inside, losing suction with every gasping pump of the old handle, & watching the sun slip down behind the ranges. Something lost behind *those* ranges, isn't there? Now that we are on the other side. You see what a little thing like rain does to me. Perhaps it's a good thing we don't have it more often.

This was the presence that Frost would characterize to Lesley, when Marjorie lay on her deathbed two years later, as "the same old Marj in her talk, grim ironical and noble."

At the end of his sonnet "Robert Frost" mentioned earlier, Robert

Lowell has the poet reflect, "When I am too full of joy, I think / how little good my health did anyone near me." In fact, Frost had his own share of illness, and his return from one of his exhausting reading tours often signalled a patch of invalidism. But he had the will to believe that he was healthy, and of his family only Lesley took after him. In the words given him in Lowell's poem there is the sense that his good health or high spirits were a provocation to those around him; indeed that they may have inspired their opposite, as another sort of "judgement" on him. As with everybody else, Frost played rough with his children, but certainly played with them; gave them demanding attention at times, at other times withdrew; teased them and cajoled them and worried about them. In short, he was like other parents, only more so, and one should be wary of pronouncing on the extent to which his "health" did either good or bad to those most near him.

———————

Having served his final year at Michigan, he returned not to farm-ing (except in his special sense of that activity), but to Amherst Col-lege under an arrangement which could hardly have been bettered. The course catalogue for 1926–27 carried, at the end of its section of English departmental offerings, the information that "During the win-ter Professor Robert Frost will be in residence to conduct special classes in English and to hold informal conferences with the student." This was an artfully worded piece of information, making clear that he was no ordinary professor and that students should not expect the usual thing—whatever that was—in their dealings with him. The English classes he would conduct were "special" ones (part of their specialness consisted in their not meeting very often) and the confer-ences he held with students would be "informal" ones. And he could look on this special status as corroborative of his insistence that in a classroom one should rise above issues of right or wrong, yes or no, true or false.

His sense of himself as a teacher comes through most vividly in a letter to Cox at the beginning of 1926 after Cox had failed to obtain a teaching position at Bread Loaf despite Frost's support. Frost flat-tered him by telling him what a good teacher he was, better than Frost ever was or would be. But he advised Cox to look for better things to do in class than debate and disagree:

Clash is all very well for coming lawyers politicians and theologians. But I should think there must be a whole realm or plane above that—

all sight and insight, perception, intuition, rapture. Narrative is a fear-
fully safe place to spend your time. Having ideas that are neither pro
nor con is the happy thing. Get up there high enough and the differences that make controversy become only the two legs of a body the
weight of which is on one in one period, on the other in the next.
Democracy monarchy; puritanism paganism; form content; conserva-
tism radicalism; systole diastole; rustic urbane; literary colloquial; work
play. I should think too much of myself to let any teacher fool me into
taking sides on any one of these oppositions.

This is an invitation to what, in another context, I have called "elevated play," the invitation to see around any particular idea or "ism"
by following it immediately with its opposed term, without even the
distinction of a comma between them ("systole diastole"). These
oppositions might then become the subject of a consideration which
would be detached and contemplative.

It is a mark of Frost's inconsistency as a "thinker"—or one might
say, of his liveliness as a man of contradictions—that he should be
able to give this ingenious and poetic advice to Cox, offered from the
vantage of a "special" teacher, and at the same time hold on so
proudly to the prejudices he claimed as his own. On one hand we have
(in the letter to Cox) the picture of Frost as elevated, seeing around
things, taking perspectives so long that they could embrace conserva-
tism and radicalism, systole diastole. Far above particular battles, his
effort might look like a critically disinterested one in the Matthew
Arnold sense: the ability to take any notion and complement it with
its opposite, in the faith that what results will be stronger and more
true. In his praise of "sight and insight, perception, intuition, rapture"
he might have joined hands with Arnold's praise of culture, of "sweet-
ness and light." But then we think of the canny, aggressive perpetua-
tor of his power as a poet, making sure he got good reviews or cultivating useful publicists for his theory of poetry. This un-disinterested
concern for his career was expressed most sharply in a letter written
in 1930 to a young poet named Kimball Flaccus, who had sent Frost
his own poetry. After praising the poems for being "carried high"
Frost proceeded to instruct Flaccus:

> You wish the world better than it is, more poetical. You are that kind
> of poet. I would rate as the other kind. I wouldn't give a cent to see the
> world, the United States or even New York made better. I want them
> left just as they are for me to make poetical on paper. I don't ask any-

thing done to them that I won't do to them myself. I'm a mere selfish artist most of the time. I have no quarrel with the material. The grief will be if I can't transmute it into poems. I don't want the world made safer for poetry or easier. To hell with it. That is its own lookout. Let it stew in its own materialism. No, not to Hell with it. Let it hold its position while I do it in art. My whole anxiety is for myself as a performer. Am I any good? That's what I'd like to know and all I need to know.

This is probably as vehemently final a statement as Frost ever made setting the record straight on his feelings about "the world." In four words: "To hell with it," or if not to hell, then to poetry with it: "let it hold its position while I do it in art." This looks less like disinterestedness than what from a humanitarian perspective might be called callousness or selfishness. "Am I any good?" is the real question, the only question, and that question makes concern about the state of the world, for better or worse, irrelevant. Of course part of the intent here was to tease the idealistic Kimball Flaccus; but the result shows in a curious way how, though superficially unlike his advice to Sidney Cox to "get up there high enough," the pieces of advice are equally firm in rejecting any ameliorative attempt at social change—at reform of anything in the name of something else. He put it succinctly in a couplet later on: "I own I never really warmed / To the reformer or reformed." The only reformation he cared about was that which he could effect by lines of poetry which took the material of the world and, in Emerson's words from "The American Scholar," made it soar and sing.

The exaggeratedly personal thrust of Frost's insistence, in the letter to Flaccus, that his sole anxiety was for himself as a performer, would later be generalized into the claim that such anxiety was the universal human condition—but benign and life-giving in its nature. In his "Letter to *The Amherst Student*," written in March of 1935 to the college newspaper which had saluted him on what they thought was his sixtieth birthday, Frost attacked the notion that the twentieth century—the present age—was any worse than previous ages for which writers, like Matthew Arnold and Wordsworth, had claimed such honors. He pointed out that it was impossible to "get outside the age you are in to judge it exactly," and that those who tried to do so ended up "gaping in agony" and writing "huge shapeless novels" bellowing with pain. (So much for literary naturalism, 1930s style.) If all ages are bad, and if we can't know how bad our own age is because we can't get outside it, then at least

> There is at least so much good in the world that it admits of form and the making of form. And not only admits of it, but calls for it . . . Anyone who has achieved the least form to be sure of it, is lost to the larger excruciations . . . The artist, the poet, might be expected to be the most aware of such assurance. But it is really everybody's sanity to feel it and live by it.

This asserting of form he calls "velvet," and the forms are made by an individual effort: "a basket, a letter, a garden, a room, an idea, a picture, a poem. For those we haven't to get a team together before we can play." There is really no difference between the brash claim to Flaccus and this later, more suave presentation of poetry, of "form," as "everybody's sanity." They are equally set against the demand that poetry try to make the world a better place; against what in the *Amherst Student* letter he referred to as "raw sincerity" trying to effect the kind of reformation or salvation that can only be effected by the artist in us. And, he says, we are all artists, if minor ones.

Such insistence, especially as it informed the poems in *A Further Range* (1936) with their sceptical treatment of social concerns, provoked the harshest criticism of his poetry Frost had ever received. But this volume was still some years off when in the summer of 1928, with *West-Running Brook* delivered to the publishers (it would appear in November of that year, his fifth book of poems) he decided to go to France and England with Elinor and Marjorie. The latter's illness had been a prolonged one, issuing in general psychological depression ("nervous prostration," as it was called). A specialist at Johns Hopkins was consulted; finally it was decided that Marjorie's health might be given a boost if she were able to realize her desire of learning to speak French. The idea was to arrange, through the offices of a Vermont neighbor, Dorothy Canfield Fisher, for Marjorie to live with a family in Sèvres while her parents went back to England to visit old haunts and friends.

As may be gathered from the tone of a long letter to Lesley, written in August after they had arrived in Paris for some looking around, Frost's responses combined uneasiness with disgust at the spectacle of tourist America confronting exploitative France. He says that if it were not for the family with whom Marjorie was to stay, "not all our conviction that all nations are alike would have kept us from thinking France was a little worst [sic] than America." It was a pity, he added,

Passport photo, Robert and Elinor, 1928.

that they had chosen to visit in August "when the races were both at their terriblest in each others embrace." There follow some accounts of unfortunate scenes with taxi drivers and theater ushers. But the real anguish came from being caught out in something that looked like tourism: "We ought not to be in France after all we said from the platform and the throne against tourism literal and metaphorical." This interesting remark goes deep, since metaphorical tourism could be thought of as a smooth trafficking in literary monuments, an easy, on-good-terms relationship with all styles, and a belief that if one has the proper guidebook one will know what to admire and to what degree. To be either a literal or a metaphorical tourist was, for Frost, to lose whatever individuality one possessed, foregoing self-consciousness and inhibition in favor of immersion in the great stream of people following the instructions of a group voice. It was this principled antitourism, even more than the suspicious Anglo-American reaction to sophisticated Paris, that explains Frost's deep dislike of his situation there. (Although suspiciousness surely had something to do with it, when in the same letter to Lesley he managed to make France triumph over New Hampshire in the ignobility sweepstakes: "Upon my soul I never saw anything to match this summer Paris for ugliness not even a White Mountain Resort.")

The antipathy to Paris was combined with and heightened by his concern not only about Marjorie but about Elinor. In a letter to Haines quoted earlier, he rather melodramatically pronounced that something radical would have to be done and that he would be the one to do it, since Elinor was past doing anything for herself. Far from doing anything, Frost extended his stay in England from early in September to middle of November, then confessed to Haines that he felt guilty about having made "Elinor unhappier keeping her on than I think I ever made her before." As might be imagined, what had happened was that Frost was having an exciting time visiting old friends and acquaintances like Haines, Abercrombie, Flint, Harold Monro (who took him to dinner with T. S. Eliot); calling on Robert Bridges, meeting Edward Garnett, visiting Gloucestershire, Edinburgh, and Leeds; traveling on his own to Dublin and socializing with AE (George Russell). In a letter to Lesley he recorded his responses to recent writing by English poets and implied that he was in England, in part at least, to see how well these fellow competitors were holding up. In almost every case he found nothing to make him envious or newly admiring. Gibson's "stock as a poet is quoted very low now"; de la Mare was recovering from a serious operation; W. H. Davies was still jealous of de la Mare; John Freeman was just dull; Abercrombie had written a play which "raised my gorge at its stilted vernacular" and had fathered "several more children than when we last heard!" It is as if Frost had to confirm how far he had moved beyond them in reputation and in the production of a substantial body of distinguished lyric and narrative verse. Eliot of course was something else, and Frost may have been unaware that six years previously, in the *Dial,* Eliot had characterized him as the poet of "New England torpor," finding his poetry uninteresting and unreadable. As for his opinion of Eliot, he would write Lesley a few years later about *The Waste Land:* "Waste Lands—your great grand mother on the grand mother on your mothers side! I doubt if anything was laid waste by war that was not laid waste by peace before." Their dinner together under Monro's auspices must have been a fairly guarded affair.

He had spoken about the bad health of both his daughter and his wife, but he too was less than well, suffering as always the consequences of too many successive social and public appearances. Elinor, who was surely not one to understate the matter, wrote to Lesley in November that he had been in bed for two or three days with sinus headache and hoarseness, that he should have a complete rest, but that with all his engagements that would be impossible: "He cannot seem to stop and I don't know just what to do." She also noted that it would no doubt be a "rather nervous period" for Lesley, what with her father's book coming out. (Recently married to Dwight Francis, Lesley was running a bookstore in Pittsfield, Massachusetts.) The book, *West-Running Brook,* was published in November as the Frosts were sailing home, each of them badly seasick; and if Lesley ever fretted about the reception of her father's books, she might have had cause to do so with this one, at least insofar as it was relatively ignored by the reviewers. No other book Frost published met with so little interesting response—which was odd, since *New Hampshire* had won the Pulitzer and there was nothing to suggest that fashions had changed in the intervening five years, nor that Frost was out of favor either with reviewers or the reading public.

By treating *West-Running Brook* in a cursory way here, it may seem that I also think it a book to be overlooked. It does strike me as the weakest of the five books Frost had published by 1928, also as clearly inferior to the two which would follow it. Yet this relatively "weak" collection (and, for Frost, especially slim, the shortest of his books except for *A Boy's Will*) contains lyrics as strong and as delicate as "Spring Pools," "Bereft," and "Acquainted with the Night"; sonnets as well-turned as "Once by the Pacific," "Acceptance," and "A Soldier"; charming miniatures like "Fireflies in the Garden" or "Atmosphere" or "Devotion"; plus the largely ambitious title poem, one of his last efforts in the dialogue form. (Later, the disturbingly private "The Lovely Shall Be Choosers," a poem about Isabelle Frost, was added to the collection.)

The poem "West-Running Brook" works hard to assert in the husband's long peroration to his wife, that though "existence," as figured in the example of the brook, seems to "run away," and is

> . . . substance lapsing unsubstantial;
> The universal cataract of death
> That spends to nothingness . . .

nevertheless there is a "strange resistance" in the stream:

> Not just a swerving, but a throwing back,
> As if regret were in it and were sacred . . .

This "backward motion toward the source," affirmed by an individual's and the race's sense of history, is a metaphysical enlargement of what was always Frost's insistence, as early as "Reluctance," that it is a treasonous betrayal of our humanity to accede, without regret, to the "drift of things": "To yield with a grace to reason, / And bow and accept the end / Of a love or a season." "West-Running Brook" is eloquent, perhaps rather too much so near its end as Frost seems to address the reader, presenting in an unironic, "inspiring" and somewhat vague way, an affirmation of the human:

> It is this backward motion toward the source,
> Against the stream, that most we see ourselves in,
> The tribute of the current to the source.
> It is from this in nature we are from.
> It is most us.

Faced with such impressive talk, the unnamed spouse of "Fred" is pretty much reduced to silence and assent, while her husband is given all the fine words. She might justifiably have wondered what came over Fred that he could suddenly rise to such heights or depths of profundity. A reader of Frost who had absorbed his poetics of the sentence sound, and who remembered his fondness for gossip which had the "actuality and intimacy" of talk, might be similarly at a loss to know just what to say in response to the prophetic, timeless voice which takes over in this poem. And having experienced the passionate speech of different female characters in *North of Boston,* this reader may be disappointed by the perfunctory and rather "feminine" language given the wife in "West-Running Brook."

Reviewing the book in the New York *Herald Tribune,* Babette Deutsch noted that Frost had moved away from dramatic poetry toward a more "personal" or philosophical lyric, and she also expressed a not altogether happy surprise at the dark tone of some of those lyrics. A month or so later in the *Times,* Untermeyer pointed out, perhaps in response to her review, that personal lyric as it was seen in Frost's first book, *A Boy's Will,* was as much a part of his style as the more objective, longer dramatic poems. At any rate, the "dark" lyrics which impressed and troubled Babette Deutsch are mainly contained in a section from the volume headed "Fiat Nox" ("Let there be Night"), with its motto taken from the last two lines of "Acceptance," in which a little bird attains its perch as night comes on and pronounces itself "Safe," saying

> Let the night be too dark for me to see
> Into the future. Let what will be, be.

But the speaker's perch in "dark" lyrics like "Bereft" ("Word I was in my life alone / Word I had no one left but God") or "Tree at My Window," with its precarious and ironic analogy between the "outer weather" which buffets a tree and the "inner weather" of the storm-tossed man, is very much a threatened perch. "Acquainted with the Night," in its acceptance of "what will be" goes so far as to employ a toneless, repetitive recitation of what happened on a night walk:

> I have been one acquainted with the night.
> I have walked out in rain—and back in rain.
> I have outwalked the furthest city light.

These sights and sounds are registered by a consciousness but provide no clues or provocation to significant action, as the sonnet concludes with observing how

> And further still at an unearthly height
> One luminary clock against the sky
>
> Proclaimed the time was neither wrong nor right.
> I have been one acquainted with the night.

He ends where he began, the poem establishes no progression, is—for one of Frost's—extraordinarily undramatic, even mesmerized and mesmerizing in its sound.

The "dark" poems assume prominence in *West-Running Brook,* not because they are the habitual form Frost's expression took in that volume, but because they stand out from the surrounding poems, which are simply not weighty, witty, or memorable enough to provide a counterforce. (The reader may experiment by scanning the table of contents to *West-Running Brook* and seeing how many poems he recognizes by title.) Too much should not be made, however, of any change in prevailing mood, any "maturing" into a grimmer view of the universe and our place in it than Frost had held earlier. After all, "Bereft" carried the afterthought "As of about 1893," and "Once by the Pacific," in which "There would be more than ocean-water broken / Before God's last *Put out the Light* was spoken," was "As of about 1880." The attempt to insist on continuities between the finished poems of 1928 and earlier feelings and circumstances in the poet's life, is a way of saying that these poems issue from permanence, not change: from permanent states of the soul, rather than the newly gloomy musings of an aging man.

---

Frost returned from England to two daughters, Irma and Lesley, who were unhappy in their marriages and contemplating the possibility of divorce. But the subject of divorce was already on his mind, as is seen from letters he wrote Untermeyer from England with respect to his friend's marital confusions. Untermeyer had divorced Jean Starr, married Virginia Moore, then divorced her and remarried Jean Starr whom he would again divorce. This activity produced an energetic response from Frost, not so much in favor of marriage—although his prejudice on its side is pretty clear—as against any possible literary exploitation of divorce and its turmoils. Frost's advice was that rather than "scoring off it," Untermeyer should "write a court drama of the IVth Dynasty." But deeper than that playful suggestion was Frost's need to put himself in opposition to liberal cant about the maturing or "learning value" to be gained from such experience:

> What I dread most now is that you will go on the assumption that, though it was folly and landed you in tragedy [Untermeyer's son, Richard, had committed suicide] it was on the way somewhere and somehow prepared you for greater and fuller things. Shut up. The hell with such comforts. It was all time and energy lost, as I have said before.

What comes through here, certainly in part, is the depth of Frost's friendship with Untermeyer, his trust that the latter will trust him to have said "Shut up" in the right tone, after he has alluded to the tragedy of his son's death. It is a Calvinist response which rejects with some animus the possibility of forgiving oneself, of not being as hard on oneself as the case may require. His contempt is directed at the cliché that we learn from our mistakes, that "somehow" we even become better because of them. To this piece of self-cheering-up, his response is those two terse words.

The advice was a moralistic bid for Untermeyer to behave himself and triumph at least this once over volubility, but Frost also spoke to himself here, or at least spoke out of the principles he saw his own poetry as honoring. On another occasion he wrote Cox that "Everybody knows something has to be kept back for pressure and to anybody puzzled to know what I should suggest that for a beginning it might as well be his friends, wife, children and self." Although the impulse in this suggestion may seem mainly like concealment, a blow against "confessional" poetry, it is equally a recognition of necessity, of the need to "keep something back for pressure." For it is out of this pressure that the measured poem is generated: "Poetry is measured in more senses than one: it is measured feet but more important still it is a measured amount of all we could say an we would. We shall be judged finally by the delicacy of our feeling of where to stop short." It is unlikely that he ever read Eliot's "Tradition and the Individual Talent," but we may be reminded of the latter's insistence that poetry is an escape from rather than an outpouring of emotion. "But, of course, only those who have personality and emotions know what it means to want to escape from those things," added Eliot. Frost advised Untermeyer to write a court drama about the IV Dynasty, rather than write about his recent marital career, and we may remember his insistence years before, apropos of *A Boy's Will,* that a poem should have doors, though he wouldn't want to leave them open. In the decade to come—the 1930s—Frost would undergo the severest testing of his declared necessity to stop short, to *not* say "all we could say an we would."

That decade began auspiciously with the publication in November 1930 of his first *Collected Poems,* for which he again received a Pulitzer. The book's appearance was occasion for reflection on his virtues and (in one instance and really for the first time) his limitations as a poet. These limitations were spelled out in the *New Republic* by Granville Hicks, a critic of strong "social," indeed Marxist leanings, who felt (referring to the end of "Acquainted with the Night") that to proclaim the "time was neither wrong nor right," as the clock proclaimed to Frost, was an inadequate proclamation, since for Hicks the time was decidedly wrong. He argued that Frost's poetry created a world of its own which kept its own time, and although it was recognizably related to "the real world" it failed to deal with three significant aspects of that world and of modern life: industrialism, the disrupting effects of scientific hypotheses, and Freudianism. Hicks did not deplore their absence, but said—in terms whose meaning is not immediately clear—that, lacking them, Frost could not "contribute directly to the unification, in imaginative terms, of our culture." Since he did not give us a sense of "belonging" to the modern age, he could not be considered a great poet. But, Hicks added, the age was so bad that probably no poet could do that, and so he allowed Frost a "relative greatness" for doing about as well as could be done in creating a world less impossible. For someone who showed as little responsiveness to language as Hicks did in this review, and considering his own social and political inclinations, the judgment of Frost's merits is fairminded, even winning. Indeed he appeared to be almost charmed out of his principles by Frost, liking the poems despite his better judgment that they were not sufficient. This acceptance with reservations of the *Collected Poems* will be seen to contrast sharply with the rougher reception accorded his next book of poetry six years later.

Along with the Pulitzer award he was elected to the American Academy of Arts and Letters in 1930. And he solidified his situation as a property owner with two new purchases. In his efforts to put the sights of Paris into their proper perspective, he had written home in a Mark Twain-like fashion about how good, by contrast, a mountain in South Shaftsbury called Bucks Cobble looked in his mind's eye. At Christmas of 1928 he bought a new farm, christened "The Gully," within throwing distance of that peak. In 1931 he purchased a handsome, roomy house of obvious distinction located on Sunset Avenue in Amherst. These gestures toward rootedness and permanence, however, were very much at variance with the Frost family situation. In the summer of 1931, before he purchased the Amherst house, Lesley—in the main a healthy person—was ill in a Long Island hospital where eventually her second child was born (she was now divorced from Dwight Francis). Carol and Lillian had moved to California for health reasons. Her husband away studying architecture, Irma was plagued with nervous ailments; while Marjorie had been forced to give up her nursing studies at Johns Hopkins and enter a sanatorium in Colorado, after she was diagnosed as a tuberculosis sufferer. Writing to Untermeyer from his new Amherst home in February of 1932, Frost took a rather King Learish attitude toward trouble, recognizing that one may not be at the worst when one says "This is the worst":

Yet I refuse to match sorrows with anyone else, because just the moment I start the comparison I see that I have nothing yet as terrible as it might be. A few of our children are sick or their spouses still in college. I and my wife are not well, neither are we young; but we mean

Frost's home on Sunset Avenue, Amherst, Massachusetts, 1936.

to be both better and younger for company's sake. That is to say we mean well, though we aren't well.

It was as if he prophesied. Through much of 1933 he himself was ill with—in the testimony of Elinor's letters—prolonged periods of fever, "prostration," a permanent-sounding cough, and the possibility of tuberculosis always held out. His ailment was mitigated by the happiness he took in Marjorie's news that she had fallen in love with a young man named Willard Fraser. "He is a dear, kind, and considerate man, another real Victorian, papa, with the beautiful ideals that I had feared no longer existed," Marjorie wrote home from the sanatorium in Boulder. Although the Frosts were unable to attend Marjorie's wedding held in Montana in May of 1933, they visited Carol, Lillian and grandson Prescott in California in late summer of that year, driving back across country in their new car. In March of the following winter Marjorie gave birth to a baby girl, and was recovering in a normal way from the delivery when she contracted puerperal fever. Elinor had visited her in Montana during the end of her pregnancy and birth of the child; now both Frosts took the train to Montana to witness the agonies of their daughter's final struggle. From the hospital in Billings she was flown to the Mayo Clinic after having been sick for a month and frequently not in her right mind. With blood transfusions every other day, her system still could not withstand the poison, and she died a few days after entering the Minnesota hospital.

The story is an unbearably sad one, a bearing out of Frost's definition of tragedy as something terrible happening and nobody to blame—although in his grief after the event he did lay a "curse" on what he thought might have been medical neglect in guarding against the septicemia which set in after childbirth. What brings it home all the more sadly to us is the eloquent poignancy of the words Frost put to this unspeakable event. To Untermeyer, just after arriving at the Mayo Clinic, he wrote that they were going "through the valley of the shadow" and that, along with blood transfusions, "Marjorie's tenacity and Elinor's devotion and the mercy of God are our hopes." Even so, and whatever the outcome, he predicted that they would be "changed for the worse for the rest of our days," and in a postscript said that his favorite poem, "long before I knew what it was going to mean to us" was Arnold's "Cadmus and Harmonia." That poem, the most beautiful of Callicles's songs from *Empedocles on Etna*—a long poem in which the sage, worn out by the evils of life, plunges into the volcano—celebrates a benign transformation of the suffering man and wife into a pair of aged snakes who "Bask in the glens or on the warm sea-shore / In breathless quiet, after all their ills." Callicles sings of how

> . . . the billow of calamity
> Over their own dear children roll'd,
> Curse upon curse, pang upon pang,
> For years, they sitting helpless in their home,
> A grey old man and woman; yet of old
> The Gods had to their marriage come,
> And at the banquet all the Muses sang.

In Arnold's poem the transformation had taken place ages and ages past. When Frost wrote Untermeyer from Amherst, two weeks after Marjorie's death, it was from an untransformed and unreconciled state, for which his only consolation was expressiveness such as is seen in these excerpts:

Well, the blow has fallen. The noblest of us all is dead and has taken our hearts out of the world with her. It was a terrible seven weeks' fight—too indelibly terrible on the imagination. No death in war could more than match it for suffering and heroic endurance. Why all this talk in favor of peace? Peace has her victories over poor mortals no less merciless than war . . . The only consolation we have is the memory of her greatness through all. Never out of delirium for the last four weeks her responses were of course incorrect. She got little or nothing of what we said to her. The only way I could reach her was by putting my hand backward and forward between us as in counting out and saying with overemphasis *You*—and—*Me*. The last time I did that, the day before she died, she smiled faintly and answered "All the same," frowned slightly and made it "Always the same." Her temperature was then 110, the highest ever known at the Mayo Clinic . . . The classical theory was not born out in her case that a fine and innocent nature released by madness from the inhibitions of society will give way to all the indecencies. Everything she said, however quaint and awry, was of an almost straining loftiness.

And after the passionate, though of course ineffectual fist shaken against "doctors" who may have been careless, he rises to a higher level: "We thought to move heaven and earth—heaven with prayers and earth with money. We moved nothing. And here we are Cadmus and Harmonia not yet placed safely in changed forms."

Frost liked to say that the point about a college was to show students there was a "book side" to everything. What is so extraordinary, so heroic about this letter, is that in the face of the most awful, senseless, heart-piercing personal loss—the death of a child, which is terrible enough, but this one the youngest and the favorite (Untermeyer refers to her as "the Frosts' dearest jewel")—Frost refuses to give up poetry also. Instead, the culminating moment of his account to Untermeyer of the event is the allusion to Arnold's poem. And there is a further twist to that allusion, insofar as "Empedocles" was excluded by Arnold from the 1853 collection of his poems on the grounds that "no poetical enjoyment" could be derived from it, since it showed a "continuous state of mental distress . . . unrelieved by incident, hope, or resistance." It was painful rather than tragic, Arnold insisted, since in tragedy there was enjoyment—"the more tragic the situation, the deeper the enjoyment." But the uses of poetry were more various than Arnold foresaw, and the remembered poem served Frost as a stay, as something (in the words of "Choose Something Like a Star") to "stay" his mind on. Reading the letter today, we experience something like a profound enjoyment, even as the tragedy of Marjorie's death is given full poetic expression in the sentences written for Untermeyer, but surely as much for Frost himself—or the sake of expression, purely. Elinor Frost's words were simpler but no less affecting, as she wrote to her friend Edith Fobes that June: "Poor darling child—it seems too heart breaking, that after achieving good health, and finding perfect happiness in life, she had to lose it all so soon."

Frost later told Raymond Holden that it was Marjorie's death "that killed my wife," and although Elinor lived four more years her spirits never recovered. In October of 1934 she suffered a severe heart attack, and for the first time that December she and Frost went to Florida, living at Key West for the winter. Key West was the opposite of elegant, but still different enough from Amherst or South Shaftsbury to be of interest to Frost, who described it to Untermeyer this way: "There is no sanitation. The water is all off the roofs and after it goes through people I don't know where it goes. Everything is shabby and even dilapidated. There are as many stinks as there are nymphs who rule o'er sewers and sinks (Delete sewers). There are mosquitoes. But there is no Yellow Fever any more . . . The air is balm." All in all, Key West in its shabbiness came off a trace better than Paris in its opulence.

That winter he turned to assembling his next book of poetry, but when Edwin Arlington Robinson died of cancer in April he agreed to write a preface to Robinson's posthumously published long poem, *King Jasper*. He had originally been admiring of Robinson and eager to meet him; they had exchanged books with mutually friendly comments. But during the 1920s when Robinson's *Collected Poems* won a Pulitzer and his long poem *Tristram* enjoyed large sales, Frost kept his distance, declining to contribute to a fiftieth birthday tribute to him, and increasingly criticizing—to Untermeyer's ears—Robinson's "romantic" temper as it was combined with a fondness for whiskey:

> How utterly romantic the enervated old soak is. The way he thinks of poets in the Browningese of "Ben Jonson"! The way he thinks of cucolding lovers and cucold husbands in "Tristram"! Literary conventions! I feel as if I had been somewhere on hot air like a fire-balloon. Not with him altogether. I haven't more than half read him since "The Town Down the River." I simply couldn't lend a whole ear to all that Arthurian twaddle twiddled over after the Victorians.

This rather violent dismissiveness toward the "enervated old soak," has, as usual with Frost's less-than-disinterested criticisms, its point. *The Town Down the River* was published in 1910, and though Frost forgets that *The Man Against the Sky* (1916) contained some of Robinson's best poems (Robinson had sent him the volume, but Frost never acknowledged it) he makes a telling point against the later, longer poems, in which literary convention and something very much like "hot air" mix unsatisfactorily. But he didn't dismiss Robinson—at least the early Robinson—altogether, and when Untermeyer in 1932 was thinking about doing a severe review of one of the later poems, Frost remonstrated with him ("Way down in my heart I don't know about your doing that to Robinson") and suggested that silence would be "severe enough in the cause of art."

Writing prose—at least the prose of a preface or an essay—did not come easy to him, probably less easily than did a poem. With the exception of the talk to Amherst alumni, "Education by Poetry," a revised version of which appeared in the college alumni magazine in 1931, he had not published prose utterances of any length or importance on the subject of poetry in general or his own in particular. As for declaring himself in public about the worth of a contemporary, and therefore a competitor, his only effort had been the few short paragraphs written after Amy Lowell's death—guarded and minimal praise, as noted previously. Although he took Robinson a good deal more seriously than he did Lowell, that only made it more difficult for him to behave disinterestedly, since the anxiety of rivalry entered the picture. As a consequence he decided to write mainly about poetry, rather than about Robinson's poetry, and to engage in a defense of "the old fashioned way to be new" Robinson had stayed content with. The preface began by ticking off various qualities that, in the "quest of new ways to be new" Frost says poetry has been tried *without:* without punctuation, capital letters, metric frame, audial images, "dramatic tones of voice," content, phrase, epigram, coherence, logic, consistency—and indeed without ability. More recently, he says, poets have decided to add to rather than subtract from poetry, and what they have added is ideas, politics, "thinking."

That winter he had taken up the cudgels against an article by Archibald MacLeish, called to his attention by Untermeyer, which argued that poetry should be "untimely" in its originality and critically disturbing of present social and economic arrangements. Returning to the article in the second of two letters, he called it a "Pound-gang editorial" and disparaged MacLeish's plea for originality as a "hitting 'em where they ain't and won't be for a hundred or two years at least." By contrast, the artist's way (Frost's preferred way) was to "tell people what they haven't as yet realized they were about to say for themselves." This was of course a restatement of the "common in experience, uncommon in writing" maxim he had invented many years before at Pinkerton. Now, writing a preface to Robinson's last book, he generalized the MacLeish idea into an observation that the most recent new way to be new was to import grievances into poetry, to use it as a "vehicle of grievances against the un-Utopian state." He was ironic about the belief that poetry should prompt one to action: "How soon?" he asks the prototypical young poet who is said to have informed him that it should.

The "old-fashioned way to be new" is rather to write a poetry of griefs rather than grievances. "Grievances are a form of impatience. Griefs are a form of patience," and we must not disarm ourselves of our patience. In a moment of condescension or superiority to the medium in which he was currently engaged, Frost says he would restrict grievances to prose, "leaving poetry free to go its way in tears"; and Robinson is skillfully brought into these Frostian ruminations by figuring as "the prince of heartachers" whose poetry was full of griefs, of tears. In its original form, the preface then closed with a vaguely specified memory of meeting Robinson at a place called "The Place of Bitters" near Boston Common, where the two of them, Frost says, looked out "without bitterness" at the "welter of dissatisfaction and experiment in the world around us." After this romantically drawn portrait of the two old-fashioned non-experimenters, who cared only that they should "lodge a few poems where they will be hard to get rid of," Frost concluded by saying that Robinson "lodged more than his share."

It was an abrupt conclusion, and Macmillan, Robinson's publishers, felt their poet deserved somewhat more by way of particular reference than Frost had given him. Although he was "bothered a little" (so he wrote Untermeyer) by having to extend the preface in order to quote from some of Robinson's poems, Frost complied—and it was fortunate that Macmillan pushed him. For in addition to obliging them with allusions to the poetry and with the amusing story of how he and Pound, years ago, had laughed at how felicitous was the fourth "thought" in "Miniver Cheevy" ("Miniver thought, and thought, and thought, / And thought about it"), he surprisingly turned round and complicated the dictum that poetry should be made up of griefs. Here was Robinson, "prince of heartachers," who yet could make Frost and Pound laugh with that fourth "thought" which surprised them. More than surprise, it was "mischief," and after speaking of Robinson's art as "playful" even "humorous," Frost develops a notion thrown out to Untermeyer ten years previously. Style was the man, or rather the way the man took himself, "and to be at all charming or even bearable, the way is almost rigidly prescribed. If it is with outer seriousness, it must be with inner humor. If it is with outer humor, it must be with inner seriousness. Neither one alone without the other under it will do."

This insight paid tribute to Robinson's poetry in an original way, and it came out of Frost's mature sense of himself as a poet wide enough in range not only to compass both grave and not-so-grave feelings or situations, but to bind them together intimately as "outer" and "inner," humor and seriousness, one "under" the other. It is possible that the terrible loss of his daughter in the previous year stimulated him to make the binding together of opposite feelings more strong, and to state more extravagantly the intensity of each feeling. Poetry is made up of tears, griefs made just bearable for the length of the poem by what he referred to (like that fourth "thought" in "Miniver Cheevy") as "the intolerable touch of poetry"—by the playfulness that turned griefs into something else. Those unrelenting words from his letter to Kimball Flaccus about not wanting to make the world any better, not caring to alleviate its materialism or its poverty or its injustices, but only to take it as it was in all its awfulness, then "do" it in poetry, are extended in the Robinson preface from an individual preference or prejudice on Frost's part into the universal condition. Any poet's life must be if it is to be worth anything, "a revel in the felicities of language," as Robinson's was. So Frost ended the revised preface by practicing what he preached, by behaving in the most playful manner about his serious subject:

> Give us immedicable woes—woes that nothing can be done for—
> woes flat and final. And then to play. The play's the thing.
> Play's the thing. All virtue in "as if."
> > As if the last of days
> Were fading and all wars were done.
> As if they were. As if, as if!

The sequence of "woes . . . woes . . . woes" followed by an equal number of "plays"; the offhand allusion to Hamlet's bright idea, then its immediate transformation into something larger; the graceful nod at

Robinson's lovely lines from "The Dark Hills," then the final tribute to the speaking voice as it invites us to take on different special postures while saying "As if," is as inventive and moving a sequence as can be found in Frost's prose.

Having said as much is doubtless to reveal something about one's own politics, or at least politics of poetry. For it was possible in 1935—as surely it is today—to find Frost's insistence that griefs not grievances were the only subject of poetry, a historical as well as a moral distortion of reality. One might ask whether the poems of Blake or Shelley, or of Frost's contemporary, W.B. Yeats, can be accounted for accurately in such terms. Or one could find, as indeed one of the reviewers of the preface did find, that the griefs–grievances distinction as wielded by Frost was a bald rationalization of an individual temperament's refusal to concern itself with anything but poetry—and a cruelly circumscribed poetry at that. Reviewing *King Jasper* in the *New Republic* at the outset of 1936, Newton Arvin seemed less disappointed by the mediocre quality of Robinson's last work than by the insensitivity shown in Frost's preface to it. Speaking from a Marxist point of view, Arvin said that the preface's attitude with its acceptance of "woes flat and final" that nothing could be done for, placed Frost at an "astronomical distance from the rest of us" (at least from readers of *The New Republic*). And Arvin pointed out, in censuring Frost, that there was a "cant of scepticism, the complacency of the pessimist" lamentably embodied in his preface. Arvin failed to comment on the complementary emphasis Frost had made of the necessity for "play" in poetry, and probably the critic found such an emphasis inappropriate as a way of thinking about poetry's essential function. But I think his charge that not only enthusiasts for social schemes could be guilty of cant and complacency, that accepters of the world's way might incur a similar accusation, was as shrewd a criticism of Frost's temperamental politics as had been or was ever to be made. The review indicated how provocative and provoking Frost's formulations could be, and it also refused to be overwhelmed or charmed into submission by the eloquence of the Robinson preface.

---

In the spring of 1936, four decades after he had enrolled there as a special student, Frost was invited to give the Charles Eliot Norton lectures at Harvard. Although the lectures (six in number) were traditionally supposed to be published eventually, they were never gotten into publishable shape by Frost; and even though a typewritten manscript, made from stenographic records of the talks, was sent to him by the Harvard University Press, no copy has survived. Thompson assumes that Frost burned it, and that he did so out of a lazy disinclination to do whatever revision or expansion might have had to be done. "Prose costs me a great deal," he said when declining an invitation to write a eulogy for Robinson for the American Academy of Arts and Letters. Although laziness should not be undervalued as a motive for Frost's disposing of the typescript rather than revising it, in this particular case something more than laziness may have been at work. From the titles of the first two lectures, one can see why he might have been reluctant to proceed further in readying them for print: "The Old Way to be New" was a reworked version of the preface to Robinson, with poems of Frost used as examples instead of Robinson's; "Vocal Imagination: Merger of Form and Content" spelled out the theory of sentence sounds and the "audile imagination"—his "never-ending consideration" (as he called it to Untermeyer) for the past twenty and more years. Both these lectures, as well as the succeeding ones, were heavily attended, beyond anything the authorities at Harvard had anticipated, and the lectures practiced what they preached; that is, they depended for their "play," for their "merger of form and content," on the performing voice of Frost the speaker. *There* first and last was the repository of whatever wisdom and theory he had to convey. His expressiveness and inventiveness, his humor and tone, were what the audience went away remembering. In turning these utterances (some of them doubtless improvised on the spot) into the orderly sentences and paragraphs of a respectable looking document bearing the imprint of Harvard, much of their play would be lost. Frost probably knew how much, with the result that he gave up the project.

The Harvard lectures symbolized a deepening split between those who by this time thought of Frost as the century's greatest American poet—as *the* poet for many who did not consider themselves connoisseurs of poetry—and those who (partly because of his popular reputation) condescended to him by allowing him limited merit, far less than what they accorded Eliot or Yeats or Pound, or than they would accord Stevens or Auden. Frost recognized this split between popular and highbrow responses to him when he wrote Untermeyer after the lectures were over that he hadn't "made too big a hit with the dignitaries and authorities" at Harvard. He was probably fooling himself, so he said, to have thought that some sort of official appointment was in the cards ("There was a moment . . . when I thought perhaps they were giving me back my father's Harvard"), and anyway he was "academic" only up to a certain point: "I may be wrong in my suspicion that I haven't pleased Harvard as much as I have the encompassing barbarians. My whole impression may have come from the Pound-Eliot-Richards gang in Eliot House here." The encompassing barbarians were those outside the Harvard literary culture, and many of them packed the room in New Lecture Hall to capacity and responded vigorously to the performing poet. The "Pound-Eliot-Richards gang," rather sinisterly located in Eliot House, heart of Harvard literary culture, refers to those of "modernist" taste who took *The Waste Land* to be the century's prime example of poetic greatness. They were those who assumed generally—taking their cue from Eliot's pronouncements and work—that greatness in the modern world and in modern poetry was impossible without a high degree of poetic difficulty and complexity, exactly what to their eyes Frost's work did not possess.

Only a year previously, F.O. Matthiessen's pioneering *The Achievement of T. S. Eliot* had been published. It would have been in the forefront of the "gang's" consciousness since Matthiessen was associated with Eliot House, and Frost went on in his letter to Untermeyer to develop and widen the conspiracy theory against his reputation:

> I had a really dreadful letter of abuse from Pound in which he complains of my cheap witticisms at his expense. I may have to take him across my page like this: It is good to be back in communication with you on the old terms. My contribution was the witticisms: yours the shitticisms. Remember how you always used to carry toilet paper in your pocket instead of handkerchief or napkin to wipe your mouth with when you got through? Etcetera.—I suspect the same dirty sycophant of having reported me to him as reported me to Wallace Stevens. I think its Mattheson. Never mind. Peace hath her victories no less renowned than war.

The last sentence echoes one he had written Untermeyer just before Marjorie's death ("Peace has her victories over poor mortals no less merciless than war") and suggests that despite the injunction to "Never mind," he was full of strong anxieties about people getting together to do him in. Frost's fantasy extended to presuming that Matthiessen was in communication with Pound (wholly unlikely, considering their political differences) and that he would be eager to pass along damning testimony against Frost. (In fact, Pound's informant about the lectures most likely was James Laughlin, a Harvard undergraduate at the time who would be Pound's publisher at New Directions.) What Pound had heard, and wrote the offending letter to Frost about, was that he, Frost, had said Pound believed only in visual images and denied the importance or presence of "tone" in poetry. Pound also accused him of having "let off a lot of cheap senile witticisms," of having an inferiority complex, of perpetrating a "deliberate damned lie," and of generally being "in the swine class." He told Frost to keep his trap shut, not to lie to the young, and ended with the following fierce sentences: "You always were dominated by envy, but you shdn't let it get the better of you on the edge of the grave. I recognized your limitations are [sic] a writer, but had hitherto considered you a man, not a shit." So the abusiveness of Frost's own response can be understood; but his need to use Pound's private blow-off as occasion for linking all sorts of other poets and Harvard litterateurs into a "gang" devoted to undermining him, indicates the range of his suspicious fears.

Poirier has put succinctly the motive for Frost's reaction, pointing out that from the late 1920s until his death, he thought of himself "as the necessary enemy of two forces in American cultural life which had formed an unexpected and perplexing alliance: the political left and the modernist literary elite." This "alliance" could be seen in the representative case of Matthiessen, who had written with deep appreciation about the poet of *The Waste Land,* and who was committed to a Marxist-socialist analysis of capitalism's ills. Frost, who thought of himself as a purveyor of "wisdom" only in the most indirect, oblique and ironic ways (all poetry could ever issue in was a "momentary stay against confusion," against "immedicable griefs") was determined that whatever wisdom was, he "will not have it systematic" ("Boetian"). Marxist or modernist systems were really, to his mind, alternative metaphors and ones which he opposed, since users of them did not seem to know when to let them go, did not know their limits or where they broke down. By contrast, Frost thought of himself as—in a phrase from "The White-Tailed Hornet," one of the poems in his new collection *A Further Range*—"dangerously skeptic." In that poem the rather inefficient, even incompetent, instinctual behavior of a hornet as he fails to catch a fly, is grounds for this reflection: "Won't this whole instinct matter bear revision? / Won't almost any theory bear revision?" The poem comes out in favor of "upward" comparisons with gods and angels rather than downward ones with dogs and hornets; other subjects in the new book on which the poet exercised his "dangerously skeptic" wit were Darwinism ("At Woodward's Gardens"), industrial regimentation ("A Lone Striker"), the right of the needy to a job ("Two Tramps in Mud Time"), the virtues of taking the long view toward things ("In Time of Cloudburst"), bureaucratic efficiency ("Departmental"), and sympathetic identification with other people ("On the Heart's Beginning to Cloud the Mind").

When, in January of 1938, Bernard DeVoto, Frost's Harvard friend and supporter at that time, published a polemical counterattack ("The Critics and Robert Frost") at reviewers of *A Further Range* who found the poetry less than admirable, he defended Frost in exactly the terms provided by the poems. What the reviewers had done, said DeVoto, was to interpose "between their eyes and the page systematic theories about the nature of poetry." In other words, they refused to look at what was in front of them and see it for what it was; instead they condemned it on theoretical principles which insisted it be something else. DeVoto was particularly annoyed by R. P. Blackmur's review in the *Nation,* calling it the most "idiotic" piece of writing he had ever seen, and provoking—as if Frost had foreseen it all in his fantasy—a letter in Blackmur's defense written by Matthiessen. But Blackmur and Newton Arvin and Rolfe Humphries, all of whom reviewed *A Further Range* adversely, were serious literary men who believed in standards and who cared about poetry. Their discomfort and annoyance with the new book was surely preferable to the placidity with which *West-Running Brook* had been greeted—or at least so we may judge in retrospect. Furthermore they were responding to the most combative book Frost had written. They heard the accents, not just of impersonal sentence sounds, but of a personal voice which for all its official embracing of scepticism was not notably sceptical about its own prejudices and the weight of authority they carried.

This personal voice was not a voice expressive of psychological depths in the poet, especially in the first section of the book titled "Taken Doubly" (each poem has a subtitle inviting us to infer a wider, ulterior meaning from the particular situation). Rather it was moralistic and didactic in its bent, often with a sharp edge of dissatisfaction or superiority. It was closer to the voice heard often in Frost's letters— teasing, bantering with, one-upping an opponent—than had been the case in most of his previous poems. One of the things Arvin objected to in his *Partisan Review* account, was the voice's fondness for uttering "oracularities," one of which Arvin found at the end of "Two Tramps in Mud Time":

> But yield who will to their separation,
> My object in living is to unite
> My avocation and my vocation
> As my two eyes make one in sight.
> Only where love and need are one,
> And the work is play for mortal stakes,
> Is the deed ever really done
> For Heaven and the future's sakes.

If this is oracularity, one wonders what Arvin could have made of Yeats's "Byzantium" or Eliot's just-published "Burnt Norton." Compared to these, and to a good many other modernist utterances, Frost's oracular mode was pretty mild, except perhaps when (as in the long dialogue "Build Soil") it was directed against socialism, and the reviewer happened, like Arvin, to be of leftist persuasion. Yet there is a problem in "Two Tramps . . ." and in other poems from the first section of *A Further Range* which doesn't so much involve the use of an "oracular" mode, but rather the feeble or tenuous way it arises out of the particular incident Frost has worked up in the poem. In this case we have the man chopping wood, the tramps appearing and observing him critically, as if he were doing for love the work of which they had need. The poem has wonderful particularities and felicities of expression which are exercised—in the middle three stanzas—as "background" material like the April weather or the appearance of a bird:

> The sun was warm but the wind was chill.
> You know how it is with an April day
> While the sun is out and the wind is still,
> You're one month on in the middle of May.
> But if you so much as dare to speak,
> A cloud comes over the sunlit arch,
> A wind comes off a frozen peak,
> And you're two months back in the middle of March.
>
> A bluebird comes tenderly up to alight
> And turns to the wind to unruffle a plume.
> His song so pitched as not to excite
> A single flower as yet to bloom.

Lovely, musical observations such as these have eventually to give way
to large triumphant talk about "love" and "need" being one. Amidst
such oracularities, the earlier delicacies of expression feel less than
inevitable; they are too wayward and stubbornly themselves to be
swept up into the concluding assertions.

In some notes he made on the poems, Rolfe Humphries (whose *New
Masses* review was sarcastically titled—though perhaps not by him—
"A Further Shrinking") referred to the poems from the "Taken Doubly" section of *A Further Range* as "didactic idylls," and Humphries
said that in them "the dramatic and sympathetic almost disappears."
No doubt he was thinking back to *North of Boston,* where both those
qualities were abundantly present, and in this sense he made a good
point about Frost's "shrinking." Frost was no longer to command—or
he no longer attempted or wanted to command—the range of impersonal sympathy extended to the New England characters who made
up that "book of people." And insofar as he had set himself against
certain tendencies in modern society and literature, as by the middle
1930s he very much had, the personal edge of his un-disinterested attitude could be felt. Thus the further range claimed by the book's title
might look, from another angle, like a diminishment.

But the loss was also a gain, at least a redirection of Frost's skills,
toward the mode we may call Light Verse. In his introduction to the
recent *New Oxford Book of English Light Verse,* Kingsley Amis characterized one of its forms in a way that comprehends Frost's practice:

> We are dealing with a kind of realistic verse that is close to some of the
> interests of the novel: men and women among their fellows, seen as
> members of a group or class in a way that emphasizes manners, social
> forms, amusements, fashion (from millinery to philosophy), topicality,
> even gossip, all these treated in a bright, perspicuous style.

When Humphries complained that "sympathy" and "the dramatic"
had disappeared from the first section of *A Further Range,* and that
the "lyric element" had disappeared from the shorter poems in the
"Taken Singly" section which followed, he was in fact describing necessary absences if the poems were truly specimens of good light verse.
While not suggesting that Frost consciously set out to produce such
specimens (so far as I know he didn't think in terms of "light verse"
at all), much of his compositional practice in poems written during the
first half of the 1930s and beyond bears out Amis's criteria, including
centrally the "bright, perspicuous style" which offended Arvin and
Blackmur.

The poem of Frost's which comes to mind immediately in connection with light verse is "Departmental," with its bright, perspicuous, smartly-rhymed observations on the bureaucratic efficiency with which ants conduct their funeral obsequies. It is easy to take the poem "doubly," by making the wider application to human societies and institutions (a former president of Amherst College, Charles W. Cole, who worked for the O.P.A. during World War II, was particularly fond of it), and "Departmental" is clever, almost too appealing in its inclinations toward cuteness:

> Then word goes forth in Formic:
> "Death's come to Jerry McCormic,
> Our selfless forager Jerry.
> Will the special Janizary
> Whose office it is to bury
> The dead of the commissary
> Go bring him home to his people . . . "
> And presently on the scene
> Appears a solemn mortician;
> And taking formal position
> With feelers calmly atwiddle,
> Seizes the dead by the middle . . .

Other poems from "Taken Doubly," like "A Drumlin Woodchuck," "In Time of Cloudburst," or the especially expert "A Record Stride," exhibit similarly brisk, fast-moving inventiveness. But some of the best poems in the second, "lyric" section of the volume—"Taken Singly"—are also brisk, exhibiting the stripped-down simplicity of vocabulary and rhythm appropriate to light verse.

One thinks particularly of "Provide, Provide" and "Neither Out Far Nor In Deep," poems which owe much of their current reputation to the admiration lavished on them by Randall Jarrell. In his fine appreciation of Frost, "To the Laodiceans," Jarrell chose these poems, along with "Design," "The Most of It," and "Directive," as five relatively unfamiliar examples of Frost's work which would be useful, he said, in removing the slightly "sugary" taste from readers' palates who had been brought up wholly on "Birches." Jarrell's way of approaching "Neither Out Far Nor In Deep" (and "Provide, Provide" also) was to say, in effect, "look how simple this seems, but look how complex it really is":

> The people along the sand
> All turn and look one way.

> They turn their back on the land.
> They look at the sea all day.
>
> As long as it takes to pass
> A ship keeps raising its hull;
> The wetter ground like glass
> Reflects a standing gull.
>
> The land may vary more;
> But wherever the truth may be—
> The water comes ashore,
> And the people look at the sea.
>
> They cannot look out far.
> They cannot look in deep.
> But when was that ever a bar
> To any watch they keep?

In his engaging way, Jarrell shows—or asserts—how subtle the poem is: "the deepest tact and restraint" in its symbolism; "flatter, grayer, and at once tenderer and more terrible" than a comparable poem by A. E. Housman. He finds the watchers in the poem to be foolish and yet heroic as well; we must feel them as both because of the tone of the last lines, "or rather, their careful suspension between several tones." So the poem as a whole is a "recognition of the essential limtations of man, without denial or protest or rhetoric or palliation"—and that recognition is the usual thing, he says, we encounter in Frost's poetry.

Jarrell's appreciation of "Provide, Provide" is similarly engaging, also large in its claims for the poem; yet one should notice how hard he must work to prove that Frost's surface simplicity in "Neither Out Far Nor In Deep" is really a deep complexity, description of which necessitates language similar to what would be appropriate for a Shakespearean soliloquy, or for Dante, or for any passage in which a Matthew Arnold might find "high seriousness." In the terms of Frost's own title, Jarrell both looks out far and in deep to characterize the poems. But perhaps their "careful suspension between several tones" is, in fact, a way of forbidding our attempts to do what he does so eloquently. For Frost's serious commitment to a verse which is "light" in its behavior, makes it all the more difficult and risky to proceed as if the poem were something more than a neatly-turned piece of entertainment. This is why Rolfe Humphries's complaint—that Frost's lyrics in the new book lacked "lyric" quality, and that the longer poems lacked sympathy and drama—was an excellent recognition, if in neg-

ative terms, of a style which puts the reader in a more uncertain relation to the poem than was the case in Frost's earlier work. (Although
if Humphries had thought of "The Road Not Taken" he would have
noted that the mischievous element had been there all along.)

Remembering his own warning about the importance of knowing
where a metaphor breaks down, it may be best not to carry the light
verse rubric any farther in describing these poems from *A Further
Range*. But it is worth recognizing that, in Frost's phrase about Robinson, they "forbid encroachment" even as they entertain and sparkle
with their witty invention. So the critic should be advised to travel, in
his speculation about them, neither out far nor in deep. In hearing
Frost read "Provide, Provide," which he was almost too eager to do at
the drop of a hat (then repeat it once or twice in case anyone failed to
"get" it), one knew that what gave him most pleasure was the way he
could growl out—or mock-growl out with theatrical exaggeration—
the final command:

> Better to go down dignified
> With boughten friendship at your side
> Than none at all. Provide, provide!

("Or somebody else'll provide *for* ya," he would add.) Jarrell treats
the poem as a subtle example of how the "Wisdom of this World . . .
demonstrates to us that the Wisdom of this World isn't enough." For
this demonstration to convince, there must be a minimal presentation
of non-worldly wisdom, which he finds in the fifth stanza:

> Some have relied on what they knew,
> Others on being simply true.
> What worked for them might work for you.

And he asks, "was restraint ever more moving?" while alluding to a
line from Rilke as apt commentary. I would argue rather that the
manner, the *sound* of Frost's lines is such that Rilke doesn't belong in
the equation at all; that "Provide, Provide" like "Neither Out Far . . ."
is a louder, more opportunistic poem whose effects are broader, less
refined than Jarrell's subtle reading suggests. The pleasures and sat-
isfactions of both poems are more theatrical, less humanly and mor-
ally profound, than he claims.

It would be wrong to overstate the case and say that either out of
choice, or out of lack of further lyric resources Frost turned in the
1930s to writing a lighter kind of verse. Although *West-Running*

*Brook* is less full of distinctive lyrics than were his previous volumes (excepting of course *North of Boston,* which was almost wholly narrative) it contained "Spring Pools," "Acquainted With the Night," and "Tree at my Window." *A Further Range,* while characterized by a prevailing light verse atmosphere, nevertheless contains "Desert Places," "The Strong Are Saying Nothing," and "Design" (which was published in final form as early as 1922, and for some reason not put into a volume until fourteen years later). But whether one calls it a further range or, as Humphries did, a further shrinking, the originality and newness of the book comes out not in these strong, traditional Frost lyrics (though "Design" is exceptional in any terms) nor in the reach outward into social-political, playful or cantankerous opinionating. In fact one need not be a committed socialist like Arvin or Horace Gregory, to find that examples of the latter mode, like "Build Soil"—the "political pastoral" dialogue between two Latin-named farmers—or "To a Thinker" ("At least don't use your mind too hard, / But trust my instinct—I'm a bard"), are simply not very rewarding poems to read through more than once.

If asked to locate through the example of a single poem the freshness displayed by *A Further Range,* I would cite "The Bearer of Evil Tidings," one of three "mountain" poems Frost included in the volume, giving a further twist to the "range" motif. Its mountains are the Himalayas, and its proverbial hero is introduced as follows:

> The bearer of evil tidings,
> When he was halfway there,
> Remembered that evil tidings
> Were a dangerous thing to bear.

Having remembered, he is led by the poet away from his mission, into the mountains:

> He ran through the Vale of Cashmere.
> He ran through the rhododendrons
> Till he came to the land of Pamir . . .

where he meets and marries a princess who explains to him her tribe's religion and how it was founded and why they have settled "There in the land of the Yak." The explanation concluded, the poem also concludes:

> And that was why there were people
> On one Himalayan shelf;

And the bearer of evil tidings
Decided to stay there himself.

At least he had this in common
With the race he chose to adopt:
They had both of them had their reasons
For stopping where they had stopped.

As for his evil tidings,
Belshazzar's overthrow,
Why hurry to tell Belshazzar
What soon enough he would know?

Although one needs the entire poem to appreciate its superbly paced movement, these stanzas may suggest how far away from both personal lyric revelation, or public opinion-filled satire, is "The Bearer of Evil Tidings." It is the sort of poem which some serious readers of modern poetry would dismiss as simply not in a league with their favorite one by Stevens or Auden or Yeats; a poem strictly of the fancy rather than the imagination, mildly entertaining perhaps but quite exhausted by such a description. On the contrary, it seems to me essential Frost, nicely representative of the kind of virtues for which he praised Robinson in the preface to *King Jasper* when he singled out the fourth "thought" in "Miniver Cheevy" as making "the intolerable touch of poetry." This intolerable touch—or mischief, as he also put it—is there in the first stanza of the poem when the figure out of legend, "the bearer of evil tidings," is converted before our eyes into an ordinary fellow who reflects upon what he is doing and decides it's a dubious business. Mischief is there in the way Frost takes apart his identity by rhyming "evil tidings" with itself, and turns his identity as "bearer" into the more sinister verb "to bear." It is also there in the penultimate stanza when he reflects again, this time on his affinities with the tribe that had landed up on that "Himalayan shelf": "They had both of them had their reasons / For stopping where they had stopped," a reflection which does not invite feeling or deeper reflection on the part of bearer or poet, or reader. It is there finally in the final stanza, with its first cool mention of Belshazzar, almost a parenthesis, and with its sensible breakdown of another legendary event into a plausible sounding reason for letting history take its course without the individual prompting:

As for his evil tidings,
Belshazzar's overthrow,

> Why hurry to tell Belshazzar
> What soon enough he would know?

Frost had said of Robinson that his was a poetry of griefs rather than grievances, but "The Bearer of Evil Tidings" shows that there can also be a poetry of good fortune, at least a momentary celebration of the individual talent for making, in this case, the fortunate decision. Anti-apocalyptic in essence, it is as un-modernist a poem as could have been published in 1936.

He received his third Pulitzer for *A Further Range* the next spring. In October, Elinor was operated on for a cancer of the breast, and Frost wrote Untermeyer from a hotel in Springfield, Massachusetts, that "You can see what a difference this must make in any future we have. She has been the unspoken half of everything I ever wrote, and both halves of many a thing from My November Guest down to the last stanzas of Two Tramps in Mud Time—as you may have divined." Here the move from Elinor's condition to his own poetry, specified by titles, may seem disconcertingly rapid, even as the final sentence to this letter—which he later asked Untermeyer to destroy—sounds disconcertingly callous: "I have had almost too much of her suffering in this world." But he was to have more of it, even more perhaps than he reckoned for. Elinor recovered from the operation but died a few months later after a series of heart attacks. Her death was both a shattering blow to him, and a loss that precipitated some of the best and almost the last significant lyrics he was to write, in a range beyond any he had previously explored.

# VII

## Witness to Dark Circumstance

The death of Frost's favorite child, Marjorie, in 1934, called up from him a response both desolate and magnificent; here was an example, in a pure form, of tragedy—something terrible happening with nobody to blame. The two further deaths he lived through over the next six years—that of Elinor in 1938, after a series of heart attacks, then of Carol two years later, a suicide—could not similarly be dealt with as instances of nature operating without collusion from the human survivor. The guilty conscience provoked in a parent by an off-spring's suicide is wholly imaginable; but the guilty agony provoked in Frost by his wife's death is deeper and harder to fathom. A year or so after the event he wrote Lesley from his newly occupied residence on Mt. Vernon Street in Boston, that he had found an old letter of Elinor's written to Lesley when the latter was a student at Wellesley in 1917. It provoked him to a realization:

> My, my what sorrow runs through all she wrote to you children. No wonder something of it overcasts my poetry if read aright . . . She colored my thinking from the first just as at the last she troubled my politics. It was no loss but a gain of course. She was not as original as I in thought but she dominated my art with the power of her character and nature. I wish I hadnt this woeful suspicion that toward the end she came to resent some thing in the life I had given her. [Four lines deleted.] It seems to me now that she was cumulatively laying up against me the unsuccess of the children I had given her.

He then hastened to assure Lesley that her mother was wrong on that score, and that she and Carol and Irma would "come out all right." Reading the letter now, with the editor's ominous "four lines deleted,"

213

directly after mention of Frost's "woeful suspicion," one feels anything but assured that he was confident the children would come out all right. In a sense his remark to Lesley is insensitive, though it is also remarkable in its openness. At other moments he blamed himself not only for his children's "unsuccess" but, as far as Elinor was concerned, for the fact of their very existence and the toll it had exacted on the childbearer. He had "given" her a life, and given her these children— and yet, somehow, especially in later years, she had not been happy. Was he not to blame? In partial defense of him, we can say that it was probably also true that the unhappiness, the "sorrow" Frost perceived in Elinor's letter to Lesley, existed prior to and was more profound than any particular cause or occasion for it; that it was ingrained in the poetic sadness of his wife's nature or had something to do with living only for her husband and children; that no external cause could fully account for it. Thus the resentment Frost says he came to suspect in her may have been all the deeper for its inexpressibility.

Elinor was operated on for breast cancer in October 1937, and Frost immediately wrote Untermeyer the short note mentioned in the previous chapter, which contained a tribute to her but also a closing sentence that seemed almost to have slipped out, yet by its placement suggests he had been "not undesigning" in writing so: "I have had almost too much of her suffering in this world." With that final sentence on his conscience and its more than a hint of complaint (and at such a time to complain), he wrote Untermeyer again the next day, asking him to burn the letter—which Untermeyer did not do. The cancer had not spread, however; Elinor recovered and the Frosts proceeded to Gainesville, Florida, to spend the winter with their children settled near them, indeed with Lesley and her two daughters occupying the ground floor of their house. Frost and Elinor lived upstairs, a living arrangement chosen so that Frost would not have to be disturbed by the patter of feet above him. But that arrangement was ironically to disturb him much more seriously later on. For while climbing the stairs to their apartment, Elinor suffered the first of the seven heart attacks from which she was two days later to die.

As she lay in bed during this time, subjected to these natural shocks, Frost waited to be summoned to her side, but no summons came. When he did enter her room she was either unconscious or asleep, and Elinor died without any final words passing between her and her husband. Frost's feelings during this time and the anguished guilt he felt afterwards, were reported by Thompson from the evidence of a conversation they had in 1940. There is no reason to discount or question the severity of Frost's judgment on himself, nor of the pain and sadness in his recollection of the time. Yet one feels less than at ease with the way Thompson describes his thoughts as Elinor lay on her deathbed: "He wanted her to say at least with her eyes that she forgave him; that all the pain and suffering he had caused her had been more than offset by the joys and triumphs of their forty years together." Could it be that the desire here, the "want," lay mainly or at least partly in the poet looking back and suggesting to his biographer the "figure" in which he would like those last moments to be described? Or in the biographer's own need to make those moments almost unbearably affecting? Surely nothing Elinor could have said or done or expressed "with her eyes," could live up to the eloquent demand with which both Frost and Thompson later invested the situation, trying to make the abruptness and silence of her final hours somehow more bearable to their imaginations.

In any case it is undeniable that whatever guilty responsibility he felt was sharpened by an unhappy exchange with his eldest daughter, who, when asked by her father about the possibility of his living with her, angrily refused, while accusing him of selfishness, of disastrously affecting Elinor's life and of hastening her death (the stairs she was forced to climb were the case in point). Ill and in bed with influenza himself (he did not attend the cremation ceremony), Frost's situation was a grim one. It will be remembered that when Marjorie died he quoted as consolatory—or perhaps rather as heightening of the grief he felt—some lines from Arnold's "Empedocles" about the fate of Cadmus and Harmonia, who had lost their children and were not yet transformed out of their pain. Now, after the novelist Hervey Allen (with whom he had become friends in Florida) visited him in his bereavement, Frost wrote him the shortest of notes of thanks, quoting lines from Tennyson's "Morte D'Arthur" spoken by Sir Bedivere to King Arthur after Bedivere had survived the last battle: "And I the last go forth companionless / And the days darken round me." Then, as if the word "darken" had, even at this hour of impoverishment, struck off a spark and implied another poem, he quoted a single line from *In Memoriam:* "Let darkness keep her raven gloss."

These bits from sad moments in Tennyson were attempts to fix and memorialize this grief, his aloneness, and they were not the last he was to make. To DeVoto, who had just published his onslaught on the anti-Frost reviewers, he wrote that

> I suppose love must always deceive. I'm afraid I deceived her a little in pretending for the sake of argument that I didn't think the world as bad a place as she did. My excuse was that I wanted to keep her a little happy for my own selfish pleasure. It is as if for the sake of argument she had sacrificed her life to give me this terrible answer and really bring me down in sorrow. She needn't have. I know I never had a leg to stand on, and I should think I had said so in print.

This was another way of alluding to Elinor's sorrow, as he later called it in the letter to Lesley (his early "My November Guest" began, "My sorrow, when she's here with me"). Evident also, in the reference to "my own selfish pleasure" is a carefully turned apology for the vigorous life of poetry and publicity (and the vigorous fathering of six children) he had been living. This life had now received its comeuppance with the "terrible answer" of her death, and Frost goes so far as to utter the grimly playful rebuke to her that she needn't have died in order to show him how bad a place the world was. It is another extravagant "as if," even at this moment of pain.

Five days later, now nearly a month after her death, he sent without comment the following poem to Untermeyer:

> Age saw two quiet children
> Go loving by at twilight,
> He knew not whether homeward,
> Or outward from the village,
> Or (chimes were ringing) churchward.
> He waited (they were strangers)
> Till they were out of hearing
> To bid them both be happy.
> "Be happy, happy, happy,
> And seize the day of pleasure."
> The age-long theme is Age's.
> 'Twas Age imposed on poems
> Their gather-roses burden
> To warn against the danger
> That overtaken lovers,
> From being overflooded
> With happiness should have it
> And yet not know they have it.

> But bid life seize the present?
> It lives less in the present
> Than in the future always,
> And less in both together
> Than in the past. The present
> Is too much for the senses,
> Too crowding, too confusing—
> Too present to imagine.

Published later in *A Witness Tree,* "Carpe Diem" is special because it was written (or at least finished and sent out to another person) after Elinor had died. If it is a shade conventional or artificial in the opening personification of Age viewing the "quiet children" and bidding them (while out of hearing) to seize the day, it is also a poem *about* a convention, and it plays ingeniously and freshly with the "burden" of poetry, its call to live in the present by seizing the day of pleasure. (Later he would begin his ambitious poem "Directive" with a similar look toward the crowding, confusing present: "Back out of all this now too much for us.")

The poignant application to Frost's newly taken-up life is surely that with a poem such as "Carpe Diem," or in the prose sentences to DeVoto quoted previously, he had begun to imagine the life he and Elinor had led together for forty-three years. The irony was that it took something as terrible as her death to make it possible for him to do so: the "too much" of life as it goes on and on in its present-ness, is such that whatever exists in a marriage cannot be known, named, appreciated, until it no longer exists—or rather, exists in the past where it can be recaptured in the imagination of the bereaved, of the poet. This is the hard paradox on which the little poem unsentimentally bases itself; and it is continuous with a reflection he sent Untermeyer a month later from Amherst, where he was dismantling the house in which he and Elinor had lived for the last few years:

> I don't know myself yet and won't for a long time, if I ever do. I am so quickened by what has happened that I can't touch my mind with a memory of any kind. I can't touch my skin any where with my finger but it hurts like a sad inspiration. In such like condition I spent all of yesterday packing deadly personal things in the desolated house on Sunset Ave.

That street, which has a claim to being as beautiful as any tree-lined, spaciously roomy one in New England, couldn't have helped him at such a moment, or rather could only, on that May day, have made the "sad inspiration," the "quickening" of himself, even more palpable. Yet the precision of language here is notable, though not unexpected; the sad inspiration which comes from touching his skin with his finger, his mind with memories, is but a larger, graver instance of what he had called "the pang that makes poetry." "Carpe Diem" was an example of such poetry, and there would be more of it to come. The only alternative to it was self-laceration and recrimination, as in the following words from August 1938 written to the artist, J.J. Lankes, who had designed woodcuts for some of Frost's books: "I'm afraid I dragged her through pretty much of a life as frail as she was. Too many children, too many habitations, too many vicissitudes. And a faith required that would have exhausted most women. God damn me when he gets around to it. I refused to be bowed down as much as she was by other deaths. But she has given me a death now that I cant refuse to be bowed down by."

Bowed down he may have been, but his way of showing it, in the months after Elinor's death and beyond, was to be actively difficult in his behavior, rather than passively submissive. From his Mt. Vernon Street apartment he wrote Untermeyer in November 1938, urging that Untermeyer participate with him in the Bread Loaf conference the following summer. Allowing that he sometimes took it hard to "be left in a city apartment alone with the night," he nevertheless assured him that he was in control:

> Don't think I haven't myself well in hand, though, and beyond the need of psychoanalysis. As I have said, I cut up no ructions but with design to gain my ends even as aforetime when I was a child in San Francisco I played sick to get out of going to school. There's a vigorous devil in me that raises me above or drops me below the level of pity. Nevertheless I sometimes weep internally with sorrow (but not as often as externally at the eyes with cold weather).

One might think it an odd way to have oneself "well in hand" that involves cutting up "ructions" like a clever and ruthless child intent on gaining his ends. Here is the "vigorous devil" speaking, who has refused to be bowed down by loss and allows, so he says, but a limited space for internal weeping. It was this devil who had vigorously performed at Bread Loaf the preceding summer, behaving erratically in public, demanding to be driven to the far end of Vermont—where his daughter Irma and her husband were living in a house Frost had purchased at Concord Corners as antidote to the hay fever season—then demanding transportation back when he was displeased with the room his daughter had assigned him. It was the devil who, while Archibald MacLeish was reading his poems at Bread Loaf that summer, had managed to set fire to some paper, thus diverting attention away from the author of "Ars Poetica." The devil also took to strong drink, in an effort to thwart memory, or to assure those concerned about him that he was as "bad" a man as he claimed to be.

After telling Untermeyer about the vigorous devil housed within, Frost went on to make the surprising confession (surprising to himself, also) that he had come to value his poetry "almost less than the friendships it has brought me." And he proceeded to explain:

> I was thrust out into the desolateness of wondering about my past whether it had not been too cruel to those I had dragged with me and almost to cry out to heaven for a word of reassurance that was not given me in time. Then came this girl stepping innocently into my days to give me something to think of besides dark regrets. My half humorous noisy contrition of the last few months has begun to die down.

He concludes by wishing that "in some indirect way she could come to know how I feel about her." One wonders whether he is being disingenuous with Untermeyer, or with himself as well, since Frost had reason to believe that "this girl"—who was by that time his secretary, Kathleen Morrison—knew very well how he felt about her. She and her husband, Theodore Morrison, had entertained Frost during his Norton Lectures at Harvard, and after the memorial service for Elinor Frost, held in Amherst in April of 1938, they invited him to make use of them and their facilities when he was in the Boston area. Frost called the Morrisons in June when they were about to leave for a summer at Bread Loaf, then visited Mrs. Morrison where she was staying near that place with her two young children. Thompson asserts that Frost proposed to her that summer that she should divorce her husband and marry him; the proposal, we are told, was firmly rejected and the assurance given him by Mrs. Morrison that even if she had been free of marital ties she would not have married him.

The exact degree of intimacy between Frost and Kathleen Morrison at that point is unknown, although there has been, as is to be expected, rumor and conjecture. (A letter from Frost to Lesley written in February 1939 says that "I came through the two weeks with the Morrisons pretty well considering all there was on all sides to dissemble.")

Washington, D.C., 1940.

Frost with Kathleen and Theodore Morrison, 1950.

In her book, Mrs. Morrison chooses not to discuss the situation beyond saying that as a compromise she agreed to become Frost's secretary and general manager partly because—her own father having recently died—the job of taking care of Frost would help make up for this loss as well as provide the challenge of looking after a fascinating, difficult character. She was to take on the management of his correspondence, his schedule of readings, all the details of his life and—as she might have guessed at the time—the troubles of his spirit. Looking back, Kathleen Morrison wondered that she had the "temerity" to agree: "No woman can mother me with impunity," Frost once growled threateningly.

But as can be seen from the letter to Untermeyer quoted above, the unexpected had happened to him. He had fallen in love, his spirit had been newly quickened, and not with the pain of guilty memory. It was of course extravagant, typically so, to assume that Kathleen Morrison would live up to his poetic image of her, forsaking husband and children to take up life with the sixty-four-year-old poet (Mrs. Morrison was in her early forties at the time). But even as a secretary and a companion, she saved him from desolation. From wondering whether his life "had not been too cruel to those I had dragged with me" (clearly referring to Elinor, although she is not named) he had been recipient of the "word of reassurance," if not from "heaven" then from "this girl," Kathleen Morrison, who stepped into his days and gave him "something to think of besides dark regrets."

Frost needed all the help he could get, for there remained one major trial to be suffered, in a way the most hopelessly unsettling one: Carol's suicide, by shotgun, in October of 1940. From Florida, Frost had written to him in Vermont late in the month his mother died, urging him to take pleasure and pains at his farming: "You'll be getting new trees and baby chicks and I suppose putting on the dormant spray. There was nothing Elinor wanted more than to have you take satisfaction out of that home and farm. I wish you would remember it every day of your life." If Carol remembered, it gave him little satisfaction. He brooded over his mother's death, slipped into paranoia, heard voices, and eventually—while his wife was undergoing an operation in a Pittsfield hospital—put an end to himself, with his fifteen-year-old son, Prescott, upstairs. The especially bitter taste of the event for Frost—as if the suicide weren't enough in itself—was that just a few days previously he had visited Carol at his farm, tried to convince him he was not a failure and that he must never take his own life.

"You always win an argument, don't you?" was the final, ominous thing Carol had said to him.

It was not as if this last-ditch attempt to shore up Carol was the first one Frost had made. As suggested earlier, no matter how difficult to satisfy he was as a parent, Frost—at least as revealed in the letters to his son—tried hard to strike a believable tone of support and encouragement, not just with respect to Carol's attempts as a farmer, but to his attempt at poetry. In contrast to Elinor's ready sympathy for her children's verse-making efforts, Frost was convinced that if any of them were to succeed at it they must do it on their own, as he had done. But when Carol, who had previously asked his father (in the letter quoted earlier) how he should express his "ideas" in a poem, sent Frost in 1935 a poem he had just written, the response began

> We both liked the apple-crating poem for the genuine satisfaction it takes in the life you are living. It has a great deal more of the feeling of real work and country business than anything of mine could ever pretend or hope to have. Your true way is straight ahead as you are going in farm work as it affects you in thought and emotion . . . You are in a very strong position on your apple farm to make dashes out from it into poems.

This was a thoughtful attempt to help keep somebody going without stooping to egregious flattery; even the rash compliment that Carol's poem has more "real work and country business" in it than one of his father's could hope to, sounds as if Frost meant it. Two years before he had said about one of Carol's poems that "You have hammered it close and hard and you have rammed it full of all sorts of things, observations both of nature and human nature—and humor and picturesqueness too." If, that is, to be a child of such a poet as Frost made it all the more difficult to write verse, there was also real responsiveness on the father's part. It cannot be easy to write a letter to one's child about how good a poem he has written.

But none of it was enough for Carol. In writing to Untermeyer after the event, Frost was unsparing of strong words to express his own failure as a parent: "I took the wrong way with him. I tried many ways and every single one of them was wrong. Some thing in me is still asking for the chance to try one more. There's where the greatest pain is located." He saw himself, ironically, as the presumedly wise poet who in his "barding around" spent his days telling people how to live, and ever once more how to live; now with Carol's death in his mind, he disqualified himself from giving such counsel—although, of course, he was not to stop giving it. The final paragraph of the letter expresses a terrible finality of judgment, a last word said about his son and his fatherly relation to him:

> I failed to trick Carol or argue him into believing he was the least successful. Thats what it came down to. He failed in farming and he failed in poetry (you may not have known). He was splendid with animals and little children. If only the emphasis could have been put on those. He should have lived with horses.

As an epitaph, it is both touching and chilling.

To his grandson Prescott, he had already written ("Disaster brought out the heroic in you"), praising the boy for his presence of mind—Prescott discovered his father's body, called the police and his grandfather, then waited until the police came. In an attempt to point him toward a hopeful future, now that the "cloud" of his father's suspiciousness and despair had been removed, Frost spoke out in favor of "the healthy clearness of ordinary plain people" which, he said, Prescott shared with his mother and with his grandfather: "Lesley is that way too. So also is the Kathleen who has set me on my way onward again. We are the tough kind." Here the dead spirits, especially Carol's and Elinor's (remembering the "sorrow" she was overcast by) are dismissed, with the hope that they will not turn into ghosts; and the "healthy" continuers of life—into which group Frost puts himself by an effort of the will to believe—are to inherit the future.

That it took such an assertion of the will to turn himself momentarily into an "ordinary plain" person is shown when about a year later he passed through a spiritual crisis of undetermined origin, at least as far as it can be named by any words of his. He alludes to it in a letter written to Untermeyer in January 1942, when he sent him a third version of a poem with which he had been fiddling over the years. Beginning "To prayer I think I go," it proceeded, with more irregularities of line-length and rhyming than were usual for him, to portray a man in the act of abasement:

> I wear a halter-rope about the waist.
> I bear a candle end put out with haste.
> For such as I there is reserved a crypt
> That from its stony arches having dripped
> Has stony pavement in a slime of mould.

> There I will throw me down an unconsoled
> And utter loss.
> And spread out in the figure of a cross.—
> Oh, if religion's not to be my fate
> I must be spoken to and told
> Before too late!

The letter which followed said in explanation

> You had the first of this from me long ago and I recently had a copy
> of it back from you. You never saw the end of it. You never saw how
> it came out. There was no end to it till now that I could write that I
> *had* been spoken to and told—you know by whom . . . I believe I am
> safely secular till the last go down—that's all. I decided to keep the
> matter private and out of my new book. It could easily be made too
> much of. I can't myself say how serious the crisis was and how near I
> came to giving in.—It would have been good advertising.

Although he did not know the details of the "crisis," Thompson
assumes that the poem is about suicide, and he treats it as yet another
instance of Frost's "spoiled-child" attitude to anything that thwarted
his own wishes. In editing the letters, Thompson added a bracketed
[death] after the "It" in "It would have been good advertising," thus
dampening the wit of Frost's remark by emphasizing the portentous
reference.

In fact the poem does not speak of death by suicide, but by "religion" rather, casting Frost in the unlikely role of a repentant sinner
who desperately embraces his fate in the most abject possible manner.
And his allusion in the letter to believing now that he will be "safely
secular till the last go down," doesn't suggest that the alternative to
being secular was death by suicide, but religious faith rather. Whether
death or religion, though, is less important than the large and largely
melodramatic terms in which he contrived the whole thing. We are to
believe, as was Untermeyer, that the "crisis" was more serious than
could be known, and that—as the now completed poem asserts—he
needed to be "spoken to and told" something, if a dire something else
were not to ensue. (This need recalls the desire for a "word of reassurance" Frost had written Untermeyer about three years previously,
and which he said Kathleen Morrison had given him.) No wonder, as
Thompson says in his headnote to the letter, the details of the crisis
"are not given." To give them would have been to render the whole
business more comprehensible than Frost's imagination wanted it to

be, even by his good friend Untermeyer. And if his faithful biographer to whom he confided so much didn't know the details, who could? Kathleen Morrison perhaps, whom we might suppose to have been privy to his inmost feelings at the time; yet the final volume of Thompson's biography (which was read in manuscript by the Morrisons who, as R.H. Winnick says, made "substantial improvement" in it) says only in a note about the crisis that it "may somehow have involved Kathleen Morrison."

Just as the account in the letter is melodramatically ominous and elusive, so the poem is one of Frost's least attractive productions, undistinguished in its rhyme and rhythms, hardly the sort of thing to be expected from the poet who at the same time was writing "The Silken Tent" and a number of other excellent new ones. No wonder he decided to leave "To prayer I think I go" out of his next book. It had little of the sound of sense he had been writing about and achieving for so long; it was humorless in its Gothic trappings and self-pitying in its appropriation of the crucifixion. If there is parody in it, it is hard to see how the parody works to benefit anything. Perhaps the most we can say is that the completion of this piece which had been hanging around for so many years, in slightly different forms, came after he had suffered grievous losses of his wife and children, after he had—at least since 1938—been plagued by guilty conscience, and when he had at last been "spoken to" by a "you know . . . whom" one assumes to be Kathleen Morrison rather than God. But the experience of these events was not capable, at least given the withholding reticence of Frost's mind, of "successful" conversion into a poem or a letter. After all, had he not written to Untermeyer that a good rule for the artist was to hold something back "for pressure" and that what was to be held back should principally include "friends, wife, children, and self"? "We shall be judged finally by the delicacy of our feeling of where to stop short"; this is the side of him which checked the equally strong impulse to confess, or startle the listener with confidences about his inner life. The result was a crisis the nature of which will not be plumbed; indeed Frost may never himself have known what hit him so hard and why.

At any rate by 1942, the crisis past, he had stabilized his living arrangements into the way they were to remain pretty much until the end of his life. In the summer of 1939 he purchased the Homer Noble Farm in Ripton, Vermont, and worked out an arrangement with the Morrisons whereby they would occupy the main house during summers, while he would live in a nearby cabin. In 1941 he left his Boston apartment, moving into a purchased house on Brewster Street in Cambridge, a most handsome place for living during the fall and spring, even though his connection with Harvard (he was Ralph Waldo Emerson Fellow in Poetry beginning in 1939) ended in 1943, at which time a new association with Dartmouth as Ticknor Fellow in the Humanities replaced it. For winter living he had built a house called "Pencil Pines" in South Miami. On another front, he was more successful in finding the right tone to take with his grandchildren than he had been with his children, although they did not invariably accede to his will. After Carol's death, Frost wrote his daughter-in-law, Lillian, that he wished his son could have died fighting the Germans instead. Nor was he content merely to commit the indelicacy of telling Lillian how her husband should have died. His belief in the rightness and inevitability of war as the final resolution of differences between nations—which he believed were just individual differences writ large—prompted him to suggest to her in 1942, as America entered World War II, that Prescott might prepare himself for the war by attending a military school. Frost was disappointed in Lillian's response, for she wrote back that Prescott had picked up a good many hours of "shop work" at Bennington High School, thus could perhaps become one of the ground crew in the air force (he wound up in the Signal Corps). Frost wrote Lesley with barely concealed sarcasm about what he considered a less than heroic aspiration:

> Not that he would avoid duty at the front. Only of course he would want to be where his abilities and training would help most. He had been out hunting and killed a grey squirrel. I shall say nothing more on the subject. Not everybody can be expected to like war.

But mainly he paid increasing and delighted attention to his grandchildren, to Lesley's two daughters, Lesley Lee and Elinor, to Prescott, to Marjorie's daughter Robin Fraser to whom, at Christmas time 1940, he explained why he was sending her a check instead of a particular gift:

> I cant buy you a hat because I dont know what size your feet are. I cant buy you glasses or a handkerchief because I dont know how long your nose has grown. I can't buy you any funny toy because I don't know how much of a joke it takes to make you laugh. So I'm stuck unless you'll take the enclosed check and buy for yourself just what will do you the most good for the shortest time.

After receiving the Pulitzer for *A Witness Tree,* he wrote Lesley Lee, enclosing twenty-five dollars and explaining that "I have had it [the Pulitzer] three times before and it never before occurred to me that it would be more fun and make the occasion more memorable if I spread some of the prize over other people." After a short, humorous meditation on originality, he asks her how important she thinks it is, and how original she is getting to be: "I feel sure I must be getting more original every ten years. How else would I have thought up the idea of letting other people in on my prize?"

The friendly sentiment is not the sort of thing Frost was likely to express outside the family. Ironically, he was awarded his fourth Pulitzer only because the judges at Columbia overruled the majority verdict of the prize committee, who had voted 2-1 (with Untermeyer in the minority) to give it to Jose Garcia Villa, even though all the judges agreed that Frost's was the best book of poetry in 1942. Out of some liberal, aspiringly democratic sentiment, they judged that enough was enough, that a three-time Pulitzer winner was acceptable, but not a four-time one. Needless to say, and after the verdict was overturned, the eventual winner had no scruples about accepting his award, and with unabashed pleasure, telling Untermeyer that his only objection was that it made it difficult for him to criticize Roosevelt, should he run for a fourth term. Like Roosevelt, Frost wanted to win all the prizes, all the elections. As he remarked to a friend, late in life, "I need all the honors I can get."

---

Published two years before Frost's seventieth birthday, *A Witness Tree* is the last book of poems in which his lyric genius is substantially present. On the basis of its first ten poems (the short, introductory "Beech" and "Sycamore" function as epigraphs), plus a few which occur later in the book, it is comparable in fullness of ambition and execution to his earlier collections, and—although such distinctions are less than crucial and according to one's taste—it seems to me the best one he had published since *New Hampshire* nearly twenty years previously. Or rather—since we noted that *A Further Range* was filled with many expert performances in a mode which approached light verse—we can call the opening sequence of poems from *A Witness Tree,* by contrast, as weighty and sustained an expression of Frost's "inner weather" as is to be found anywhere in his poetry.

In the typical plot of an earlier Frost lyric, the protagonist goes forth into nature, encounters somebody or something, is moved to consider its significance, and ends with a balanced reflection—a composed version of the "wisdom" in which (he said) the figure a poem makes should end. The only one of the first ten poems from *A Witness Tree* which follows that pattern is "Come In," where the invitation to enter the dark woods is resisted with the gracefully witty "But no, I was out for stars: / I would not come in. / I meant not even if asked, / And I hadn't been." Instead, the poems largely forsake the convention of the central "I," a man who sounds suspiciously like a poet, who makes maximum use of his sensations and is endowed with a resourceful language. They ask us instead to move rapidly from one situation to another, as mainly unidentified figures move and speak in landscapes which have little in common with the carefully set-out ones of the earlier "New England" Frost. Often the voice of the poet can be heard speaking from no place in particular, establishing the weight of his concerns in language independent of a concretely realized dramatic situation. What seems evident, if not easy to demonstrate, is the depth of the note these poems cumulatively strike. They show "the pang that makes poetry" and write it large; they ache with the tears of things. Frost once said in one of his monologues about poetry, that it was always saying to us, in effect, "If I could only tell you . . .," and these ten poems from *A Witness Tree* say it more than once.

Except for *New Hampshire,* which was dedicated to his two current states of residence in 1923—Vermont and Michigan—all Frost's books had been dedicated to Elinor, and he said after her death that he could not imagine dedicating a book to anyone else. Nevertheless, *A Witness Tree* bore the inscription "TO K.M. FOR HER PART IN IT," and "The Silken Tent," which is given pride of place in the book as its first poem after the short introductory ones, celebrates a "She" who is "as in a field a silken tent." When he presented the poem to Kathleen Morrison (it was first published in the winter of 1939) he titled it "In Praise of Your Poise." Practicing what his original title preached, Frost wrote probably the most poised sonnet of his career, a virtuoso filling-out, over the course of the single sentence which is the poem, of the lineaments of graceful firmness:

> She is as in a field a silken tent
> At midday when a sunny summer breeze
> Has dried the dew and all its ropes relent,

So that in guys it gently sways at ease,
And its supporting central cedar pole,
That is its pinnacle to heavenward
And signifies the sureness of the soul,
Seems to owe naught to any single cord,
But strictly held by none, is loosely bound
By countless silken ties of love and thought
To everything on earth the compass round,
And only by one's going slightly taut
In the capriciousness of summer air
Is of the slightest bondage made aware.

Lesley Frost remembers typing out this poem for her father while Elinor was still alive, so although Kathleen Morrison was eventually its recipent and was celebrated in its original title, there is no reason to think of her as the unique inspiration for "The Silken Tent." Indeed the poem is "strictly held by none," and it stands at the beginning of the volume as if to set forth an ideal image of poise, a perfect relation (as in the silken tent) between being free and being bound; between its plethora of "countless" affiliations and a particular tug felt (as in the "capriciousness of summer air") in one direction.

In the early "Bond and Free," written well before it was published in *Mountain Interval,* Frost came out in favor of the former condition, represented in that poem by Love as opposed to Thought. Thought made spectacular flights into space, cleaving the "interstellar gloom," while Love stayed home, clung to earthly things and built walls against fear. Even though Thought made impressive "gains in heaven"

Yet some say Love by being thrall
And simply staying possesses all
In several beauty that Thought fares far
To find fused in another star.

By 1942 though, when he wrote "Beech," the longer of the two short poems serving as epigraphs to *A Witness Tree,* Frost considered the notion of being "bound" in a less fervently affirmative way. In "Beech" he bends an "imaginary line" into a woods, stakes out a corner with some rocks, and then directs attention to the beech tree, announcing that

One tree, by being deeply wounded,
Has been impressed as Witness Tree
And made commit to memory

My proof of being not unbounded.
Thus truth's established and borne out,
Though circumstanced with dark and doubt—
Though by a world of doubt surrounded.

This dark utterance can be read as a further report on the early tribute
to Love in "Bond and Free": "Yet some say Love by being thrall /
And simply staying possesses all / In several beauty . . ." If we read
"Beech" as an allusion, however unspecified and generalized it is, to
Frost's recent losses of those he loved, then the deeply wounded tree
is symbol of what is left him—"My proof of being not unbounded."
To speak of the marking as establishing or bearing out "truth" is as
much as can be claimed for it, and it is with an ironic twist that
"truth" yields immediately to the "dark and doubt" of circumstance,
then is followed with the re-echoing final line—"Though by a world
of doubt surrounded." In this extremely muted and chastened setting-
forth of his human condition, Frost practices an old activity of simul-
taneous revelation and concealment; holding back any particular reference to his private sorrows while bidding us to respond to the voice
of a man who has been acquainted with grief.

Both "The Silken Tent" and "All Revelation," the powerful piece
of ingenuity which follows it and whose sexual force has been well
commented on by Poirier, are relatively impersonal utterances. If
objectively more considerable, they lack the personal accent heard in
two poems which were the first ones Frost published after Elinor's
death. Appearing together in the *American Scholar* in the fall of 1938,
"Happiness Makes Up in Height for What It Lacks in Length" (after
the epigraphic ones, the third poem in *A Witness Tree*) and "Carpe
Diem" (the sixth, which he had sent to Untermeyer a month after
Elinor died), complement one another in their discreet but poignant
allusion to the fact of loss and the nature of what remains. "Carpe
Diem" is sadly ironic about that advice, saying, in effect, that although
one must suffer the present one can't seize it, since imagination—the
imagination of love, for instance—can only work on what is past or
what is to come. "Happiness Makes Up in Height . . ." begins by evoking the "stormy stormy world" (the "dark and doubt" which "Beech
says we are "circumstanced by") not only as characterizing the present but as being the remembered condition of most days in the past,
when "the sun's brilliant ball" was "in part or all / Obscured from
mortal view—." Such is the way he remembers it, yet there remains

to him "the lasting sense /Of so much warmth and light," which he accounts for thus:

> If my mistrust is right
> It may be altogether
> From one day's perfect weather,
> When starting clear at dawn
> The day swept clearly on
> To finish clear at eve.
> I verily believe
> My fair impression may
> Be all from that one day
> No shadow crossed but ours
> As through its blazing flowers
> We went from house to wood
> For change of solitude.

The odd word here is "mistrust," which circumstances with dark and doubt the therefore all the more precious "fair impression" enacted so beautifully by the poem's final lines. As the Witness Tree from "Beech" served to mark Frost's "proof of being not unbounded" and thus bore out "truth," so "Happiness Makes Up in Height . . ." records a witness-bearing to the lasting effect of one day's perfect weather. What makes the manner of its recording so convincing is the way a single sentence weaves through the final seven lines, and by not pressing the claim too grandly, enforces it the more. It is a perfect example of what Frost later described as happening "In a Poem":

> The sentencing goes blithely on its way
> And takes the playfully objected rhyme
> As surely as it keeps the stroke and time
> In having its undeviable say.

In "Happiness Makes Up in Height . . ." a simplicity of diction appropriate to convey the simplicity of the lovers' remembered solitude, enables the adjective "blazing" to suggest an intensity within that simplicity: "As through its blazing flowers / We went from house to wood / For change of solitude."

Those blazing flowers, quietly alluded to and not worked up into an elaborate metaphor, are recalled from long ago, from "that one day" of perfect weather when everything was clear and without shadow. Read with respect to Frost's own poetry, it takes us back to *A Boy's Will*, where a number of such moments were celebrated—as in "Rose

Pogonias," when the lovers come across a "saturated meadow" of
flowers

> There we bowed us in the burning,
> As the sun's right worship is,
> To pick where none could miss them
> A thousand orchises;
> For though the grass was scattered,
> Yet every second spear
> Seemed tipped with wings of color
> That tinged the atmosphere.

Then the lovers raised a prayer that the "general mowing" spare the
flowers, or that it be forestalled until they have had their day in the
sun: happiness can make up in height for what it lacks in length. Frost
dedicated that first book to "E.W.F.," and the poems from *A Boy's
Will* occupied a special place in their affections as monuments to a
time when nobody but the two of them knew about Frost's gift: "She
always knew I was a good poet, but that was between her and me, and
there I think she would have liked it if it had remained at least until
we were dead," he had written Untermeyer years previously. Now,
with only Elinor dead, *A Boy's Will* came back strongly into Frost's
consciousness as a book of poems which were made in youth, melancholy, wistfully sad, yet without the real "proof of being not
unbounded" that only worldly experience would bring to their author.

This proof is found most explicitly in "The Wind and the Rain,"
seventh in the sequence of ten poems and directly following on "Carpe
Diem." In the first half of this two-part poem "a season-ending wind"
signals the destruction of things:

> That far-off day the leaves in flight
> Were letting in the colder light.

The man remembers how, as a young poet, he gave himself to the
destructive element and "leaned on with a singing trust," willing to be
driven "deathward too" along with the leaves. "Reluctance," the last
poem in *A Boy's Will,* had concluded with an exclamation of resistance—for all its powerful attractiveness—to the "drift of things":

> Ah, when to the heart of man
> Was it ever less than a treason
> To go with the drift of things ...

Now, in "The Wind and the Rain," the older poet looks back upon his younger self just setting out, and finds something disturbing in the way that self courted disaster and destruction in song, before it had to suffer them:

> I sang of death—but had I known
> The many deaths one must have died
> Before he came to meet his own!
> Oh, should a child be left unwarned
> That any song in which he mourned
> Would be as if he prophesied?

There is no more naked an exclamation or unanswerable a question to be found in Frost's poetry, while its personal reference seems unmistakable. "Song," the act of poetry, is seen as an indulgence, an unwitting prophecy of one's fate that Frost superstitiously suggests—although the lines don't go so far as to say it—somehow incurs that fate. As the concluding first part of the poem has it:

> And yet 'twould seem that what is sung
> In happy sadness by the young,
> Fate has no choice but to fulfill.

Shakespeare's song from *Twelfth Night* is lurking in the background here, in its rueful celebration of coming to "man's estate" and finding that "The rain it raineth every day."

But Frost's effort in the poem's second half is as waywardly elusive of any large, clear assertion about human life as is the Shakespearean song, even though the "Wind" part of the poem provoked such assertions. In part II, the "Rain" part, the speaking "I" becomes fantastic, a Whitmanesque giant who would "pick up all ocean less its salt,"

> And though it were as much as cloud could bear
> Would load it on to cloud,
> And rolling it inland on roller air,
> Would empty it unsparing on the flower
> That past its prime lost petals in the flood . . .

This rainmaker aspires to a good drenching, calls for "water heavy on the head / In all the passion of a broken drought," then pulls back in a line which is isolated by white spaces (a quite untypical practice on Frost's part) and announces, oracularly, that " . . .there is always more than should be said." That "more" is to be found only in the white spaces, and Frost ends this strange poem in an "Acquainted with the Night" mood, while hinting at how much he has experienced, indeed shed, the tears of things:

> I have been one no dwelling could contain
> When there was rain;
> But I must forth at dusk, my time of day,
> To see to the unburdening of skies.
> Rain was the tears adopted by my eyes
> That have none left to stay.

The poems from this opening section of *A Witness Tree* are spoken by a voice which commands grave accents, hints at vicissitudes undergone, sufferings endured, but "always more than should be said." By way of not saying too much, too explicitly, but making it troubling and memorable to the reader, the "I" becomes metaphysical, or Whitmanesque, or fantastic, and gives poems titles like "I Could Give All to Time":

> I could give all to Time except—except
> What I myself have held. But why declare
> The things forbidden that while the Customs slept
> I have crossed to Safety with? For I am There,
> And what I would not part with I have kept.

In this third and final stanza, the ravages of Time are resisted by an ingenious poetic conceit, as Time is turned into a drowsy Customs official the smuggler has outsmarted. Nothing is specified, everything suggested: "things forbidden" (and what are they?), "Safety," most grandly the "There" attained (so it is announced) at the poem's end. What has been "kept"? No more nor less than "what I would not part with"—five monosyllables which give away nothing to the curious reader. In trying to find words for the way this poem ends, Jarrell was reduced to ultimates—"A blaze of triumph, of calm and rapturous certainty that is as transfiguring, almost, as the ending of 'A Dialogue of Self and Soul.'" Frost's art is to provoke admirers to such vague and splendid heights of speech.

"The Wind and the Rain" leaves the "I" mysteriously seeing to the "unburdening of skies," adopting rain to replace the human tears he has so completely shed. For the final three poems in the sequence we hear no more about "I"; there is instead a "he" engaged in some quite unordinary activities. In "The Most of It" he thinks he keeps "the

universe alone," and he cries out for "counter-love, original response."
In "Never Again Would Birds' Song Be the Same," he spins out a
fable about how the voices of birds were forever changed by the voice
of Eve; and in "The Subverted Flower," he encounters a young woman
under whose horrified eyes he is transformed by passion into something terrible—"the dog or what it was, / Obeying bestial laws." As
one attempts to describe what is going on in these poems one is conscious of faltering; the statements feel inadequate or ludicrously literal-minded. This is so because, in part, of what Poirier (referring to
"The Most of It") calls the "large but wavering mythological context"
each poem creates: a man alone in the universe, crying out for love
and encountering a "great buck" in response; a sonnet-meditation
about pre- and post-Edenic sound; a grim fairytale about sexual horror. The mythological context is large, but wavering insofar as one
feels uneasy in pronouncing grandly at that level ("This sonnet is
about Eve and the persistence of song"), and the poems don't unam-
biguously locate a particular speaker in a particular place. Poirier
stresses this effort not to "localize" as one characteristic of Frost's best
poems; but *A Witness Tree* surely presents that effort most intensely,
as in the implied situation of its title. And along with the unspecific,
generalizing inclination goes an interesting dependence on the pro-
noun "that," used to point at rather than explain what happens in the
poem. After the buck forces the underbrush and "stumbled through
the rocks with horny tread," "The Most of It" ends abruptly with—
"and that was all." The final couplet to the sonnet about Eve
announces that

> Never again would birds' song be the same.
> And to do that to birds was why she came.

And in "The Subverted Flower," "A girl could only see / That a
flower had marred a man." The word "that" serves to point at intimate and ultimate matters, playing with but refusing to gratify the
reader's impulse to want to hear more about what exactly "that"
involves: *What* was "all"? To do *what* to birds? *How* was the man
marred by the flower?

Poirier speaks of them collectively as "three great poems," and so
they may be. Yet when we put them alongside other poems from this
century which have been called great—Yeats's "Easter 1916" perhaps, or Stevens's "Sunday Morning," or Eliot's "East Coker," or
more recently Lowell's "For the Union Dead," or Larkin's "The Old

Fools," one notes (and I have not rigged the list to make a point) how the subjects of Frost's poems do not conform to certain expected models for the "great poem": eloquent meditation on heaven and hell, beauty and death, as in Stevens; complex, tortured, public-private conflict, as in Yeats or Lowell; symbolic expression of dark, ancestral wisdom, as in Eliot; the passionate fear and contempt of Larkin responding to old age. None of these models serves to take in the extremely individual, even perverse-looking aspects of the three Frost poems. Their peculiar effect derives partly from the highly artificial, "unnatural" treatment of the central situation of each. For example, when, in "The Most of It" we hear of the man that

> Some morning from the boulder-broken beach
> He would cry out on life, that what it wants
> Is not its own love back in copy speech,

it is useless to imagine a lone figure on some beach or other, California Pacific or Maine Atlantic. The "he" who "would declare and could himself believe" in "Never Again . . ." is little more than an amusing echo of Horatio's answer to Hamlet—"So have I heard, and do in part believe it." And in "The Subverted Flower," if we try to think of a "real" young man or woman caught in the coils of sexual desire and sexual loathing, the narrator's presentation jolts us with the weird fairy-tale cast it gives the action, removing it to some level other than the realistic:

> It was then her mother's call
> From inside the garden wall
> Made her steal a look of fear
> To see if he could hear
> And would pounce to end it all
> Before her mother came.

Pat rhymes and short lines tumbling one into the next add to the prevailing artificiality.

There is also a tilt in these poems toward a wild humor. In "The Figure a Poem Makes," written in 1938 and for many years prefacing his collected poems, Frost said that the "second mystery" was "how a poem can have wildness and at the same time a subject that shall be fulfilled." These poems fulfill their subjects in most surprising yet seemingly inevitable ways, just as the buck crashes through the underbrush and appears, if only for a moment, as a surprise package delivery to the human cry for "counter love, original response." What happens to the protagonist of "The Most of It" is in the nature of a large joke, one which turns grim or sick in "The Subverted Flower," as the passionate imploration of the male—"If this has come to us / And not to me alone—"never gets a chance to complete itself. For the woman hears and sees his plea as something quite different:

> So she thought she heard him say;
> Though with every word he spoke
> His lips were sucked and blown
> And the effort made him choke
> Like a tiger at a bone.

The man is reduced to a "brute" obeying "bestial laws," and there has been, to put it mildly, a misunderstanding. But in blowing up and simplifying the "action" into brief cartoon-like sketches—unaccompanied by sensitive, sympathetic commentary on a narrator's part, or lacking the expressive voices in conflict of a "Home Burial"—"The Subverted Flower's" wildness is more than the reader can comfortably bear; and its strangeness, even its garishness, refuses to go away even after repeated readings. The whole affair is a dreadful joke. And though it is probably wrong to speak either of wildness or a "joke" in relation to "Never Again Would Birds' Song . . .," still the "eloquence so soft" with which Frost unrolls this quietest and most discreet of his sonnets, has about it the air of a tour de force. Like his heroine Eve, he has added "an oversound" to the world of created sounds—bird calls, love calls, sonnets, in which he lives. The sonnet's cunning phrasing, with its artfully polite phrases—"Admittedly," "Moreover," "Be that as may be," all at the beginning of lines—suggests the impressive blend of delicacy and firmness with which the case is made for Eve's persistence in song:

> Moreover her voice upon their voices crossed
> Had now persisted in the woods so long
> That probably it never would be lost.
> Never again would birds' song be the same.
> And to do that to birds was why she came.

In "The Figure a Poem Makes" Frost designated "wildness" along with "sound" as the poem's "better half." But "Just as the first mystery was how a poem could have tune in such a straightness as meter, so the second mystery is how a poem can have wildness and at the same time a subject that shall be fulfilled." A way of at least partly understanding the first mystery, was to strike "dramatic tones of meaning" across the meter ("Never Again Would Birds' Song . . ." speaks of the birds' song as having "her [Eve's] tone of meaning but without the words"). The second mystery is even more mysterious, since Frost refuses to define wildness, though he asserts that "If it is a wild tune, it is a poem," and also speaks in favor of a "wildness of logic" rather than one of "inconsequence." More important than what "wildness" may mean, is the fact that he wanted to use the word—and more than once—to suggest a freedom that poems must exhibit if they are to be true poems. He used the word about his life as well: a letter to Cox after Elinor's death in 1938 says that he is managing— "But I am very wild at heart sometimes. Not at all confused. Just wild—wild. Couldn't you read it between the lines in my Preface nay and in the lines?" How can a poem have both wildness and a fulfilled subject, he asks, and answers the question (in his "Preface") by beginning a new paragraph: "It should be of the pleasure of a poem itself to tell how it can. The figure a poem makes." Then the paragraph proceeds through the famous sentences:

> It begins in delight and ends in wisdom. It begins in delight, it inclines to the impulse, it assumes direction with the first line laid down, it runs a course of lucky events, and ends in a clarification of life—not necessarily a great clarification such as sects and cults are founded on, but in a momentary stay against confusion.

This formulation about delight and wisdom has made Frost seem, to some, a much more reassuring, even complacent poet than at his best he is. But it should be pointed out that there is no "wisdom" in the shape of a nugget somehow extractable from the sequence of the whole poem—from its figure. And as he so pointedly adds, in case we missed the metaphor, "the figure is the same as for love."

We may speak of him as a love poet, through he is seldom treated in those terms (Poirier's book is a notable exception to the rule). But the first ten poems from *A Witness Tree* represent his last great effort in that direction: to make "love" look and sound as excitingly different as it does in reading "The Most of It," then "Never Again Would Birds' Song . . .," then "The Subverted Flower," is a mark of the poet's originality, the mark of his wildness. In his final two books, *Steeple Bush* and *In the Clearing,* Frost was not again to touch such heights and depths. And indeed, the remainder of *A Witness Tree* reads as a comparative relaxation of the powers displayed at its outset. Two fine sonnets, "The Gift Outright" and "Time Out"; an early, lovely poem from *A Boy's Will* days called "The Quest of the Purple-Fringed" ("To a Moth Seen in Winter," also in the book, is similarly an early poem); a crisply argued, ironic tribute to a fellow poet who gave his soul to politics ("The Lost Follower"); and the incidental felicities of "November" and "The Rabbit Hunter" are about all, except for the short, mainly two- and four-line poems in the "Quantula" section. These squibs are clever enough so that one tends to find them too clever, though it is invigorating to come across a poem titled "An Answer" and find this:

> But islands of the Blessèd, bless you, son,
> I never came upon a blessèd one.

Surrounded by much white space, occupying one page of the old *Complete Poems* volume, the utterance took on an added point.

Frost felt that *A Witness Tree* contained some of the best poetry he had written, and the approach of his seventieth year may have helped to prompt that insistence on him. He was, in fact, absolutely right about the book, which reveals a range of feeling and atmosphere beyond what he had conveyed in his previous one, *A Further Range*. But even beyond that, it is compelling evidence that he wrote poems in his sixties every bit as distinctive, as "wild" as those he had published thirty years before in *North of Boston*. There was no decline from the peak of achievement that early volume showed; rather a movement on to a different terrain, no less difficult of attainment. If *North of Boston* reveals the narrative Frost at his best, *A Witness Tree*—so it seems to me—does the same thing for lyric Frost. The best of these poems bear witness to his conviction, tragically confirmed by the deaths he had suffered over the years just past, that he was—in the words from "Beech"—"not unbounded." And in the face of this knowlege, the truth of the poems he had written established and bore out his spiritual persistence:

> Though circumstanced with dark and doubt—
> Though by a world of doubt surrounded.

# VIII

## Deeper Into Life

Frost received his fourth Pulitzer for *A Witness Tree* in May 1943; he died in Peter Bent Brigham Hospital in Boston, in January 1963, age eighty-eight. The final two decades of his life were those of a man whose productions as a poet, for the first time in his career, took a position secondary to his life as a public figure, a pundit, an institution, a cultural emissary. He had become the goodest greyest poet since Walt Whitman. *Steeple Bush* was published in 1947, and Randall Jarrell told the truth about it in the *New York Times Book Review* (1 June) when he noted that "Most of the poems merely remind you, by their persistence in the mannerisms of what was genius, that they are the productions of someone who once, and somewhere else, was a great poet"—although Jarrell rightly excepted "Directive" from his stricture. Frost did not see this review of *Steeple Bush* (Kathleen Morrison assured him that it was "all right") but did see one in *Time* which said the book "did nothing to enlarge his greatness." He promptly went into a tailspin, suffering pains in his wrists and chest. The review almost literally went to his heart; he was treated by a doctor who found no evidence of an attack, but who diagnosed the strain Frost was under and elicited from him the reasons for it.

It is fair to say that from that point on, his writing, or at least his publishing of poetry, became occasional rather than habitual. After the appearance of the *Complete Poems* in 1949, he managed to produce about one a year, and did so under the pressure of sending out his annual Christmas card, consisting of a new poem. But as the poems dried up, his reputation expanded: let the poet be sent to Brazil and to Israel; let him receive degrees from two ancient English universities. Make him Poetry Consultant at the Library of Congress. Let him read a poem at the inauguration of a president. Send him to the Soviet Union and let him talk with Premier Krushchev. Make various films about him in which he pauses by a stone wall, or shoulders an axe, or putters around the stove in the kitchen of his Vermont cabin. Make sure that everyone knows America possesses, in Jarrell's phrase (from his essay "The Other Frost"), the Only Genuine Robert Frost in Captivity.

It is difficult not to regard Frost's later years—in which the poems written were relatively few and relatively minor—with mixed feelings. The series of triumphs of the public figure may be celebrated for the honor they brought him; alternatively this increasing publicization may be regretted or even deplored. Surely there was something less than heartening in the spectacle of an old man being listened to too often, by too many people—most of whom cared little about poetry and cared about his only because they thought it wholesome country-American. At certain moments Frost spoke with candor and wry self-knowledge about what had happened to him, and on one such occasion, in an interview with Randall Jarrell at the Library of Congress in 1959, he mused on the difference between private and public, on what might be lost in moving from one realm to the other. "I'm a bad man to have around at a wedding," he said. "What begins in felicity and privacy, ends in publicity—and maybe really ends there. A wedding is the end of it." And he continued, thoughtfully: "What begins in felicity and a career like mine, you know, could end . . . Someone might say mockingly, what began in felicity and all the privacy and secrecy and furtiveness of your poetry is ending in a burst of publicity." Yet the fact was that over the course of his life he had devoted intense energy toward making sure that his work did not lack publicity, and of the most favorable kind.

Since on occasion he was able to view what had happened to him with perspective, even with a touch of irony (as in the play on the phrase "ends in publicity"), we should likewise be of two minds about his romance with fame and publicity. The weakness of the late poems is partly a matter of Frost's disregard for his own principles. After the eloquence with which, in the preface to Robinson's last book, he had insisted that poetry be left free to "go her way in tears," that her subject was "griefs, not grievances," *Steeple Bush,* a decade or so after the preface, was full of grievances against phenomena such as "the guild of social planners" ("The Planners"), or the revolutionary figure (in "A Case for Jefferson") who wants America "Made over new"

("He's Freudian Viennese by night. / By day he's Marxian Musco-vite"), or against other prophets of disaster (one poem is titled "The Prophet of Disaster"). Frost felt compelled to respond to earthshaking world events like the dropping of the atomic bomb; but his response was so heavily underlined, in its attempted playfulness, that the reader fidgets uneasily. In the sonnet "Bursting Rapture," for example, he goes to the physician to complain that there's so much "science" around these days that "the discipline of farming" is too stern a one to be practiced:

> It seemed as if I couldn't stand the strain.
> But the physician's answer was, "There, there,
> What you complain of, all the nations share.
> Their effort is a mounting ecstasy
> That when it gets too exquisite to bear
> Will find relief in one burst. You shall see.
> That's what a certain bomb was sent to be."

In this untroubled move from a trumped-up personal complaint to the assertion that it is one shared by all nations, and that relief is just a burst away as—in the unfortunate final line—that "certain bomb" fulfills its mission, there is a failure of taste and of scale. The sonnet form is trotted out once more and given only the smallest rhythmic interest, the sentence sounds are undistinguished—yet the homemade apocalypse joke is supposed to be rousing.

This sort of thing occurs too often in Frost's late verse, especially when the poet is so programmatically mischievous, his eyes all a-twin-kle with disillusioned, clever-tough patter. When for a time it looked as if America, Britain, and Russia were the three powers in the post-war world, Frost wrote a sonnet ("No Holy Wars for Them") mocking the little states ("Good is a thing that they, the great, can do, / But puny little states can only be"). In the poem's sestet he turned to God for His word on the whole matter:

> God, have You taken cognizance of this?
> And what on this is Your divine position?
> That nations like the Cuban and the Swiss
> Can never hope to wage a Global Mission.
> No Holy Wars for them. The most the small
> Can ever give us is a nuisance brawl.

Amusing enough perhaps, but complacent as well: herein speaks the Big Voice of the hugely successful poet who has seen them come and

244 · FROST: A LITERARY LIFE RECONSIDERED

go. If the career which began in felicity were to end in publicity and in poems like "No Holy Wars for Them," maybe—the reader feels—it had better really *end* there. Yet to complain that Frost's late poems are inferior to the others, is to indulge in the complacency one has identified in the poems. Instead, they should be put in their place, which is a small one, and seen as relatively weak manifestations of what on other fronts still revealed itself—never more so—as a quite unbelievable energy of performance.

In Robert Lowell's sonnet, mentioned earlier, this performance is referred to as "the great act." It begins, "Robert Frost at midnight, the audience gone / to vapor, the great act laid on the shelf in mothballs, / his voice is musical and raw . . .," and proceeds by artfully deploying a conversation between Lowell and Frost in which each man subtly and significantly misunderstands the other, thus making for unexpected and vivid jumps in their exchanges. Lowell's poem probably originated from a remembered, late-night conversation, and Lowell is different from others only insofar as he was able to summon up and shape the memory into art. For countless people who remember their conversations with Frost, remember him *talking,* moving from subject to subject, pausing over something, turning it around, playing with it, varying his tone from gentle to harsh to scarcely definable—so that the listener would feel afterwards, "How did he mean that"? We recall the woman accusing her husband in "Home Burial": "*You*—oh you think the talk is all." At this late stage in Frost's life, the "talk" had indeed become just about "all." And it seemed to more than one listener, that such talk had never been heard before and probably never would be again—that was the extent of the spellbinding.

At Amherst College, to which he returned in 1949 with an appointment for life as Simpson Lecturer, his only function was to talk. For roughly two weeks in the fall and a similar period in the spring, he came to town, gave a single large public reading in the chapel, then made a few smaller appearances. He would read some poems and talk to students at a fraternity; he would go out to dinner at one or another faculty member's house, and after dinner hold the floor until the people with classes the next day made their apologies and left. When he was accompanied home, usually on foot, to the inn where he stayed, he would offer to walk the accompanier back a ways in the other direction, then having reached a certain point would suggest that the accompanier walk *him* back toward the inn. This game could go on

Eightieth birthday celebration, Amherst, 1954.

for some time. As long as he commanded the power of his speaking voice, no evening would have to end.

In a sense he had always acted as if he could say anything and get away with it; his friendship with Bernard DeVoto was a case in point. At Bread Loaf in the summer of 1938 after Elinor's death, Frost had behaved in erratic, destructive ways, drinking and talking wildly, testing the limits of his friends' patience. DeVoto's patience was tried to the extent that he made the remark (to Frost's ears) about how he was a good poet but a bad man. Some years later they found themselves together at a writer's conference at Bloomington, Indiana, where Frost engaged DeVoto in intimate conversations, then after the latter left town told faculty members at a dinner that DeVoto was under the care of a psychiatrist who had warned him not to associate with Frost, since the latter's strong personality had a bad effect on him. This tale got back to DeVoto, who then wrote Frost a sharp letter telling him in no uncertain terms to desist. Frost responded with a long letter beginning "Benny, Benny!", referring to himself as a "disappointed novelist" and

With Amherst professors Theodore Baird and G. Armour Craig, 1958.

defending the "story" he had told by saying "I wouldn't have thought it hurt either of us and it makes us both more amusing." The presumption behind this claim which, so the logic ran, DeVoto had not been quite big enough to accommodate to, was that the power of the storyteller rendered questions of truthfulness, privacy, or confidentiality insignificant; such matters were of little weight when compared with the inclination, the necessity to be "amusing," and by invention to render both the teller and his subject more interesting. One could term Frost's response a rather desperate attempt to save face; yet there is in his letter a truly surprised note that DeVoto could have failed to be amused by the inventive—at least invented—story which "the disappointed novelist" had been telling about him.

In the words from Auden's poem about Yeats, Frost "became his admirers," sometimes, as in the difficulty with DeVoto, "becoming" them in enthusiastic ways they could not live up to, having other concerns in their lives besides admiring Frost. The final volume of the Thompson biography is devoted mainly to enumerating Frost's honors, as one by one this medal or that degree was bestowed on him. His

With students at Mount Holyoke, 1959.

remark that he needed all the honors he could get, is understood by his biographer as further confirmation of his insecurity: "The doubters now were all believers, but the old inner doubts remained. Only the steady influx of objectified praise could quiet the fear he had that everything he had achieved would somehow slip away." But if this way of understanding Frost's need is supposed to distinguish him from other artists, it does not so distinguish him from Samuel Johnson, who when a friend tried to assure him that there was already sufficient evidence for the existence of a spiritual world, replied "I LIKE TO HAVE MORE." Like Dr. Johnson, Frost knew firsthand the "hunger of imagination which preys incessantly upon life" *(Rasselas),* and the need to have all the honors he could get became more intense as the poems grew less frequent, less substantial; as other people became or were transformed into listeners and admirers; and as the thought of death—when everything does indeed slip away—became more present.

One of the most imaginative things Frost did with all those honors was to have the hoods from his various honorary degrees made into a quilt. But the quilt was presented to him before it could have included the most coveted and impressive of the academic prizes he received in his last years—the award of degrees from both Oxford and Cambridge, in 1957. As with so much else in his career, this welcome tribute did not just happen but was actively sought out by the poet, who let it be known that he would be visiting England as a "distinguished representative of the American cultural scene." This language, used in a letter from Secretary of State Dulles, was prompted by Frost through the offices of his friend in power, Sherman Adams, Assistant to President Eisenhower. Oxford and Cambridge duly responded by inviting him to receive a degree, and thus he could look upon the going back in triumph to England as icing on the cake: "I have had about everything I can have in my own country. Now for the mother country," he wrote Lawrance Thompson, who was to accompany him.

Although unwell at certain points during this exciting and exhausting month's stay in England and Dublin (besides the Oxford and Cambridge degree visits he went to Durham, Manchester, and once more his old Gloucestershire haunts of 1914), the whole venture was a triumph. Perhaps its high point occurred when at a London dinner, the toastmaster, T.S. Eliot, saluted him as "perhaps *the* most eminent, the most distinguished, I must call it, Anglo-American poet now living." This, from the Eliot who thirty-five years previously in his "London Letter" for the *Dial,* had characterized Frost as "specializing in New England torpor" and had regretted that "his verse . . . is uninteresting, and what is uninteresting is unreadable . . ." Perhaps Eliot slowly or suddenly changed his mind about Frost's merits; or perhaps at the public level that both poets had now achieved, talk about eminence and distinction was simply the currency of the realm. Frost responded in kind, acknowledging the remarks by insisting that there was nobody living in either England or America from whom he would rather hear such praise. This from one who had been repelled by Eliot's obscurity, and whose attitude toward *The Waste Land* was contemptuous.

It is a relief, amid one triumphant occasion after another, to find a single occasion on which something untoward happened. At a Savile Club dinner, he was invited by Stephen Spender to reminisce about his stay in England early in the century. Frost began to oblige, but was soon bothered by the smiling and chuckling of one of the guests whose name he had not caught. Taking matters into his own hands, he challenged the man by asking him what he was "giggling" at. The unidentified guest, embarrassed, fell silent. Later as the party broke up he was identified as E.M. Forster, whose feelings had evidently been hurt by Frost's challenge. Informed of this, Frost wrote Forster a letter of apology, and later visited him at his King's College rooms. But there is a symbolic satisfaction in the awkward occurrence at the dinner table. Here was a moment when Frost was invited to speak, to a table surrounded by ready admirers, and something went wrong; one of them responded in an inappropriate way, out of motives which cannot be named with any certainty. Was Forster genuinely amused, and unable to control his vocal expression of pleasure? Was he indeed out of control, tipsy, or on the edge of senility? It matters less than that he managed to discomfit Frost, indeed to provoke him into aggressive behavior, unusual at the Savile Club. And then to find afterwards that the giggler was in fact E.M. Forster, defender of the liberal imagination and of tolerance, good humor and sympathy! It seemed to show that even under the most auspicious circumstances it was possible to have an imperfect fit between American and English culture, between the farmer-poet and the apostle of civilization from Kings, between roughness and urbanity, between two kinds of humor. Not even Frost's speaking voice was able, on this occasion, completely to reconcile the antinomies.

The degrees from Oxford and Cambridge were looked upon by him as "sort of round[ing] off my rather great academic career in general." In putting it this way, with the strategically placed "rather," he made with humorous style an audacious claim, and as with others he had made, the claim was a mixture of seriousness and joking. It was a "rather great academic career" because so completely unlike anything that could claim to be considered as a truly great academic career. Here he was at his old trick of formulating something which wouldn't quite formulate; of making an academic career out of asking things like "Why do they have classes?"; or of giving a student an "A" for an examination on which he had written nothing. Never did one see him more warmly received by students, and by college presidents, than when he would turn his wit to mocking the professors, those literal-minded, humorless souls who kept trying to turn "Stopping By Woods . . ." into a poem about suicide, or committed other offenses against good taste and good sense. To poke fun at the academy, its procedures and its discourse, to disparage the very idea of a classroom and the teachers who insisted on explaining everything, and then to receive so many honorary degrees from colleges and universities that one had to have them made up into a quilt—this surely was a superb way to "round off" an academic career.

But it was not merely on the academic stage that Frost was convinced he had a role to play. His part in the release of Ezra Pound from St. Elizabeth's Hospital in Washington was an example, so it seemed to him, of how successfully public events could be shaped and important people moved to change their position, if only they would listen to his advice. The move to secure Pound's release from St. Elizabeth's, where he had been confined since 1946, was engineered by Archibald MacLeish, who in 1957 had the effective idea of putting Frost's name on top of a list (also containing Hemingway and T.S. Eliot) of distinguished American men of letters requesting that Pound be released, since he was a distinguished poet and had suffered enough for his ill-advised broadcasts from Italy during World War II. A meeting was arranged between Frost, Sherman Adams and Attorney General William Rogers, whose position on releasing Pound had become less intransigent. In fact by the time Frost visited Rogers (Hemingway and Eliot did not come to Washington—MacLeish knew that Frost was his strongest card) the mood of the Eisenhower administration had swung round toward dismissing the charges against Pound, who had already been judged incompetent to stand trial for treason. The whole carefully orchestrated procedure was a triumph of MacLeish's astute planning, but what is interesting for purposes of Frost's portrait is the way in which he convinced himself and told others how sweepingly and abruptly the deed had been effected. "I've dropped in to see what your mood is in regard to Ezra Pound," he said he had announced to Rogers at their meeting, to which the Attorney General had replied, "Our mood is your mood, Mr. Frost." "Well, then, let's get him out right away," said Frost.

Whatever else the Attorney General may have told him during their conversation, the punch line—"Our mood is your mood, Mr. Frost"—perfectly epitomizes the way Frost understood the situation and was surely the way he wanted to have it understood by those to whom he told it. MacLeish's elaborate planning was forgotten in the ease with which, in Frost's story, Washington red tape was cut through by directness ("I've dropped in to see what your mood is in regard to Ezra Pound") and no-nonsense clarity ("Well, then, let's get him out right away"). This is not to imply that his part in effecting Pound's release was not significant, but that the ground had been fully prepared. Here was the quintessential American poet, whose magnanimity could be displayed as a convincing reason for letting Pound go. Immediately after the success with Pound, he was offered a job succeeding Jarrell as Consultant in Poetry at the Library of Congress, for nine months beginning in the fall of 1958. In an interview with the press the day the appointment was announced, he referred to his recent "success" in Washington, saying humorously that his reputation was now more for "politics" than "poetry." He allowed that he possessed "wiles," and finally remarked, apropos of Pound's release, "All I did was the whole thing." One recalls again the earlier ditty—"I only go/When I'm the show."

What begins in felicity ends in publicity. Those who thought of themselves as serious admirers of Frost's poetry were inclined to wince at this sort of self-congratulation carried on in front of people, most of whom couldn't have told a sonnet from an epic. When, in fact, the Library of Congress job turned out to have little of the importance Frost imagined it might have, he joked about it: "I wondered if I hadn't come down here on a misunderstanding. I thought I was to be poetry consultant in everything—poetry, politics, religion, science. I'll tackle anything." Of course he would have, as he had been doing for years. But his light tone should not obscure the seriousness of this fantasy of power, the dream of a boy's will grown old but retaining its youthful capacity for demanding that the world come round to it. In a line from a poem ("Escapist—Never") published in 1962, the year before he died, "His life is a pursuit of a pursuit forever." Yet a sinecure at the Library of Congress was not the situation in which Frost could begin to live up to his imagined version of heroism—of tackling anything and by so doing making a real difference to the nature of things.

It is all too easy to look back upon these last years of public, international acclaim in the 1950s and early '60s, and regret his being taken in by the hoopla, his having succumbed to the now authentically public figure's relishing consciousness of himself. This impulse toward patronizing him may be checked by reminding ourselves that there were moments of weariness, of doubt, of the suspicion that there must be something specious about at least part of the celebration, now joined in on by all parties. What, for example, were the feelings, if any, which lay behind his response to the Vermont State Legislature's passing a bill designating him "Poet Laureate of Vermont," when acknowledging the honor Frost produced this four-line poem:

> Breathes there a bard who isn't moved
> When he finds his verse is understood
> And not entirely disapproved
> By his country and his neighborhood?

There is nothing in these artful lines which suggests he was not pleased at getting one more honor. Yet is it not possible to imagine him somewhat less than "moved" by the idea that those Vermont legislators "understood" and approved of his poetry, even if such humorous or sceptical comment was confined to his private thoughts?

The public occasion on which something more like the full range of his personality was expressed was the famous eighty-fifth birthday party held in 1959, when Lionel Trilling gave a speech saluting Frost as "terrifying": a "tragic poet" whose work conceived of a "terrifying universe." Trilling made heavy use of D.H. Lawrence's *Studies in Classic American Literature* in order to ally Frost with what Lawrence said classic American writers had done. They were radicals committed to sloughing off the old European consciousness, and they did this not by affirming old virtues and pieties, but by representing "the terrible actualities of life in a new way." Frost's response to Trilling's salute was somewhat halting and uncertain. He may well have had difficulty hearing it all, or putting it together consecutively, and he was surely disturbed by being praised in Lawrentian terms. Also, he confessed to being especially "nervous" that night. But the next day he met Trilling for a friendly chat, and later when Trilling published the speech in *Partisan Review* and sent him a copy—with the hope that his remarks hadn't "distressed" him—Frost replied, "Not distressed at all. Just a little taken aback or thrown back on myself by being so closely examined so close by." And he praised Trilling for "departing from the Rotarian norm in a Rotarian situation."

When Trilling published the speech, he prefaced it by an introduction describing the outraged reaction to it from some quarters (J. Donald Adams's contemptuous account of it in the *New York Times Book Review* drew forth angry letters from people who hadn't heard the speech but didn't want their image of Frost disturbed), and subtitled it, "A Cultural Episode." Perhaps it was in fact a cultural episode, rather than the close examination Frost felt he had been given. For Trilling mentioned only two particular poems, and those only in passing, to illustrate that Frost conceived of a "terrifying universe." The poems were "Design" and "Neither Out Far Nor In Deep," both of which Jarrell had selected and analyzed at length a few years before, as indications of the "dark" Frost. At the risk of being ungenerous to Trilling, it looks as if, asked to give a speech for the birthday celebration, he remembered the Jarrell essay and used it to build a case for Frost as a "radical" critic of American life. But in this lively departure

from the "Rotarian norm," he made his own simplification of Frost's
art into a melodramatic rendering of terrifying, terrible darkness. In
so doing he discounted, or at least did not pay serious attention to, the
humor, the irony, the mischief, the teasing, the playfulness. It is probably true, as Poirier points out, that Frost was committed to "rein-
state" rather than obliterate the old virtues and pieties which Lawrence had said the important American literary tradition was out to
destroy. But it is certain that he was a harder figure to pin down than
Trilling imagined, as he went about pinning Frost down to the
"tragic" mat. One can imagine that Frost perceived something of this
when he was made "nervous" by the talk.

Whatever one thought of Trilling's speech as an adequate description of Frost's poetry, it was important for the way it stimulated argument about the poetry at a time when it was mostly receiving pious
accolades. If the speech's simplifications about how "terrifying"
Frost's poetry was, were just exciting and uncomplex enough to allow
people to latch on to them, they were also salutary in that they encouraged looking at him as something other than an affirmer of American
pieties in the 1950s. It may well have been that Trilling's rather sen-
sational version of things made Frost more interesting to himself; at
any rate, he continued to act as if there were great felicity in all the
publicity. As poetry consultant at the Library of Congress he had
insisted that he was ready to tackle anything, and at a press conference on the morning of the day which would close with Trilling's birthday speech, he was asked by a reporter about New England—was it
in decay? In reply, Frost adduced the vitality of Harvard and Yale,
predicted that the successor to Secretary Dulles (who was dying)
would be from Boston (Undersecretary Christian Herter), and that
the next president would also be from Boston. When pressed by the
reporters to say whom he meant, he eventually produced the name of
John Kennedy, a "Puritan from Boston." The headlines made by this
pronouncement were sufficient to elicit a note from Senator Kennedy
and later, after the 1960 elections, an invitation to participate in the
inaugural ceremonies.

What happened is a familiar but still inspiriting story of disaster
transformed into triumph. Frost had worked feverishly on a new poem
in couplets (and the occasional triplet): seventy-six lines in celebration
of America's history, of how "our venture in revolution and outlawry
/ Has justified itself in freedom's story / Right down to now in glory
upon glory." The poem spread on the glory pretty thick, with such un-

sublime events as Kennedy's recent election squeak-through against Richard Nixon becoming, in Frost's tribute, "The greatest vote a people ever cast, / So close yet sure to be abided by." About the mood of the moment he declared, "Courage is in the air in bracing whiffs," and the poem ended in a mood as exalted and exultant as Dryden's "Astraea Redux" or Pope's "Windsor Forest," poems prophetic of the English "Augustan" age. Frost called for a life that would be "sterner," "braver," with "more preoccupation with the sport," and he declared that

> It makes the prophet in us all presage
> The glory of a next Augustan age
> Of a power leading from its strength and pride,
> Of young ambition eager to be tried,
> Firm in our free beliefs without dismay,
> In any game the nations want to play.
> A golden age of poetry and power
> Of which this noonday's the beginning hour.

In these lines the boy's will came full circle, if in a slightly disturbing way. As Frost had pretended, at the beginning of his career, that the will could make circumstances other than they are, so the career culminated in a fantasy of willing the realities of modern power politics into an alliterative "golden age of poetry and power." In this age, America, heroic as she would become, was ready to play any "game" the nations wanted to play (one thinks now, unavoidably, of the Bay of Pigs invasion). In this inaugural poem, Frost presented himself as laureate of the new age, by projecting on it the vocabulary of prowess and performance and play he now used as second nature. It was some kind of ultimate finding of felicity in publicity.

Except that, on the occasion, he was unable to read more than a few lines of the poem, troubled as he was by the sun's glare that bright, cold January day, but at least as much by the poem's newness to him, his unfamiliarity with and uncertainty about the way it went. Or perhaps, as he had been wont to say about himself, it was a sort of judgment. He had been tempted to believe that it was a great occasion at which he would perform—not just a transfer of power from one party to another, both of which were filled with politicians. Like many others, he conceived the new president as Young Lochinvar, the perfect combination of spirit and flesh, passion and toughness, poetry and reality, Harvard and Irish. It was almost as if, in the language of his poem "Kitty Hawk," Kennedy had been sent "As a demonstration / That the supreme merit / Lay in risking spirit / In substantiation." And Frost wrote the extravagant words about the "next Augustan age," as if by proclaiming them he could help it come into being, could substantiate it. But the poet was old, the flesh was weak, and he could not utter the words he had written. At this moment of disaster, he called on some resource and rose to a level in every way superior to the pumped-up one of the new poem's advertisement. Putting behind him the stumbling uncertainties of voice and tone which characterized his attempt to deliver the new poem, he fell back on an old one he knew perfectly, and in the most splendidly commanding of voices read "The Gift Outright" impeccably: "The land was ours before we were the land's." His performance thus attained a dramatic, even a heroic quality, which it would otherwise have lacked if things had gone off perfectly. The imperfect version had more of "life" in it: in the midst of flattery and display, the sound of sense suddenly and movingly made itself felt.

If the performance at the inauguration represents victory snatched from the jaws of defeat, the trip to Russia and meeting with Krushchev must be reckoned less happily, at least in its aftermath. The final lesson appeared to be that poetry and power went together only in poems, and that to prophesy—as Frost had done—a golden age, then try to help bring it about, was a course fraught with peril. These terms for judging the event may be excessive ones, but Frost invested heavily in the notion that a meeting with Krushchev and a frank exchange of views, might contribute to a new relationship between the superpowers founded upon the principle of rivalry. Franklin Reeve, the scholar and interpreter who, along with Secretary of the Interior Udall, accompanied him on the trip to Russia in September of 1962, said that when Frost and Krushchev finally met, "he [Frost] told the Premier that there should be no petty squabbles, that there must be a noble rivalry between Russia and the United States, forcefully and magnanimously pressed by the leaders of both sides." There would be an end to propaganda and name-calling, and a forthright recognition of each other's greatness and power. Krushchev was perceived as agreeing with these sentiments.

The meeting between them was heightened by the uncertainty that it was ever to materialize and by the fact that Frost was ill. Upon arriving at Krushchev's summer home in the Caucuses, he went to bed, welcoming the premier, when eventually he arrived, in his pajamas. From Reeve's account Krushchev was at his most charming, and there is every reason to believe that the two men genuinely took to each other. (Frost liked to refer to him as a "ruffian," a name denoting qualities he admired.) After the hour and a half conversation was over and Krushchev had left, Frost dropped back on the bed and said, according to Reeve, "Well, we did it, didn't we? He knows what power is and isn't afraid to take hold of it. He's a great man, all right." He was clear that Krushchev possessed the latter of the two qualities which would figure in the "golden age of poetry and power" he had written about in the inaugural poem. Who could say that he might not rise to poetry as well, to "magnanimity" in his rivalry with the United States?

Thus he returned from Russia with the sense of having accomplished something, and with the expectation or hope that Kennedy would summon him for a conversation. As is well known, this never happened—to Frost's deep regret. It is not clear whether or not he knew he had annoyed Kennedy, but such was the case. Upon landing at Idlewild after the long flight home, he was surrounded by reporters wanting to know what he had talked about with Krushchev, and by way of answer he gave them to believe that the premier had said he feared for "us modern liberals"—"He said we were too liberal to fight." For years, of course, he had been baiting "liberals" as hesitant, over-thoughtful types who shirked the realities of power recognized by Krushchev, Kennedy, and himself. Any opportunity to tease this species was eagerly sought out; but it was a mistake to indulge himself when the stakes were international ones, and though he claimed to have a message for Kennedy from Krushchev which he was ready to deliver, an invitation was not forthcoming (Stewart Udall had reported to Kennedy that Krushchev did *not* make the remark about liberals). Thus the tale ended as a cautionary one in which Frost found that "cutting up," as he had done at the airport, was more appropriate on the poetry lecture circuit than in the theater of international relations. Still, except for its very end, the trip to Russia by the old poet in the last months of his life, still filled with the most ambitious imaginings and aspirations, is a fine thing to contemplate. He almost brought it off.

---

It may be only retrospection that makes it seem as if, in the late fall of 1962, Frost knew the end was in sight. *In the Clearing* had, after

many delays, been published in the previous March to a response
which could at best be called polite. There had been a large eighty-
eighth birthday party in Washington, at which he presented a copy of
his new book to the president; then came the Russian adventure with
its less than glorious conclusion. In late November and early December of the year, he made what were to be his last two public appearances, the first of them at the newly opened Hopkins Center at Dartmouth. There he delivered his usual blend of talking and reading from
his poetry; it was posthumously published as "On Extravagance"—
his main theme for the evening. Five days later, he made his annual
Ford Forum appearance at Jordan Hall in Boston. The Dartmouth
talk celebrated "extravagance," the extravagance of the universe, and
of man as "the most wasteful, spending thing in it—in all his luxuri-
ance." Poetry was an "extravagance about grief," springing from
great impulses such as the one to say "It sometimes seems as if" or
(and as he would repeat in the Ford Forum talk) "If I could only tell
you." After reading various poems, including "The Most of It" and
"Never Again Would Birds' Song . . ." as examples of extravagance,
he ended with a short one from *Steeple Bush* which he seldom read
aloud (first of a group titled *Five Nocturnes,* it was titled "The Night
Light"):

> She always had to burn a light
> Beside her attic bed at night.
> It gave bad dreams and broken sleep,
> But helped the Lord her soul to keep.
> Good gloom on her was thrown away.
> It is on me by night or day,
> Who have, as I suppose, ahead
> The darkest of it still to dread.

"Suppose I end on that dark note. Good night," he concluded his talk.
It was an unusual place for him to end, and carried a hint that the
foreseeing "I" in the poem had a human counterpart in the old and
tired poet.

At the Ford Forum he acknowledged that he wasn't feeling well
("I'm a little tired . . .I've been sick") but nevertheless gave a full performance. It was one final attempt to set poetry above various "con-
tentions"—like politics, the academy, religion—by thinking of it as
something "in itself"—"like a street song . . . it wants to be catchy."
Poetry should be above "satire," and it was at war with "music," since
the poem was a song in itself without being set to music (he may have

At his writing desk, in Franconia, New Hampshire, 1915.

had in mind the recent experience of hearing some of his poems in settings by the composer Randall Thompson). That night the poems he read rather pointedly went back to *A Boy's Will,* and he said about "October" (one of three he read) that it was "innocent of everything I know of." He emphasized the importance of making the individual tunes different from each other, but seemed to take most pleasure in tracing out, with his speaking voice, the expressive curve of an utterance. With animated excitement he read and repeated a six-line poem, "Questioning Faces," published in his last volume:

> The winter owl banked just in time to pass
> And save himself from breaking window glass.
> And her wings straining suddenly aspread
> Caught color from the last of evening red
> In a display of underdown and quill
> To glassed-in children at the windowsill.

Like "October," this was a poem "innocent" of just about everything; a song in itself without being set to music. It makes its own music by

At Ripton, Vermont, 1956.

the way its second couplet does not, like the first one, come full stop at its end, but continues on into the splendid "display of underdown and quill," a momentary extravagance those glassed-in children were so fortunate, whether or not they knew it, to have seen. "You remember that . . . ," Frost said to the audience about the poem, the insistence being that they had been able to share something common in experience, by virtue of the writing being just uncommon enough to illuminate it.

That night he ended, rather abruptly, with "The Road Not Taken," but then after saying good night stayed on to answer questions, the main one of which concerned his Russian trip. Having been burned once, he disclaimed the remark he had formerly attributed to Krushchev, and also disclaimed any thought that he had been "arranging" anything. He had gone over, rather, "to assert my own thinking" in the face of the premier (who was described this time as "like a great big horse-trader") and to promote a "grand rivalry" between the powers. He spoke calmly, without boasting, in such a way that the listener would be hard put not to feel that, after all, what he had done was quite wonderful—a perfect example of his tribute to extravagance in the Dartmouth talk, in which the universe was both the model of "great expense" and productive of it in the aspirations of man— "everybody trying to make it mean something more than it is."

Then somebody from the audience asked him to read from "Two Tramps in Mud Time." After saying the last stanza about work being "play for mortal stakes," he moved on to talk about life as a "gamble." It was all "gamblin'," and one had to bet nothing less than one's life; indeed, he said, one of the "sweetest" of all expressions was "You bet your sweet life." There was "nothing to life" unless one could say, "I bet my sweet life on this." "That's what takes it away from everybody but yourself," he continued; "Nobody's gonna run you." And if the bet, the gamble, turned out disastrously, well then "The most inalienable right of man is to go to hell in his own way." He spoke of his own life as a gamble: he was gambling every time he opened the day's mail, each week when some person or other changed his opinion of him. Then, in another one of those moments where he seemed to stand aside and look at things from a long way off, as if he were no longer quite a part of them, he laughed briefly and announced, "It's a wonderful world"—after which he added, evenly, "To hell with it." The audience was uncertain whether to laugh, and after one further anticlimactic question the proceedings were terminated.

So ended his last public performance. It was almost seventy years since he had been introduced by the Congregational minister to the men's club at Derry, and had had "The Tuft of Flowers" read aloud because he was too shy to do it himself. That night at Jordan Hall he read aloud "The Tuft of Flowers" on his own, insisting once more that the mower had spared the flowers "just because he liked them." In a similar vein, he wanted the audience to think of his reading that night as innocent of everything except itself: "You can't suspect me tonight of being political . . .or anything but somewhat poetical, at the risk of my life." And he read a poem from his new volume ("Away!") which felt as if it were about something besides going for just another walk and which ended with the following instructions:

> Don't think I leave
> For the outer dark
> Like Adam and Eve
> Put out of the Park.
>
> Forget the myth.
> There is no one I

Am put out with
Or put out by.

Unless I'm wrong
I but obey
The urge of a song:
"I'm—bound—away!"

And I may return
If dissatisfied
With what I learn
From having died.

The next day, December 3, 1962, after much effort by Kathleen Morrison and his doctor, he was persuaded to enter Peter Bent Brigham Hospital for an operation on his prostate.

He had predicted that if he entered there he would never leave, and such was to be the case. Even though it revealed cancer of the bladder, the operation was a success, but while recuperating from it he suffered a pulmonary embolism, causing damage to his heart. This was followed, in the first week of the new year, by a second embolism, then a rapidly weakening condition. Two weeks before he died he dictated a letter to his friend and former colleague George Roy Elliot and his wife Alma, thanking them for liking the poem he had sent them at Christmas. He told the Elliots he had been thinking about the problem of salvation, and that just that day had been saying how "Christ posed Himself the whole problem and died for it." The problem was:

How can we be just in a world that needs mercy and merciful in a world that needs justice. We study and study the four biographies of Him and are left still somewhat puzzled in our daily lives. Marking students in a kind of mockery and laughing it off. It seems as if I never wrote these plunges into the depths to anyone but you.

Earlier in the letter he had declared that "Metaphor is it and the freshness thereof." In the effort to show—despite the Gospels and their truth, despite our knowledge that we must combine justice with mercy—that we are "puzzled" about what to do, he reached for metaphor. There came the flash of poetry, as he embodied the puzzlement to his old academic colleague: "Marking students in a kind of mockery and laughing it off." In this almost offhand metaphor was revealed the confusion existing under the presumed clarity of a final grade; bitter, knowing, and wistful all at once, the metaphor was dropped as quickly as it was picked up. But it had been a plunge into the depths.

In the concluding paragraph of his letter to the Elliots, he paid tribute to Kathleen Morrison and her daughter, who he said were helping him "through these hard days in a grand and very powerful hospital." And he promised his correspondents that "If only I get well, with their help, I'll go deeper into my life with you than I ever have before." It was not to be. Yet the going deeper into life had already occurred, as perhaps the Elliots surmised, in the letter just concluded—in the freshness of metaphor, which was a plunge into the depths as well. For the last time, Frost's promise had been performed in the making of it.

# Notes

The numerals at the left refer to page numbers in this book. The words that follow the numeral indicate the beginning of the annotated phrase or passage. In the main, I have not duplicated information already in the text. The following abbreviations are used:

EY   Lawrance Thompson, *Robert Frost: The Early Years, 1874–1915.* (New York: Holt, Rinehart and Winston, 1966.)

YT   Lawrance Thompson, *Robert Frost: The Years of Triumph, 1915–1938.* (New York: Holt, Rinehart and Winston, 1970.)

LY   Lawrance Thompson and R. H. Winnick, *Robert Frost: The Later Years, 1938–1963.* (New York: Holt, Rinehart and Winston, 1976.)

SL   *Selected Letters of Robert Frost,* ed. Lawrance Thompson. (New York: Holt, Rinehart and Winston, 1964.)

Untermeyer   *The Letters of Robert Frost to Louis Untermeyer.* (New York: Holt, Rinehart and Winston, 1963.)

Family   *Family Letters of Robert and Elinor Frost,* ed. Arnold Grade. (Albany: State University of New York Press, 1972.)

Selected Prose   *Selected Prose of Robert Frost,* ed. Hyde Cox and Edward C. Lathem. (New York: Collier Books, 1968.)

## Introduction

xii   "When Helen Vendler . . . David Bromwich . . . Howard Moss": Vendler's review appeared in the *New York Times Book Review,* 6 Aug. 1970. Bromwich's review appeared in the same place, 16 Jan.

1977. Moss's comment is from *Whatever Is Moving* (Boston: Little Brown, 1981.)

xii   "offer a balanced delineation":
     *YT*, pp. xiv–xv.

xiii  "But the simple truth is that I love you":
     Thompson to Frost, 4 Dec. 1940, letter, Dartmouth College Library.

xiii  "The imagined forms of retaliation":
     *YT*, pp. xiv–xv.

xiv  "illuminating the complicated and contradictory responses":
     *YT*, p. 705.

xv   "It is touch and go with the metaphor":
     "Education by Poetry," *Selected Prose*, p. 41.

xv   "In England, there came a day":
     *YT*, p. 440.

xvi  "I have made a life study":
     Notebook, Dartmouth College Library.

xvi  "Play no matter how deep":
     Notebook, Dartmouth College Library.

xvii  "Crash there goes another young ideal":
     Notebook, Dartmouth College Library.

## Chapter I. Guessing at Myself

3   "I must have been asked once years ago":
    Reginald Cook, *Robert Frost: A Living Voice* (Amherst: University of Massachusetts Press, 1974) pp. 109–10.

6   "It may have crossed his mind":
    *EY*, pp. 176–7.

6   "listened, and thought bitterly":
    *EY*, p. 164.

8   "where Milton finished Paradise Lost":
    Frost to Susan Hayes Ward, 15 Sept. 1912, *SL*, p. 52.

8   "if he were alive as he might have been":
    Frost to Sidney Cox, 26 Dec. 1912, *SL*, p. 61.

9   "I came here to write":
    Frost to Thomas Mosher, 19 Nov. 1912, *SL*, p. 55.

10  "We have had ice (a few times)":
    Frost to Ernest Silver, 25 Dec. 1912, *SL*, p. 58.

11 Frost approached the firm of David Nutt:
In this connection see B. J. Sokol, "The Publication of Robert Frost's
First Books," *The Book Collector,* Summer 1977, pp. 228–39. See also
Sokol's "What Went Wrong Between Robert Frost and Ezra Pound,"
*New England Quarterly,* Dec. 1976, pp. 521–41.

11 "I have lived for the most part":
Frost to F. S. Flint, 21 Jan. 1913, quoted in *EY,* pp. 408–9.

12 "Out twice after eight o'clock in eight years":
William A. Sutton, ed., *Newdick's Season of Frost: An Interrupted
Biography of Robert Frost* (Albany: State University of New York
Press, 1976), p. 260.

13 "The beauty of such things":
*SL,* p. 73.

14. "I am like a dead diver":
See Thompson's discussion of "Despair" in *EY,* pp. 267, 548–9.

15 "comes pretty near being the story":
*SL,* p. 66.

17 "He is for the most part as simple":
Ezra Pound, in his review of *A Boy's Will,* in *Literary Essays of Ezra
Pound* (London: Faber, 1954) pp. 382–3.

18 "the best poetry written":
*SL,* p. 78.

20 In a journal Frost kept in England:
*EY,* p. 397.

24 "In his editor, E. C. Lathem's":
*EY,* p. 562.

24 "from people and (college)":
*SL,* p. 66.

25 "against the idea that you write poetry":
Tape, Amherst College Library.

## Chapter II. Life Before England

30 "A person of my character cannot transfer his love at will":
*SL,* p. 7.

30 "He was a long-distance swimmer":
Tape, Amherst College Library.

31 "Her frame was angular":
*EY,* p. 210.

32 "counteracting influence . . . voluble profanity":
Louis Mertins, *Robert Frost: Life and Talks-Walking* (Norman: University of Oklahoma Press, 1965) p. 9.

32 "In later life Frost was never quite able to understand":
*EY*, p. xvi.

33 "Sometimes he could hear whole sentences":
*EY*, p. 42.

33 "the sentence sound often says more":
Frost to John Bartlett, 22 Feb. 1914, *SL*, p. 113.

34 "He never read [all the way through]":
*EY*, p. 500.

36 "Very first one I wrote":
*Paris Review* No. 24, p. 117.

37 "There are not many girls I like":
*SL*, p. 18.

37 recounted by Thompson in full detail:
*EY*, pp. 103–5.

39 "Whatever may be the resources":
*EY*, p. 126.

39 It was the sort of "pang":
Frost to Susan Hayes Ward, 8 Sept. 1907, *SL*, p. 42.

40 Thompson argues that the doctrines of liberty:
*EY*, p. 136.

42 "getting past the point where I could show any great interest":
Frost to Harold G. Rugg, 20 Apr. 1915, *SL*, p. 167.

44 "Yet the consideration is hardly due me":
*SL*, p. 20.

46 "Virginia, North Carolina, and Maryland":
Frost to Susan Hayes Ward, 4 Dec. 1894, *SL*, p. 24.

48 "I stood not upon the order of my going":
Frost to LeBaron Russell Briggs, 11 Sept. 1897, *SL*, p. 30.

48 "Never be brought to take a low school view":
13 Nov. 1917, *Family*, p. 18.

49 "Whether you do or not depends":
William James, *The Will to Believe and Other Essays in Popular Philosophy* (London: Longmans, 1897), pp. 23–4.

50 "If this life be not a real fight":
James, *Will to Believe*, p. 63.

50 "The Figure a Poem Makes":
*Selected Prose,* pp. 17–20.

51 "It was only later that I found so much that was unsympathetic":
Van Wyck Brooks, *Scenes and Portraits* (New York: E.P. Dutton, 1954), p. 102.

53 Kathleen Morrison has written entertainingly:
Kathleen Morrison, *Robert Frost: A Pictorial Chronicle* (New York: Holt, 1974), p. 30.

54 The prime example of this latter mood:
*EY,* p. 308.

57 "They would see me starting out to work":
Mertins, *Frost: Life and Talks,* p. 78.

57 "I kept farm, so to speak":
*SL,* p. 158.

59 in retrospect at a Ford Hall Forum in 1960:
Tape, Amherst College Library.

60 "The general aim of the course in English is twofold":
*EY,* pp. 346ff.

62 "Its effect was startling":
*SL,* pp. 37–8.

64 "an absence of conformity . . . something earthy":
Sidney Cox, *Robert Frost, Original "Ordinary Man"* (New York: Holt, 1929), p. 30.

64 "She recalled [him] as conducting":
Recollection by Mrs. Eva Barndollar in Sutton, ed., *Newdick's Season of Frost,* p. 317.

66 "not the long deferred forward movement":
*SL,* p. 43.

66 "Two lonely cross-roads":
Frost to Susan Hayes Ward, 10 Feb. 1912, *SL,* pp. 45–6.

## Chapter III. Not Undesigning

69 "The boom is not started yet":
*SL,* p. 69.

70 "You are not going to make the mistake":
*SL,* p. 84.

70 "I want to reach out, and would":
Frost to Bartlett, ca. 5 Nov. 1913, *SL,* p. 98.

70  With Bartlett's assistance an article could be written:
    *SL,* p. 75.

72  "a man can stand being overpraised":
    Frost to Silver, 8 Dec. 1913, *SL,* p. 102.

72  "one of the few artists writing":
    *SL,* p. 88.

72  "the fact that he discovered me":
    Frost to Mosher, 17 July 1913, *SL,* p. 84.

73  "I suspected though that in praising me":
    *SL,* p. 86.

73  A presentation copy to Frost of one of Pound's earlier books:
    Elaine Barry, *Robert Frost on Writing* (New Brunswick: Rutgers University Press, 1973), pp. 170–72.

74  "You seem to be having things pretty much":
    Pound to Frost, 6 Dec. 1915, letter, Dartmouth College Library.

74  "I am looked on as someone":
    *SL,* p. 73.

74  "so very personal in this first book":
    Frost to Wilbur Rowell, 17 July 1913, *SL,* p. 85.

74  "I am made too self-conscious":
    *SL,* p. 83.

75  "kind of success called 'of esteem'":
    *SL,* p. 98.

76  "To be prefectly frank with you":
    *SL,* p. 79.

78  "Frost in 1914 wanted to believe":
    Margery Sabin, "The Fate of the Frost Speaker," *Raritan,* Fall 1982, pp. 134–5.

78  "The living part of a poem":
    *SL,* p. 107.

79  "In literature it is our business":
    *SL,* p. 111.

79  "It is so and not otherwise":
    *SL,* p. 113.

80  To speak in the review, as Pound did:
    Pound's review of *North of Boston,* in *Poetry,* Dec. 1914. *Literary Essays of Ezra Pound* (London: Faber, 1954), pp. 384–6.

80  "must always be to make his own words":
    Frost to Cox, Dec. 1914, *SL,* p. 141.

81 "We have had a good deal of him":
Frost to Cox, 18 May 1914, *SL,* p. 123.

82 "There must be a great deal to see":
Frost to Cox, 26 Mar. 1914, *SL,* pp. 121–2.

82 "I wish I could make you feel":
*SL,* p. 123.

83 "No book of verse has had as much space given it":
Frost to Cox, 20 Aug. 1914, *SL,* p. 132.

84 "Swinging is not stirring you know":
Frost to Cox, 15 Sept. 1913, *SL,* p. 93.

85 "leaves them all behind in the sublime":
Frost to Mosher, Nov. 1914, *SL,* p. 139.

85 "You and I wont believe that Gibsons":
Frost to Cox, 2 Feb. 1915, *SL,* p. 151.

86 "I hadn't a plan for the future that didn't include him":
Frost to Edward Garnett, 29 Apr. 1917, *SL,* p. 217.

87 "loveliest book on spring in England":
Frost to Cox, 18 May 1914, *SL,* p. 124.

89 In fact each of Thomas's reviews:
The three reviews are found in *A Language Not To Be Betrayed: Selected Prose of Edward Thomas,* ed. Edna Longley (Manchester: Carcanet Press, 1981) pp. 125–31.

92 "almost humorous . . . almost jokes":
*Untermeyer,* 7 Aug. 1916, p. 40.

92 "I have dropped to an everyday level of diction":
Frost to Mosher, 17 July 1913, *SL,* p. 82
"absolutely unliterary":
Frost to Bartlett, 8 Dec. 1913, *SL,* p. 102

92 "to fill a letter with tendentious confidences":
Note in *SL,* p. 158.

93 "I like the actuality of gossip":
*SL,* p. 159.

93 In the Derry version:
Found in *EY,* p. 592.

96 In the long and important review Edward Garnett wrote:
"A New American Poet," *Atlantic,* Aug. 1915, 214–21.

99 When Randall Jarrell interviewed him:
19 May 1959, tape, Amherst College Library.

103   In a recent, critically intelligent book:
      John Kemp, *Robert Frost and New England: The Poet as Regionalist*
      (Princeton: Princeton University Press, 1979) pp. 135–42.

104   "briefly possessed himself of a humane realism":
      Louise Bogan, *Achievement in American Poetry* (Chicago: Henry Reg-
      nery, 1951), p. 49.

105   "a quiet job in a small college":
      *SL,* p. 138.

106   "a small college with the chance of teaching a few ideas":
      Frost to Cox, 2 Jan. 1915, *SL,* p. 149.

106   "I ought to know by the length of your silence":
      Frost to Flint, 13 Feb. 1915, *SL,* p. 152.

## Chapter IV. Forms of Guardedness

110   Amy Lowell's admiring review:
      "North of Boston", *New Republic*, 20 Feb. 1915, pp. 81–2.

111   "That's an unpardonable attempt to do her":
      7 Nov. 1917, *Untermeyer,* pp. 62–3.

112   "quite delightful—as unspoiled as when":
      *SL,* p. 176.

113   "You have to be attractive enough":
      Notebook, Dartmouth College Library.

114   "the proper Bostonians, fashionably dressed":
      Louis Untermeyer, *Bygones* (New York: Harcourt Brace & World,
      1965), p. 145.

114   "You and I are not clever, Louis":
      11 Nov. 1915, *Untermeyer,* p. 17.

114   "an epic of dentistry":
      30 June 1919, *Untermeyer,* p. 88.

115   "one or the other with more or less":
      9 Sept. 1915, *Untermeyer,* pp. 13–14.

116   "too romantic for my tastes":
      9 Sept. 1915, *Untermeyer,* p. 15.

116   "I can't say for certain that I don't like Spoon River":
      Aug. 1918, *Untermeyer,* pp. 75–6.

117   "We've been having a dose of Carl Sandburg":
      Frost to Lincoln MacVeagh, May 1922, *SL,* p. 277.

120   "Sometime at a worse season I will tell you":
      *YT,* p. 64.

120 "These are piping times":
Frost to Braithwaite, 21 Mar. 1916, *SL*, p. 200.

120 "I think we shall enjoy our new home":
*SL*, p. 177.

121 "altogether out of health": *SL*, p. 192.

121 "out of those woods":
*SL*, p. 197.

121 "unspeakably sick":
Frost to Bartlett, 2 Dec. 1915, *SL*, p. 197.

121 "Elinor has been sick":
Frost to Bartlett, *SL*, p. 218.

121 "in such a nervous condition":
Nov. 1919, *Family*, p. 71.

121 "Elinor had a serious nervous collapse":
*SL*, p. 312.

121 "Elinor has had too much on her":
Frost to Haines, 26 Aug. 1928, letter, Dartmouth College Library.

122 "Finds Famous American Poet":
E. C. Lathem, ed., *Interviews with Robert Frost*, pp. 9–15.

123 "The boys had been made uncommonly interesting":
12 Aug. 1924, *Untermeyer*, p. 170.

124 "We found a sturdily built man":
George Whicher, *Mornings at 8:50* (Northampton: Amherst College Press, 1950), p. 159.

125 "and then told the boys about your coming":
*SL*, p. 209.

125 "The college is primarily not a place of the body":
Alexander Meiklejohn, *The Liberal College* (Boston: Marshall Jones Co., 1920), pp. 30–35.

126 "You get more credit for thinking":
*Untermeyer*, p. 47.

128 "Nothing ever so sincere":
Notebook, Dartmouth College Library.

129 "He has spoiled everything here":
*Untermeyer*, p. 54.

130 "It would be something like":
Henry A. Ladd, "Memories of Robert Frost," *Touchstone*, Feb. 1939, p. 15.

131   "I'd no more set out in pursuit":
       Frost to Wilbur L. Cross, 15 May 1920, *SL,* p. 250.

131   "I told him, 'No, *I* say it'":
       *Family,* p. 66.

132   "some thing ahead to prolong life":
       Frost to Harriet Moody, 19 Mar. 1919, *SL,* p. 234.

132   "will make things so disagreeable":
       *Family,* p. 71.

132   "While he detests my dangerous rationalistic":
       Frost to Robert Stanley Breed, 2 Feb. 1930, *SL,* p. 242.

133   "I own any form of humor":
       10 Mar. 1924, *Untermeyer,* p. 166.

134   "And now my time is my own":
       4 May 1916, *Untermeyer,* p. 29.

135   "I read The Cloister and the Hearth":
       Sept. 1925, *SL,* p. 322.

135   "She had had very little use for me":
       12 Apr. 1920, *Untermeyer,* p. 103.

136   "Pushing Things Around—things and people":
       Notebook, Dartmouth College Library.

136   "any form of humor shows fear":
       10 Mar. 1924, *Untermeyer,* p. 166.

136   "lest we grow too suspicious":
       *Family,* p. 34.

137   "Be away, be otherwise engaged":
       *Family,* p. 97.

138   "personally conducted the elopement":
       *Family,* p. 26.

138   "outbursts of writing without self-criticism":
       *Family,* p. 5.

139   "They say not, but you've got to score":
       *Paris Review* interview, Summer/Fall, 1960.

139   "My politics are wholly American":
       4 July 1916, *SL,* p. 205.

139   "I do love a country that loves itself":
       21 Apr. 1919, *SL,* p. 236.

140   "She called the janitor fool and damn fool":
       19 May 1922, *Untermeyer,* p. 148.

141 "The time is early evening":
Dorothy Tyler, "Robert Frost in Michigan, "*Frost Centennial Essays,
III*, ed. Jac Tharpe (Jackson: University Press of Mississippi, 1978) p.
54.

141 "fairly absent from Ann Arbor this year":
William R. Evans, *Robert Frost and Sidney Cox* (Hanover: University
Press of New England, 1981) p. 147.

142 "ought to have been poet enough to stay away":
17 Aug. 1923, *SL*, p. 293.

143 "is that which indicates how the writer":
10 Mar. 1924, *Untermeyer*, pp. 165–6.

144 "Dry humor is the kind that doesn't seem to appreciate itself":
Notebook, Dartmouth College Library.


Chapter V. *Mountain Interval* and *New Hampshire*

145 "were not going to get out of giving":
Frost to Harriet Monroe, *SL*, p. 206.

148 "I doubt if you intended any reference":
16 Nov. 1916, Evans, *Frost and Cox*, pp. 130–1.

148 "exaggerating the importance of a little sententious tag":
*SL*, p. 208.

153 "Like a person hard pressed in an argument":
Notebook, Dartmouth College Library.

155 "something he *cared* about instead of something":
Kemp, *Robert Frost and New England*.

156 "the public figure's relishing consciousness":
Randall Jarrell, "The Other Frost," *Poetry and the Age*, 1953, p. 31.

160 "a satisfaction so smug":
Richard Poirier, *Robert Frost: The Work of Knowing* (New York:
Oxford, 1977), p. 242.

165 "One of the greatest changes my nature has undergone":
Frost to Bernard DeVoto, 13 Oct. 1938, *SL*, p. 482


Chapter VI. Further Rangings

171 "return to print hurling fistfulls":
*SL*, p. 240.

171 "The strength of a teacher's position":
*SL*, p. 275.

171 "All that makes a writer":
*SL*, p. 327.

172 "just the right dubious note":
*SL*, p. 293.

172 "We reached an agreement that most":
12 Aug. 1924, *Untermeyer*, p. 170.

173 "All metaphor breaks down somewhere":
*Selected Prose*, p. 41.

174 "Amherst goes sadly, I'm afraid":
*Untermeyer*, p. 167.

175 "Nonsense and charlatanry":
*Untermeyer*, p. 107.

175 "a little compunctious prose to her ashes":
20 June 1925, *Untermeyer*, p. 174.

175 "The water in our eyes from her poetry":
"The Poetry of Amy Lowell," *Selected Prose*, p. 72.

176 "come to Ann Arbor to make some show":
*Untermeyer*, p. 178.

179 "You can get in a kerosene can":
14 Oct. 1920, *Family*, p. 105.

179 "crush the poetic instinct":
Holden's reminiscence is in the Dartmouth College Library.

179 "I don't under[stand] the system of blank verse":
17 Dec. 1932, letter, Dartmouth College Library.

180 "Dear Moma and Papa. A wonderful rainy night":
ca. 1932, letter, Dartmouth College Library.

180 "the same old Marj in her talk":
20 Apr. 1934, *Family*, p. 166.

181 "Clash is all very well for coming lawyers":
*SL*, p. 324

182 "You wish the world better than it is":
*SL*, p. 369.

184 "There is at least so much good in the world":
"Letter to 'The Amherst Student,'" *Selected Prose*, p. 106.

184 "Not all our convictions that all nations":
*Family*, p. 120.

186 "Elinor unhappier keeping her on":
*EY*, p. 342.

186  Gibson's "stock as a poet":
Frost to Lesley Frost, 11 Sept. 1928, *Family*, p. 124.

186  "Waste Lands—your great grand mother":
*Family*, p. 163.

187  "he cannot seem to stop":
*Family*, p. 134.

190  "write a court drama of the IVth Dynasty":
11 Oct. 1928, *Untermeyer*, p. 191.

190  "What I dread most now is that":
24 Oct. 1928, *Untermeyer*, p. 192.

191  "Everybody knows something has to be kept back":
19 Sept. 1929, *SL*, p. 361.

191  "Contribute directly to the unification":
Granville Hicks, "The World of Robert Frost," *New Republic*, 3 Dec.
1930, pp. 77–80.

192  "Yet I refuse to match sorrows":
*Untermeyer*, p. 220.

193  "He is a dear, kind, and considerate man":
*SL*, p. 384.

194  "through the valley of the shadow":
*Untermeyer*, p. 240.

194  "Well, the blow has fallen":
*Untermeyer*, pp. 241–2.

196  "Poor darling child":
*SL*, p. 409.

196  "There is no sanitation":
10 Jan. 1935, *Untermeyer*, p. 250.

196  "How utterly romantic the enervated old soak is":
6 June 1930, *Untermeyer*, p. 200.

197  "Way down in my heart":
*Untermeyer*, p. 221.

197  "the old fashioned way to be new":
This and further quotations from the preface to Robinson's *King Jasper* may be found in *Selected Prose*, pp. 59–67.

197  "Pound-gang editorial":
18 Feb. 1935, *Untermeyer*, p. 257.

201  "made too big a hit with the dignitaries":
9 May 1936, *Untermeyer*, p. 277.

203 "let off a lot of cheap senile witticisms":
Pound to Frost, 10 Apr. 1936, letter, Dartmouth College Library.

203 "as the necessary enemy of two forces":
Poirier, *Frost*, p. 226.

204 "The Critics and Robert Frost":
Bernard DeVoto, *Saturday Review*, 1 Jan. 1938, pp. 3–4.

204 Arvin objected to . . . "oracularities":
"A Minor Strain," *Partisan Review*, March 1936, pp. 29–30.

206 Rolfe Humphries, whose *New Masses* review:
"A Further Shrinking," *New Masses*, 11 Aug. 1936, pp. 41–2. Humphries's preliminary notes for the review are in the Amherst College Library.

206 In his introduction . . . Kingsley Amis:
Introduction to *New Oxford Book of English Light Verse* (New York: Oxford, 1978), p. xviii.

207 In his fine appreciation of Frost:
Randall Jarrell, "To the Loadiceans," *Poetry and the Age*, p. 39.

212 "You can see what a difference this must make":
*Untermeyer*, pp. 295–6.

## Chapter VII. Witness to Dark Circumstances

213 "My, My, what sorrow runs through":
*Family*, pp. 209–10.

215 "He wanted her to say at least with her eyes":
*YT*, p. 494.

215 "And I the last go forth companionless":
*SL*, p. 470.

216 "I suppose love must always deceive":
12 Apr. 1938, *SL*, pp. 470–1.

216 "Age saw two quiet children":
17 Apr 1938, *Untermeyer*, p. 307. There were minor changes made when "Carpe Diem" was published in *A Witness Tree* (quoted here).

217 "I don't know myself yet":
*Untermeyer*, p. 308.

218 "I'm afraid I dragged her through":
Quoted in *YT*, p. 511.

218 "Don't think I haven't myself well in hand":
*Untermeyer*, p. 314.

219 "I came through the two weeks":
3 Feb. 1939, *Family*, p. 203.

221 "No woman can mother me with impunity":
*LY*, p. 370.

221 "You'll be getting new trees":
*SL*, p. 469.

222 "We both like the apple-crating poem":
*Family*, p. 183.

222 "You have hammered it close":
18 Mar. 1933, *SL*, p. 390.

222 "I took the wrong way with him":
26 Oct. 1940, *Untermeyer*, pp. 232–4.

223 "Disaster brought out the heroic":
12 Oct. 1940, *Untermeyer*, p. 218.

224 "You had the first of this from me":
*Untermeyer*, p. 391. Thompson's remarks about "To prayer I think I go" are in *LY*, p. 391.

226 "Not that he would avoid duty":
8 Oct. 1942, *Family*, p. 235.

226 "I cant buy you a hat":
*Family*, p. 224.

227 "I have had it [the Pulitzer]":
20 May 1943, *Family*, p. 242.

229 "Lesley Frost remembers":
"In Aladdin's Lamp Light," *Frost: Centennial Essays*, III, p. 314.

234 "A blaze of triumph":
Jarrell, *Poetry and the Age*, p. 51.

238 "but I am very wild at heart sometimes":
Evans, *Frost and Cox*, p. 228.

238 "It begins in delight and ends in wisdom":
*Selected Prose*, p. 18.

## Chapter VIII. Deeper into Life

242 "I'm a bad man to have around at a wedding":
Taped interview with Jarrell, Amherst College Library.

246 "I wouldn't have thought it hurt either of us":
10 June 1943, *SL*, p. 510.

247   "The doubters now were all believers":
      *LY*, p. 215.

248   "distinguished representative of the American":
      12 Feb. 1957, *SL*, p. 562.

248   "I have had about everything":
      *SL*, p. 565.

248   "specializing in New England torpor":
      T. S. Eliot, "London Letter", *The Dial*, April 1922.

249   "sort of round[ing] off my rather great academic career":
      Frost to Thompson, 16 Aug. 1957, *SL*, p. 565.

252   "not distressed at all":
      Frost to Lionel Trilling, 18 June 1959, *SL*, p. 583.

255   "he [Frost] told the Premier":
      F. D. Reeve, *Robert Frost in Russia* (Boston: Atlantic Little Brown, 1963), p. 112.

256   "'Well, we did it, didn't we?' ":
      Reeve, *Frost in Russia*, p. 116.

257   he made what were to be his last two public appearances:
      The talk at Dartmouth, "On Extravagance," is in *Robert Frost: Poetry and Prose*, ed. Lathem and Thompson, pp. 447–59. The Ford Forum appearance is on tape, Amherst College Library.

261   "How can we be just in a world that needs mercy":
      12 Jan. 1963, *SL*, p. 596.

# Index